P9-BYN-008

My Own Medicine

My Own Medicine

A DOCTOR'S LIFE
AS A PATIENT

Geoffrey Kurland, M.D.

TIMES BOOKS
Henry Holt and Company   New York

Times Books
Henry Holt and Company, LLC
Publishers since 1866
115 West 18th Street
New York, New York 10011

Henry Holt® is a registered trademark of
Henry Holt and Company, LLC.

Library of Congress Cataloging-in-Publication Data

Kurland, Geoffrey.
  My own medicine : a doctor's life as a patient / Geoffrey Kurland.—1st ed.
    p. cm.
  Includes index.
  ISBN 0-8050-7171-7 (hb)
  1. Kurland, Geoffrey—Health. 2. Leukemia—Patients—Pennsylvania—Pittsburgh—
Biography. 3. Pediatricians—Pennsylvania—Pittsburgh—Biography.   I. Title.
RC643 .K87 2002
362.1'9699419'0092—dc21
[B]   2002019025

Henry Holt books are available for special promotions and
premiums. For details contact: Director, Special Markets.

First Edition 2002

Designed by Kelly S. Too

Printed in the United States of America

1   3   5   7   9   10   8   6   4   2

To my mother and to the memory of my father. To the memory of Michael E. "Spike" Miller, M.D., mentor and colleague. To my friends and family who watched me live through my illness and recovery. To Kris, whose encouragement and support allowed me to write about the experience.

"It is quite true what Philosophy says: that Life must be understood backwards. But that makes one forget the other saying: that it must be lived—forwards. The more one ponders this, the more it comes to mean that life in the temporal existence never becomes quite intelligible, precisely because at no moment can I find complete quiet to take the backward-looking position."

—Søren Kierkegaard, journal entry, 1843

"Pain is inevitable; suffering is optional."

—anonymous ultrarunner

CONTENTS

True autobiography cannot contain direct quotes, unless one constantly carries an instrument like a tape recorder. Instead, this is a memoir, a recollection, and a remembrance. I do not intend the quoted statements in this book to be taken as absolute truths. Their essence, however, is true to my memory. I have elected to change the names of many of the people in this book. For some, it is to protect their privacy. As individuals, however, they will see themselves in these pages.

My Own Medicine

1

I awake to the night as out of a bad dream, suddenly aware of the darkened room around me. The soft lights in their louvered recesses along the baseboard filter a reluctant glow into the darkness, allowing me to see the bare wall beyond the bed, the blank ceiling above me. I can hear, from behind the partially pulled curtain between us, the stuttered snoring of my elderly roommate. I try to raise my left arm and feel the pull of the adhesive tape, which secures my intravenous line. The door to the small bathroom on my right sways in the half-light, and I feel myself quietly weakening as I will myself into sleep. But there will be no sleep, at least not now. The jolt that has ripped me from sleep is my fever, now rocketing once more to the upper reaches of the thermometer, the sweat building beneath my skin, my muscles about to start the shivering that has been the focal point of my nights now for more than two weeks. With my free hand I reach for the cord and press the small button to summon the nurse. Lying back, I mentally prepare myself for what I know will happen in the next several minutes. As if to mock my preparation, my teeth begin to chatter, now in small spurts, then within moments, in full throttle, threatening to break my jaw, gnash through my own tongue, while my arms, shoulders, legs all shake with a false cold, now uncontrollable even with the meager remnants of a strength that has ebbed from me on a daily basis, perhaps never to return. My roommate, oblivious to my trembling horizontal dance, sleeps deep within his own cancer-driven nightmare. I close my eyes, trying to stop the fever, the chills, the river of sweat that now pours off me, soaking into the bedsheets. The light in the room fades.

"Dr. Kurland . . ."

I look up at the nurse, dressed cleanly and efficiently. Her face is fragile, worried, her eyes somber. She'd seen me several hours ago, near midnight, as she started her shift. Back then, she'd told me to try to have a better night than the previous dozen or more. Her look now reflects our combined disappointment.

"It looks like you're having another chill . . . put this under your tongue." She hands me the electronic thermometer. I hold the palm-sized box with its digital display and put the plastic-sheathed probe into my mouth, holding my jaw as still as possible to avoid biting the thing. I curl down into a ball, pulling the sheets around me and watch the light on the dial spin madly, as the reading screams past the normal 37 degrees Celsius before slowing and finally stopping well above 40, which is 104 degrees Fahrenheit, pretty warm for a baby, but downright hot for a forty-two year old. I take the plastic protector off the thermometer tip, holding it as if it were some prize I've won (highest temperature on the ward tonight?), and hand the rest of the device back to the nurse. She gives me some medication and a glass of water, and I blandly take the tablets.

For an unknown reason (the fever? delirium?) I brighten: "Hey," to the nurse, "do you know the difference between oral and rectal thermometers?"

She looks blankly back at me. "Uh . . . I don't know, doctor. What's the difference?"

"The taste," I cackle as she rolls her eyes upward.

"Very funny."

I am suddenly very tired from shaking, but the intermittent waves of unwanted and undirected movement continue to pass through me.

"Let's let that work," she says. "If this is like other nights, you should feel better in a half hour or so. At least they stopped ordering blood cultures every time you spiked." She talks familiarly with me, for she knows I understand that *spike* means the sudden burst of fever which, when plotted on a daily temperature sheet, gives it the look of a mountain arising from the topographic plateau of 98.6 at which we all normally live.

I lie back on the bed, feeling the medicine take hold, slowing my shivering, bringing me back to euthermy. I feel as though I've run ten miles on a humid day in June, which, in fact, it is: June of 1988. But there is to be no running for me, at least not now, not tonight, just as there has not been any for the last two weeks or more. Perhaps, I tell myself, I'll run again, later, when I'm better. Or perhaps, I tell myself, I'm not going to get better; perhaps I'm going to die from this fever that drains my body and soul, this fever that has suddenly appeared in the midst of my treatment. The soaked sheets gather me into their grip as if foretelling a shroud.

The nurse sees me in the wet white linen as she bustles quietly into the room with an armful of clean and dry sheets. "Now, if we're feeling better, perhaps we should change the sheets." Why, I wonder to myself, do nurses, and doctors for that matter, use the pronoun *we* so much? My enviable roommate still snores in his bed only a few feet from mine.

I pull myself out of bed and uneasily stand up. I try to help as my bed is stripped, but I am so weak I can barely lift the pillow.

"Gee, this stuff is kinda wet," the nurse says.

"Kinda is an understatement. Maybe I could wring them out for you. Now I finally know what patients mean when they say they have night sweats and fevers." I hobble the two feet into the bathroom, close the door, and change into dry pajamas, an act that itself takes several minutes because I have to stop after each stage of undressing and dressing just to rest. I shuffle back out and watch the final stages of new sheet placement as I suddenly began to feel better, drier, more awake. I know it's only temporary. Like all the previous nights in the hospital, my shivering has stopped almost as fast as it started; I can feel my temperature, so high a few minutes ago, drifting toward normal. I hope that I will be allowed to stay with the rest of humanity at 98.6; but, as I'd learned on many other nights, uncertainty is my constant companion.

The bed is ready for my cooler body, and I lie down slowly, carefully, as if afraid I might somehow shatter in the movement. I look back up at the nurse, then over at the pile of sheets and pajamas, looking like a misplaced snowbank against the far wall. The night is more than half over, and I just want my illness to end. I want to have something else to think about, talk about.

"How did the Pirates do tonight?" I'd moved to Pittsburgh less than four months before, yet here I am caught up in the team, its ups and downs, its young players all in such good health.

"I heard they lost. The Reds scored twice in the bottom of the eighth."

"Oh well . . . there's always tomorrow." For some, I think. Maybe I'm one of them. No, I'm probably not one of them. For me, there are only a few tomorrows left, I'm somehow sure.

"How long have you been in here, Dr. Kurland?" The nurse startles me back to the reality of the room, the hospital, the night.

"I don't know . . . two weeks? . . . two and a half weeks? . . . it's all been one long night, make that one long nightmare, for me."

"And they still don't know why you're having fevers? Haven't they done a lot of tests?" I laugh the cynical, half-hearted laugh of the condemned man told one last joke on his way to the gallows.

"No . . . they don't know . . . and it's not for lack of trying to find out. I mean, they've probably taken a quart of blood, X-rayed me to where I'll probably start glowing in the dark pretty soon, done enough nuclear scans for some third world countries to consider competitive bidding for my remains . . . all sorts of stuff . . ." I drop my voice a notch. "Maybe they'll find out when I . . . I don't know . . ."

I'm about to say *when I die.* For I am convinced that I am slowly wasting away, sweating and burning away my life, and that this, the summer of 1988, will be my last. Every day, Dr. Ellis, my hematologist, comes in with a cheery greeting, which I try, but fail, to match.

"Geoff, your blood counts look great. I'm not sure why you're still having fevers, but I'm convinced it's not your leukemia. Nothing's really turned up, but we'll keep looking. It must be an infection . . . but . . ."

"Where?" I finish his sentence. "Or what?" I offer.

He stands in silent agreement with me for a moment. "I talked to Dr. Habermann again."

"At Mayo?" Habermann is the hematologist who'd helped diagnose my disease. "He got any new ideas?"

"He's still worried about atypical TB . . . but we can't seem to find it."

Atypical TB is all too familiar to a specialist in lung diseases, even if he's a specialist in pediatric lung diseases like me. Rather than a single type of germ, atypical TB is actually a collection of microorganisms related, but not identical, to what we call tuberculosis. Atypical TB can cause severe illness in those susceptible to it, but few have been susceptible until recently, when AIDS provided a population of patients unable to fend off the normally docile atypical TB, allowing it to wreak havoc on the defenseless bodies of its victims. What's worse, atypical TB is, if anything, less treatable than tuberculosis.

Ellis sees my look; he knows that I can put two and two together. "Your HIV test was negative . . . you don't have AIDS. But your immunity has been affected by the leukemia and by the chemo. That's why we held the drug. Well, we'll keep looking. I hope you have a better night."

"So do I."

But here it is, another one of those not-better nights, another after-midnight-sweat-and-fever show, melting my flesh. The bed now is crisp, cool, and I am looking at the ceiling as the nurse carries the old sheets from the room and turns down the lights. As the room darkens I feel for the cord with the call button, just to make sure it's there. I hear again the rhythmic snoring next to my bed. Disjointed and minute parts of the previous day come wandering into my consciousness: a brief visit from a coworker, and a call from Karin, her worried and loving voice nearly cracking over the line from Sacramento as I lied and told her I would be fine, telling her she should stay there instead of coming out to be with me, to see me. I don't want anyone to see me, really. The thought of being seen in my sad sick state: my weight down several pounds, my face lined as never before, the unpredictability of my febrile shakes are all too difficult to take and nearly unthinkable to have witnessed. No, I tell myself, it's better for me to hide in my hospital bed and hope I either get back to my previous "health" in the midst of leukemia or just continue to waste away until death takes me. I drift down now into the bed, into the sleep that I so desperately wish for, into the dream that I want this whole thing to be. I can feel my past rush up to meet me, to tell me that this nightmare is in fact real, even though it began with a single quick and remarkably innocent X ray only fifteen months before, in March of 1987. I can remember it as well as if it were occurring on this very evening, another night of sweated, shivered agony in which I find myself trapped, a prisoner of my own illness.

I enter the large room that holds the massive X-ray equipment and remove the long, white coat containing my two stethoscopes, symbols of my physicianship. I strip off my shirt and tie and stand, far more than half-naked in my own mind, before the film holder in the room. The technician has raised the holder so that the top is just at the level of my upwardly thrust jaw.

"Put your chest against this," she says, indicating the box holding the film. The X rays will enter me from behind, go through my chest, and hit the film contained within the holder. She hides herself behind a shielded screen within arm's reach of the control panel.

"Take a breath . . . now let it out." I do as I am told. "Take another . . . hold it." I hear the sound of a soft bell as the X ray is taken. I am turned sideways, with my arms out of the way of the X-ray beam, repeating the process for a side view. The technician takes the film cassettes into the darkroom to process them.

I hurriedly put my clothes back on, working my way back into my white coat while I wait the ninety seconds the processing takes. I still have a lot to do: lectures to prepare for a conference in a few days, rounds to make, residents to teach. And now this X ray, taking up more of my precious time. I'd already put off having the X ray taken for several weeks because I had too many patients in the clinic or on the ward, lectures to give, rounds to make. But here I am at last, hoping the X ray will reveal the cause of the recurrent sharp pain in my left chest. Maybe, I tell myself, it'll also explain that nagging cold and cough I had a few months ago. Perhaps I really had broken a rib when I coughed during one of my long training runs. As a matter of fact, I convince myself that a fractured rib would fully explain the pain, especially after the weeks of aspirin didn't do anything except make me bleed excessively every time I cut myself shaving. The bleeding, I tell myself, was only because of the aspirin, which makes it harder for the blood to clot. None of this—the pain, the cough, the cold, the bleeding—none of it had completely stopped my running. But I know something is wrong, and that something is slowing me down.

Dave, the radiology resident, had squinted sidelong at me in the near darkness of the processing room when I told him of the pain and asked for the X ray of my chest. But his brow furrowed, his gaze narrowed, and his jaw dropped when I told him that the pain had been sufficient to start to interfere with my running. Just as everyone at the medical center knows me as Dr. K., a nickname I've had since my own internship, I am equally marked as the physician who runs the year round, at night after work, carrying his beeper, in any weather. I am an acknowledged nut, running in the rain, singing on rounds, trading bad jokes with my patients, residents, and students.

Not only am I somewhat crazy, I'm tough, I keep reminding myself. It takes more than just a little pain to stop my running. Only four weeks ago, despite the pain in my chest, I did a fifty-mile run and qualified for my ultimate goal, my personal Holy Grail: the Western States Endurance Run. All the thousands of miles I've run since I first started running as a teenager have been, unbeknownst to me, the physical and mental training for that one-hundred-mile run over the Sierra Nevada mountains, on trails over peaks, into canyons, and across the icy American River. Now, after all those years, I am at last ready to face the challenge that will test my physical limits, perhaps allowing me to see a hidden part of myself. Nothing, not even the pain in my ribs or the fatigue in my legs, would be able to stop me from doing that run, I tell myself. Nothing.

Dave and I wait for the films to appear. A beeper goes off; as usual, it's mine. I pick up a nearby phone and tell the resident that I'll be up on the pediatric ward in just a few minutes, and we can see and discuss my patient together. The X-ray area is dark and quiet, and I savor the near silence, the hum of equipment, and the smell of developer fluid.

"Dr. K.," Dave revives me from my reverie, "your film is coming out of the processor. Want to take a look?"

He pulls the black pieces of film from the large, purring box. They are dark wings flapping in his hands as we cross to a view box up on the wall. Dave puts them up against the fluorescent light as we both peer at the X rays.

He is silent. I swallow hard and feel my throat suddenly become dry; my breath chokes in small bursts.

"Are you sure those are my films?"

"Donna, are these here Dr. K.'s X rays?" Dave asks hopefully.

"Only ones in there" is the reply from around the corner. They are mine and mine alone, the shadows before me flying out from the view box into my eyes, which stare with disbelief. I take a step back, then one forward, as if to erase what I see by refocusing the view. Then I look away, snatch a breath of air, and turn to Dave.

"Well, well, isn't this interesting."

"No," he says, "I don't think so."

My rib is fine. In fact, there's nothing wrong with that side of my chest, the area of the pain I've been having. But there, right there in the upper central part of my chest, is a large, fist-sized blotch of white, a mass, a *something*. It pushes my windpipe far to the right, kinking it. My spine, as if in religious devotion, genuflects with a soft curve pointing to my left, as if it were bowing toward the white mass filling the upper part of my chest.

My breath, previously in short snatches, now is frozen in my throat, and my eyes glaze over as I attempt without success to smile through the fear that grips me. What the hell is this . . . this *thing*? What is going on with me? Then, quite suddenly, I realize who I am, into whom I have been transformed at the moment I saw the white shadow on my film. And although I can't possibly know it completely, my new persona is taking over as it melds itself unalterably into my being. I am no longer the doctor. I am the person with the disease.

It is several hours later, and in the midst of the nebulous fog of fear, I stand at my desk and speak into the telephone.

"Hey, Dad, how ya doin'?" I ask in as normal a voice as I can muster under the circumstances.

"Fine. Fine, just too busy," my father says. "What's going on? How's Sacramento treating you? Why are you calling me at the office?" He senses something amiss, as I almost always call home in the evening, when I can speak to him and my mother. My mind is blank for a moment, then comes back, detouring again to the radiology department, where my X rays had been the subject of a quick discussion by the members of the faculty, including Dr. Palmer, the recognized chest expert. I had stood by his side and tried to appear clinical, as if the X rays were someone else's and I was the physician taking care of the patient.

"Well," Palmer had said in his near English South African accent, "the mass is in the anterior mediastinum. Look how smooth the borders are." He pointed at the sharp, white edges of the mass, lying, as he said, in the front part of the narrow space between my lungs, just beneath my sternum.

"It's likely to be benign, just by its appearance, something in the thymus, a benign thymoma. Of course, it's possible it's something more worrisome like a teratoma or lymphoma, but it doesn't look like that to me," Palmer continued as he turned away from the view board and looked up at me. His face softened. "What are you going to do, Geoff?" He asked, his voice a bit softer, less assured, more concerned.

"I guess I'll call my father. He's on staff at the Mayo Clinic. I think it would be easier to get it taken care of back home in Minnesota, get home cooking for the recuperation, get a few days off away from here." I smiled a bit even though I was roiling with uncertainty and fear.

Palmer and the others had chuckled. They knew that if I were a patient at the medical center I'd be inundated with visitors and wouldn't get any rest. I'd probably be expected back at work right after discharge. They knew what I knew: I did need a rest from the relentless pace of my work, where more and more patients and parents expected more and more of my time and expertise.

"From what I've heard, taking out something like this," he gestured again toward the films, "is pretty straightforward. It shouldn't be too big a deal. You'll be back at the salt mines here in no time."

I thanked him, took the films, and headed out of the department.

Moments later I have forgotten all but the barest essentials of the discussion: anterior mediastinal mass, probably benign. *Probably* is a comforting word to the physician pronouncing it, but not to the patient. I'd used *probably* all the time with patients and their parents, thinking that it would suffice to allay their fears. Now I realize how wrong I'd been all those years. Patients don't want *probably*, they want *certainly*, even if it is unreasonable to expect it. One can always hope for the unattainable rather than just accept the given. I am being forced to accept the given, and the physician in me tries to do just that: accept. The patient rebels and wants much more.

I am confused, lost, and fearful, finding it nearly impossible to concentrate on the plan I'd set out for myself, on the next steps to take, on telling my father the news. And now I have to tell him, as I look again at my desk, then at the phone in my hand, and hear the breath of my father as he waits for me to speak.

"Dad, I need your help. I've had some pain in my chest I thought was from a fractured rib. So I got a chest X ray and . . ." I pause.

"Yes? What did it show?"

"Dad, I've got an anterior mediastinal mass. I want someone at Mayo to look at me. I'll probably need some sort of workup, surgery, or something. If I need surgery, I'd rather get it back home and recuperate there." I blurt it all out in one breath. Then I hold my breath and wait for his reply.

There is silence, as if my father has been struck. Then his voice, now softer.

"Who do you want to see? I'll set it up if you tell me who."

My father is an epidemiologist, a physician who seeks the causes of a disease by searching for common factors in people affected by the disease. My father is famous, a world authority on the epidemiology of various neurological diseases, including Lou Gehrig's disease and Alzheimer's disease. But as famous as he might be in his area of expertise, my father spends most of his time with patient charts and records rather than with patients. His expertise in epidemiology is overshadowed by my own particular expertise in pediatric lung disease, and I deal daily with chest problems in children: cystic fibrosis, asthma, and tumors. It is not lost on my father that even though he could tell me how common or rare the possible explanations of my chest mass are, I probably know which Mayo Clinic physician should see me. And the irony that I, a chest specialist, have a tumor in my chest, is lost on neither of us.

"Ed Rosenow. He's my choice."

"Ed Rosenow? He's in thoracic medicine, right? Do you know him?"

"No, but I know of him. He's got a great reputation."

Both parts are true: I've never met Ed Rosenow, but I've heard enough about him to know that he is the right physician for me.

"Okay. I'll call him and set something up. I'll get back to you by this evening. You'll be home?"

"Sure. I'll be home after I . . . ," and I pause. Will I be home after I go for my run? Am I going to run? Is this . . . mass . . . going to interfere with my training for the one-hundred-mile run? My father didn't mention my running, though he may have thought that was my reason for pausing. I pull my eyes shut. "I'll be home tonight."

"Okay. I'll call you later. Let me get going on this stuff." He's all business now, just as he is when he has a paper to finish or a grant to write. Or just like I am on a training run, or when I talk with parents about a difficult diagnosis affecting their child.

"Okay, Dad. Thanks." I hang the phone up and look out the window. It's late in the afternoon. I still have a lot of work to do, and I have to let my partner, Ruth, know that she'll have to take care of the patients for me during my absence. And, saving the hardest for last, I have to tell Karin that I'll be going back to Minnesota. I turn to the room, take a breath, and decide that I'll run before my father's call tonight.

Finishing rounds, finalizing my lecture plans, and arranging for patient coverage are all relatively easy: many things are easy to do if one is numb at the time of the doing. But some things cannot be anesthetized away, and I have indeed saved the most difficult for last. I walk up to the door of the small pharmacy on the sixth floor of the medical center, as I've done so many times before. I see Karin sitting in front of the large glass-fronted sterile box known as a hood, preparing an intravenous solution for a patient. The pharmacist in charge ushers me into the small alcove of the pharmacy and leaves the two of us as alone as possible given that we are in plain sight of everyone in the pharmacy.

"Hey, Karin," I say, again in as normal a voice as possible. But it's no use, for she sees my eyes.

"What's the matter?" she asks in her clearly Minnesotan voice, itself somewhat out of place in the middle of California. She smiles as she says it, knowing that just by smiling she usually gets me to cheer up.

"I've got to talk to you. When you're finished with that." I look at the solution she's concocting.

"Okay. Just a second. Steve, I'm going to take a little break." Steve, the pharmacist, is used to her taking short breaks when I come by.

We've been seeing each other for nearly two years, since the time of her separation from her husband, which had occurred at the time Ann, with whom I'd lived for so many years, left me. Karin and I have carried within each of us the scars of those shattered relationships. With Ann's departure, I had felt abandoned, wary about any form of commitment. I still hate being alone, but I'm even more afraid of finding myself alone because of someone else's decision to leave me. This mind-set keeps me alone. Although she never told me any specifics, I could tell that Karin's marriage had been far from perfect. And although she knows that she did the right thing in separating from him, she's now struggling with a low-paying job and joint custody of two young children. Much of the time we've been seeing each other was spent just listening to each other, helping each other understand our own fears of relationships, of failure. It took a long time for both of us, finally, to trust each other and ourselves, to reach an understanding built on love, trust, and time. And it took some time for me to accept that Karin's children were more important to her than I was. Despite that, or perhaps because of it, because of the strength of her character that it revealed, I had finally seen that Karin was the woman with whom I could share my life.

"So, what's up?" She asks as we slowly walk down the hospital corridor. She places her hand in mine, and I can smell her perfume.

I am afraid to look at her. I walk with her slowly, deliberately, and tell her what's up. She grips my hand tighter, finally pulling me to a stop, turning toward me, her mouth agape, as I lay out the story of the X ray, the mass, and my decision to fly back to Minnesota for the all-too-likely surgery. She searches my face for clues, but there are none except for an awkward smile, a catching of breath. She can't feel my stomach churn or my knees quake.

"Do you want me to come with you? I could stay with my folks." In one of the ironies of fate, even though we'd met in Sacramento, Karin had grown up in Austin, Minnesota, only forty-five miles from Rochester, home of the Mayo Clinic and my parents.

"No, not now. First, we don't know what this thing is. If it's just a little benign mass, it'll take a pretty easy operation, so they say. Then I'll be right back here. I'm not going to get too upset until I've got a reason to be upset," I lie. "I think you should wait here."

"But you know I'll go there if you want. You know that, don't you?"

"Of course I do. And you know I'd ask if I wanted you to go, don't you?"

"Well, would you?"

I am silent. She knows me all too well. In every relationship I've ever been in, I've always tried to appear self-sufficient. I never asked too much of Ann, for that, I told myself, might burden her. I was always quick to provide her with her "space," as we said back in the '60s and early '70s. Initially, it could be seen as very giving, but in reality was a fantastic lie, a way to avoid true intimacy. By not taking from anyone else, including someone who had been as important as Ann or, now, Karin, I avoided having to reciprocate, to fully give of myself, to allow someone in to my thoughts and feelings. Ann had known it, and she left after so many years of being shut out of all but my surface life. Karin, herself fearful of giving too much because of the pain she'd been through, had easily seen the same fear reflected in me as we started to date. But, I tell myself, this is a different time. "Okay," Karin smiles, accepting my unspoken insecurity. "You know that I'll be here if you need me. All you have to do is ask. But what do you think is going to happen?"

"I'm not sure. Like I said, if this thing is benign, and it looks that way, I should be getting surgery, which won't be too bad. Even though the idea of having my chest cracked is not something that sounds like fun. But if that's what has to be done, then I think I should take care of it as soon as possible. And then I'll get back here to you and to work.

"I'd be lying if I said I wasn't scared. But right now I've got to see what this is going to turn out to be. I should know more in a few days."

"You won't be leaving for a while yet. You know where I am." Karin looks at her watch, signaling that she has to get back to the pharmacy to work. We walk back down the corridor, and she turns to me just before we open the door.

"I meant what I said, about coming out there if you want. Geoff, I love you. You know that, don't you?"

"Yes, I do. And I love you. Do you believe me?"

She smiles and nods even as she turns and walks back into the pharmacy with a determined step. It is true that we both hide our feelings well, for the most part, but also true that we can read each other well enough to make it difficult to hide.

I manage a half-hearted run of only a few miles in the evening and am at home when the phone rings.

"Geoff," my father says, "it's all set for next Monday morning. When will you get here?"

"Sunday. I've got some talks to give on Saturday." I tell him the flight numbers.

"Okay. We'll pick you up. Mom wants to talk with you, then I've got some other details to work out with you. Here's Mom. She's on the other line. There, Mim?" he asks.

"I'm on, Len." Her voice is soft, with bravery and fear mixed in equal amounts. "Hi, babe. How are you doing? Dad's filled me in. I've already started cooking. Any requests?"

"Hi, Mom. Yes, chicken soup. Lots of it." I want the Jewish mother's cure for everything. I want it to really work, to be magic and take away any need for surgery. And my mother's chicken soup with matzo balls, taught to her by her mother, even if not medically up to that challenge, was still the best soup in the world to my unprejudiced mind.

"Chicken soup? You know I've always got that. I meant, anything else? Brisket? Chicken? You name it, you've got it."

Speaking now, I can see my mother, her ample body in a rayon housedress, standing before the stove, the focal point of the kitchen. Her slightly graying, formerly red-brown hair (a gift from her red-haired father) no doubt pulled back in a tight bun. Her eyes, I can sense, are still cheery, although a little red, not from crying, but from worry, which seems to have a similar effect.

"Chicken soup is the only thing that comes to mind right now, Mom."

"How do you feel?" my mother asks. She wants more than physical descriptions, I know. Although my mind is confused, I try my best to supply an answer.

" 'Weird' is the word that comes to mind. I mean, I thought I'd hurt a rib, so that's why I got the X ray. I don't feel too bad. You know, I just ran tonight, and I didn't feel any pain or anything, actually. Maybe that's part of it; I just don't feel too much of anything. I guess I'm sorta numb. I tell myself that it can't be that bad. After all, I did just do that fifty-mile run a month ago."

"Do you think that's a good idea, all that running?" my father says from the other line. "I mean, do you think it might be related to this mass?"

"What? We don't even know what the mass is, Dad. It's probably benign, anyway. No, I'm not going to stop running, at least not right now."

My father, even though he swims nearly every day of his life, has never been especially in favor of my own addiction to running. He knows that I have thrown myself into it even more, have increased my training distance, and he thinks the idea of running fifty miles, not to mention one hundred miles, approaches insanity. He also, as a scientist, wonders what effect long-distance running might have on the body's ability to fight off infections, cancer, or any of the other thousands of potentially life-threatening obstacles placed in the way of daily living. But to his credit, this time he chooses not to push too hard.

"Okay. You know what's best."

"Yes," my mother agrees, "let him alone about this. First, we'll find out what this thing is," referring to the mass as if it were an inanimate object sitting within me rather than something that is actually alive, which, in fact, might be derived from my own tissues.

The three of us finish our talk about plans for my return. Then my father speaks once more.

"Geoff, Rosenow thinks you should try to get a CT scan. He says it will probably be easier for you to get it there and just bring it out with you. The scanners here are pretty booked up, you know. Anyway, do you think you can get that taken care of?"

"Sure. I talked with the chest radiology specialist here," now remembering more of that afternoon's conversation with Palmer, "and he doesn't think a CT will add much. But, if Rosenow wants it, I'll get it."

"Okay. I'll talk with you tomorrow or so. Let me know if you need help making your travel plans." My father could teach a few things to most travel agents.

"Right, Dad. Okay. I'll talk to you both tomorrow and let you know what's going on. And I'll see you soon. Thanks for the help."

"Okay, babe," my mother says. "We love you."

"Thanks, Mom. I love you, too. Talk to you tomorrow." I hang up the phone slowly, more slowly prepare for bed, and sleep fitfully, awakening at least once in the darkness to ask myself if it is all a ghastly dream.

I walk into my office and see my chest X rays sitting on my desk. The dream of yesterday stings back as reality. Carrying my X rays, I walk across the street to the medical center and into the CT scan area of the radiology department. Rich, another resident, is assigned to CT; I quickly explain my situation to him, showing him the X ray. The scan is arranged for the afternoon.

I wander up to the ward to make rounds. There is added silence around the ward desk; the nurses look at me and look away. I grab a chart from the rack. Alma, the ward resident, is sitting next to me as I scan the notes.

"Dr. K. . . ." Alma looks over at me, then down at her work.

"Hi. What's up?"

"I . . . I mean we or somebody heard that you have something . . . a chest mass or something . . ."

"Yeah. Looks benign. I feel fine. It's probably nothing. I'm going to get it taken care of and then be back here in no time. Don't worry, I'll be great. How're things with my kids?"

"Uh . . . okay . . . nothin' major overnight . . . What do they think you've got?"

"I don't know. They don't know. We'll all know soon enough when it's removed. Now, I guess I'd better make rounds."

At least I know that the greased grapevine of the hospital still works. And here I am, hiding again behind my work. Here I am, keeping my fear inside. But, I tell myself, what is there really to be afraid of? After all, this . . . mass is probably benign. They'll take it out, and I'll be done with it. Right? I tell myself. Anyway, this whole thing is so nebulous; how can I possibly know how to deal with it? And my patients await me, just as they always do. And I choose them first, just as I always do.

The business of rounds is something I've done now for years. Going from room to room, seeing each patient for whom I am the attending physician, the physician who directs the patient's treatment. Also on rounds, I see all the patients for whom I am a consultant, cases where my expertise in pulmonary problems has led the patient's attending physician to seek my advice. I look through the chart of each patient before going into the room. I speak quietly with the nurses to find out how each night has gone.

I feel suddenly tired, then just as suddenly ferociously awake, even before I start rounds. I realize how my own restless sleep of last night rekindled my memories of internship, when any sleep I got was minimal and interrupted. The sleep deprivation of last night has left me strangely and acutely awake, but I know I could just as suddenly lose my focus and fall asleep in a moment.

Before I walk into Timmy's room, I hear his cough, the hacking, repetitive, deep, ripping, and ultimately unsatisfying cough of someone with cystic fibrosis. The thick secretions in his lungs fail to yield to the cough, and he tries to raise them again and again. I enter the room, which has a predawn illumination because of the nearly closed curtains, as if Timmy were in hiding while yet spying on the brightening day of the outside world. His mother, recently awakened and wearing a worn bathrobe, lies on her side in a cot by his bed. Her son's cough is so much a part of her life that she seems to barely hear it now. Her brown hair is disheveled from her own restless sleep of the night before. She looks back and forth from Timmy to me as she rouses herself with the fatigued body of one who has lost too much sleep for too many years. Timmy is tiny, looking more like a thin five-year-old than the nine-year-old boy he is. His eyes are very blue, standing out in a face nearly as pale as alabaster beneath his thin, blond hair.

"Hi, Timmy. How you doing? How's your cough?"

"Oh, not too bad, Dr. K. I'm starting to feel better."

His mother gives me a knowing glance of only partial agreement with her son.

"Well, Timmy, you know you've only been here a few days. I know you'll feel even better after those antibiotics have had time to kill some of those germs in your lungs. How's your IV?" I ask, looking at the taped needle inserted into the skin of his dowel-thin, pale left arm.

"Oh, it's not too bad. They had to change it yesterday, but I got Margie to put it in. She's real good." He pauses, looked at his mother, then looks back at me. "Say, Dr. K., are you sick? I heard you were sick. You don't look sick."

I hold my breath. Timmy looks away again, half smiling at his mother, who flushes as she slaps a sharp look toward her son.

"Timmy!" She turns to me with a sheepish look as she sits up. "We just happened to overhear some of the nurses talking, Dr. K. I know it's none of our business . . . but you are our doctor . . . and . . . well, we just heard and . . . I'm sorry, we probably shouldn't be asking about this."

"No. It's all right. You can ask. I've got nothing to hide."

I've always tried to tell the truth to my patients about their diseases, no matter what pain the truth led to, and I've always tried to help my patients through the pain of the truth. I've always told my students and myself that honesty with patients (as with everyone) is ultimately the best policy. I've not always succeeded, either in telling the entire truth or in minimizing the pain. But, I'm not going to be a hypocrite, masking my illness in a veil of white or not-so-white lies. I turn to Timmy.

"Yes, I have a problem. It's something in my chest. I'll probably need some surgery, but I figure I'll be back here working very soon. Dr. McDonald will be taking care of you while I'm away. But as I just said, I'll be back as soon as I can." I'm not smiling, and Timmy gives me a serious look.

"Is there anything we can do?" his mother asks. "I mean, I don't know what we can do, but . . . you know, we want you to get well soon."

"It's funny," I say, looking out a corner of the window, "but I feel well. The whole thing is pretty weird because I don't really feel too sick. But," and I turn to face her son, "now that I think of it, there is something you can help me with, Timmy."

He looks up brightly, smiling at the chance to help.

"Timmy, do you have any advice for me? I mean, if I get sick and need an operation or something?"

He sits on the bed, his face lifted up, his eyes half closed, gathering the wisdom of his many hospitalizations, the burden of an unfair disease that has taken its toll from his beleaguered body. As I wait expectantly, his mother smiles gently at her son.

"Well, Dr. K. . . . I'd say," his look is as serious as the news anchorman, "you should make sure somebody good starts your IV . . . and watch out for the hospital food."

The three of us laugh at the anticlimax of the comment, at the obvious oxymoron of "hospital food." But then I look down at him, now serious.

"Okay, Timmy, thanks. That sounds like good advice to me. Now, may I listen to your breathing?" I pull out my stethoscope for the first time.

In the afternoon, I go back to radiology to get the CT scan. I strip off my shirt, don the hospital gown (one of the least flattering pieces of clothing ever designed), and lie down upon the narrow table as the technician straps me into place. I feel the hard coldness of the platform and shiver as it slowly moves into a large ring standing nearly seven feet high like an ungainly high-tech version of an upright doughnut.

CT stands for "computed tomography" and is nothing more than an X-ray picture of a thin slice of the body. The ring into which I am being moved houses the equivalent of several dozen X-ray machines and, opposite each one, a scintillation counter, or X-ray detector. For each image or slice, multiple X rays (each with a minute amount of radiation) are done and, with the aid of the scintillation counters and a very fancy computer, a thin slice of the body is reproduced as an X-ray picture. With the modern scanners, an entire slice is done in only a second or two, and a scan of the entire chest can be done in about ten or fifteen minutes. One advantage of the CT scan is that it not only shows the internal body structures but it can also show the different densities of those structures to a degree not possible with conventional X rays. It is to look at the mass in my chest, to see if it has an internal structure that might give a hint as to its nature.

I lie in the scanner, feeling cold, alone, and helpless. The lights in the room dim, and I can hear the fans cooling the computer in the next room. I can hear the air in my trachea as it twists its way past that detour, the interloper in my chest. I can hear the blood pounding in my chest, near what I know is the mass. And I hear the whooshing sound of the intercom, and the technician's voice, waking me and returning me again to the cold reality of the table, the scanner, the dimly lit room in which I cry inside for help and find myself alone.

"Dr. Kurland. Can you hear me? We're going to start now."

I mumble that I'm ready but realize they probably can't hear me very well at all.

"Take a breath in. Let it out. Take one in and hold it." It is as it was yesterday (or was it today?) when I had the simple chest X ray. The entire table slowly but smoothly moves into the scanner, the length of my chest, then just as smoothly moves out again. An initial X ray looking at my entire chest is quickly done. Then, over the next ten minutes, a series of slices, each requiring a single breath being held, each with the table a little further into the ring of the scanner, is done. And for each I hold my breath, hoping that the slice would be the last one, that it would show there is nothing wrong with my chest, that it is all a big mistake, that the initial chest X ray wasn't actually mine, that I can just get out of there and go back to work, to Karin, to running, and not have to worry about anything.

Although I know I'm trying to appear nonchalant to the CT technicians, I am paralyzed with the fear that the scan might show something unexpected, something about the mass in my chest that would suggest a more malignant diagnosis. I lie there at the mercy of the scanner, the technician, the radiologists, and the mass within me. Any importance I place upon myself is subjugated to the extra tissue hiding in my chest, and nothing that I can do will change it now. It is all beyond my power and control. As a patient, I can see that my life will be directed by my illness on the one hand and those trying to diagnose and cure it on the other. Neither of those, I am beginning to feel, have to answer to me, and there is only one side with whom I can even attempt to reason.

As I realize the lack of control I am confronted with, I see, much to my embarrassment, that even though I am a physician, my illness, if that is what it is, is very much a mystery to me. Even though I know (or think I know) that a CT scan probably won't add much information, the fact that Ed Rosenow wants me to get one worries me. Is there something I'm not being told or don't know? Is there something else to worry about? Why don't I know why the CT scan was suggested?

Then it strikes me, as I lie there in the scanner, that perhaps "they" are lying to me to be kind, to hide from me a truth I shouldn't know. I now know what patients have been talking about when they would refer to me and my colleagues at the hospital as "you doctors." For all these years, many of my patients had felt it was "them" against "us," the physicians. For the first time, I can understand where that had come from, what it meant, and, most importantly, what it feels like to feel that way.

Are they lying to me? And if so, why? I'd faced dilemmas as a physician: torn between having to tell parents the truth that their child was dying and trying to maintain hope and a positive outlook in the face of death. I would find myself asking if giving the entire story, complete with the full medical details, was in the best interests of a family. A lot of those decisions had been painful, and I usually tried to do both: tell the truth, but allow for hope. In some cases, parents thanked me for it; sometimes, they resented and hated being told any part of the truth that might hurt. Underneath it all, they may have felt I was being more than a little presumptuous to decide how best to present information to them. That last thought, the very idea that the doctor can decide just how much the parent can take, is the arrogance of power that could easily be mistaken and misused. Even the glimmer of possibility that I might be the patient on the receiving end of that power is terrifying, humbling, and, in the end, somewhat edifying. All the same, I can feel myself beginning to hate the idea of being treated like a patient.

Further and further I go into the scanner as the X ray slices down my chest. I feel shut in by the ring of the scanner and realize for the first time just how coldly claustrophobic the imposing piece of machinery is. After fifteen scans or so, the table moves me out.

I lie still in the silence, waiting for someone to come out and loosen the straps holding me to the table, to tell me I can leave. After a few minutes lying there, I screw my head around and look to my right. There, behind the thick glass in the control area, several of the staff are sitting, looking at my scan on the computer screen, talking with one another. I close my eyes feigning sleep, hoping I really will go to sleep, perhaps to awaken somewhere else. Rich suddenly appears at my side with a paper cup filled with orange liquid.

"Geoff, drink this contrast." He hands me the cup.

"What? Why?" I ask. Contrast is a liquid that appears dense (white) on X rays, and drinking it will outline my stomach and gut, nowhere near the mass in my chest. Why do they need contrast in my stomach?

"Your spleen is enlarged. We want to scan your abdomen," Rich explains.

He may as well kick me in my abdomen. The mass in my chest isn't alone. It has company in my belly: my enlarged spleen, an organ involved in diseases like leukemia, lymphoma, or a variety of unusual infections. I tell myself that we can live without our spleens, that perhaps it is enlarged because of some infection, that maybe it won't be a big deal. And then I tell myself the probable truth: that it is a big deal, that it probably means something other than just a little isolated mass in my chest, it means something else, something more sinister.

But Rich is still standing there, offering me the paper cup. He has a serious look on his face, and I try to drink. Many times I'd heard my patients complain about the taste of the contrast they had to drink for X rays. I would always nod my head, appearing to understand and commiserate. Now, as I drink the orange stuff, I know instantly what they have been talking about. The near orange taste is not quite good enough to enjoy but not bad enough to hate.

My mind is numb, and I drink slowly without thinking as I sit crosslegged on the table. After finishing the paper cup of contrast, I lie back and, strapped down again, move into the scanner, further and further until I am seemingly surrounded by the white and blue ring, surrounded now by a fate that is beyond me entirely. The lights flash with each course of X rays as I hold my breath literally and figuratively. Now, something is wrong, more than just a benign-looking mass in what was most likely my thymus, now it is a big something, perhaps more than I want to deal with, or can deal with, alone. I feel my life being pulled out of me, slowly, in the scanner, as if it is unlocking a part of my doom, as if it were the oracle of Oedipus, telling the truth of corruption that will surely lead to death. And unlike Oedipus, who solved the Sphinx's riddle, I want no part of this particular truth right now. I can only hear a small voice inside telling me to somehow get out of there, to wake up and find it all a bad dream. But instead I find myself moving further and further into the scanner until I am surrounded by its bulk and lost completely within it.

2

⚬ March 1987 and April 1974 ⚬

It is only four days after the mass in my chest was discovered and three since my CT scan. I am flying to my parents' home in Rochester, Minnesota. In a bit of self-deception, I tell myself quietly to relax, to make this trip a little vacation from my insane schedule at work. I have brought only a few shirts and one extra pair of trousers. Of course, I also have my requisite running stuff: the shoes, the polypropylene tights, the nylon shorts, the extra pairs of socks, the Gore-Tex jacket to keep me warm during my runs at home. As I board the plane, carrying my X rays and gym bag, I have no idea how the strength I've developed by running those roads and trails over the years may be tested over the next several days and weeks. As far as I'm concerned, I'll just get this mass in my chest taken care of and then get back to work, to my life, to Karin.

There is a direct flight from Sacramento to Minneapolis with a connection to catch the short flight to Rochester. Sacramento is already deep into its spring, with the heat of summer approaching. I am flying back into winter. The country below reflects the collision of the seasons: the Central Valley of California fast greening with crops, the

Rockies masked by snow, and the Great Plains a patchwork of white snow and brown green that hints at the impending eruption of the first plantings in the fields. Sitting in the plane, I feel the pull of my parents from one direction and Karin from the other. I feel the fright in my chest even as I hear the whine of the engine in my head. There are just over seven miles below to the ground, a thin-aired, spinning, freezing free fall were I to leap somehow through the window of the plane. Yet, I tell myself, I am not defeated, at least not now, not while I still have my strength. After all, I can run the equivalent of those seven miles in less than an hour. After all, I keep trying to convince myself, the mass in my chest is probably benign. A surgeon will be able to remove it. My problem will be solved. Why then, do I feel so tired, so fearful? My exhaustion, I tell myself, is from the combination of work, fear, and the additive effect of miles of running. And yet I know instinctively that something else is making me tired, sucking my strength out through my marrow and out through the mass in my chest. But I refuse to face it: in my family, acceptable reasons for being tired have always been hard work or tough exercise rather than illness and certainly not fear. I keep watch out the window, waiting for something to show me my direction, to show me a sign that I will be all right. The land returns my gaze unchanged for all my silent prayers, the engines monotonously roaring, my breath falling away on my knees, cramped between the seats of the plane.

With planning made possible only by a demonic mind or a computer, the Sacramento flight arrives on one side of the cavernous Minneapolis airport while the Rochester flight departs thirty or forty minutes later from the other side. Almost any delay in the Sacramento flight results in a mad dash across the terminal in order to make the connection. There have been other times in the past when that walk across the hundreds of yards peopled by seemingly countless other slow travelers turned into a semirun, with me carrying my baggage and hoping that the Rochester flight was delayed. I am lucky this time and make the cross-terminal trip easily and relatively unrushed. The flight to Rochester is only about twenty-five minutes long, but I somehow fall asleep just after takeoff only to suddenly awaken, with the lost feeling of one who has slept just enough to become disoriented. For the first several moments, I don't know where I am and have temporarily forgotten my destination and reason for my travel. As I look out the window of the plane, I recognize the approach to the Rochester airport, which brings me to my senses. I've made that approach many times before on other trips home and now feel the pang of knowing just how different this trip is.

My parents are waiting at the gate when I arrive. My father is in chino pants and a workaday shirt, my mother in a dark dress. Both are carrying expressions mixing smiles and uncertainty. Their heavy coats are at the ready, and my father has his winter corduroy hat with earflaps. I shake my father's hand and embrace my mother.

"Do you have any bags?" my father asks. Then, seeing the large envelope in my hand, "Are those your X rays?"

"I've got everything here," I say. "I didn't want to pack too much. Let's go home."

"Yes," my mother agrees, "let's get you home. I've got some chicken soup already made. And some brisket." She looks over at me, now smiling. The three of us, with me in the middle, walk across the small terminal toward the door.

My father looks down at the envelope. "How do you feel, Geoff?"

I look back and forth at both my parents. My father, in his midsixties, looks a bit thin. His gold-rimmed glasses frame his gently lined face. My mother, a bit younger than my father and heavier than she wants to be, has pulled her reddish gray hair back, revealing her rheumy eyes gazing with the look she'd had as I deplaned, the look ricocheting between the extremes of happiness, fear, and confusion. Neither my mother nor my father can see much wrong with me. I look the same, my step light and my voice steady. My eyes, however, cannot lie.

"Well, I really don't feel too bad. I mean, it's true that I feel a bit tired, but not much. And nothing hurts, really. This whole thing is strange. But I guess I'll know more in the next couple of days. I don't know exactly what to think or how I should feel." We are almost to the door. Coats are put on.

"I'll get the car," my father says. "You wait here with your mother."

"I don't mind walking; I feel okay."

"Wait here with me." My mother is firm. I stop and wait, watching my father walk out into the wind.

My mother turns slowly to me as my father crosses to the lot. "We're both worried about you, you know."

"I'll be okay, Mom. I'll be okay. Let's first figure out what this is."

"Sure. We'll wait . . . somehow." She turns and looks out the door.

The car approaches, and I reach out and take hold of my mother's hand, squeeze it, and lead her to the outside, feeling the cold wind whip like a rod through my shirt. But the cold I feel is not the bitter northern Plains wind-whipped arctic freeze of the heart of winter. Hiding within the wind is the spring, furtively sneaking into the air as we walk to the car. My father speaks almost as soon as we start off for home.

"You're set up to see Rosenow tomorrow morning, early. No breakfast, because he may want to get some lab work. You'll take your X rays to him, and he'll send them over to radiology."

"Sounds fine to me. I guess I'll have to eat extra tonight. Right, Mom?"

"Great. All you want."

The rest of the fifteen-minute trip is spent talking about my three brothers, my nephews and nieces, my sister who is soon to be married, the weather, anything other than my health. My family has never spent a lot of time talking about feelings, our spirits, or how we relate to each other. As I see it, we just "do" and "are" with each other, and we've always been quietly successful living our lives that way. I'm not sure if that collective silence, that union of isolation will help me through what might prove to be a long ordeal, but this is no time to try to change my family's style of communication (or lack thereof). I have the feeling that a lot of the battle I am about to face will have to be fought alone. The mass, I tell myself, is somehow a part of me, and I have to find out for myself what it is and what is wrong with me. I know it will play a role in the life of my family, but mine will surely be the life most affected. Perhaps, too, there is the morbid fascination of a chest physician with a chest mass. I have begun to develop a relationship with my personal unwanted guest.

The Rochester airport is to the south of the city, and it had been the city, seemingly anchored in its center by the tall buildings of the Mayo Clinic, that I had recognized as my flight approached the airport. We travel past cornfields waiting for the last snowmelt before the planting. The fields metamorphose into shopping malls and housing developments, the signs of the outward movement of the small city, and then suddenly we are in the residential area in which my parents live. Their house is on Plummer Circle, named for one of the great physicians hired by the visionary Mayo brothers as they watched their clinic grow in size and importance. Henry Plummer was more than a physician; he was in many respects the Renaissance Man of the early Mayo Clinic. It was he, for example, who was largely responsible for the architectural design of the first major building of the Clinic. Today, the fifteen-story-tall, brown sandstone Plummer Building dominates the center of Rochester.

My father parks the car in the driveway, and I step out into the snow and ease my mother out of the back seat. I take my bag and X rays into the house, walking into the kitchen, which is filled with the smells of hectic cooking from the previous several days and evenings.

"Are you hungry? Want some soup?"

"Sure, sure. What kind of juice do you have?" I ask, opening the refrigerator.

My mother rattles off a choice of four or five, and I grab a glass container. I sit down with my drink as she places the soup before me. The rising steam transports me to my childhood. I am staring down into the fog, not noticing my father sitting next to me, already starting to eat.

I suppose that nearly everyone has his or her version of home cooking. For me, chicken soup with matzo balls, fried chicken, brisket, and angel food cake serve as the foundation of my dietary life. My mother is such a good cook, I tell myself, that it is a wonder I didn't become obese during my childhood. I have my father to thank for protecting me from that: he made sure we exercised every day. He is religious with his swimming; even now, at age sixty-five, he swims a half mile a day, every day. When I was a kid, we'd go swimming nearly every night, even if it meant driving for miles in the Minnesota winter to do it. And after each night's swim, we'd come home to my mother cooking in the kitchen, for my mother never swam. For her, pumping iron involved pots and pans.

Fairly soon after dinner, my father, with a long day before him in the office, goes off to bed. The jet lag keeps me awake, and I sit in the kitchen with my mother, drinking hot water with milk in it: a substitute for coffee in the late hours.

"I just can't believe all this is happening," my mother says.

"That's two of us . . . probably more," I say, looking over my shoulder toward my parents' bedroom and thinking of Karin back in Sacramento.

"Is there anything else we can do? Do you need anything?"

"No. The first thing I've got to do, I suppose, is wait until Rosenow sees me and figures out what this thing in my chest is. I can't afford to get all upset over what may turn out to be nothing or at least not a big deal. All the same, I want to find out what it is. And I think I'll do fine, I really do. I guess the best thing you and Dad can do for me is what you've done: be here for me . . . and, of course, make chicken soup, Mom."

She laughs, but only briefly, and looks back at me. Her hair is down, both she and her housedress are tired and worn down without looking worn out. Her eyes are red around the edges, but she is not tearful. Her rounded face firms a bit, her shoulders square toward me.

"You know we'll always be here for you. You know that."

"Sure, Mom. And I'll do my best; you know that, too. I'm just not sure what doing my best is supposed to mean or do for me." I glance at the clock. "It's getting late, I'd better get some sleep. I'm supposed to see Rosenow at 7:30 tomorrow."

"And no breakfast either," my mother mutters with a half-wicked smirk, not sure if she should laugh or sigh. "Okay. I'll see you in the morning. Do you want me to wake you?"

"No, thanks. I've got an alarm built in to my wristwatch." I hold it up: it's one of those digital things that has a stopwatch, lap timer, alarm. It also walks the dog, delivers a pizza, entertains visiting relatives, writes prescriptions, and calls Dial-A-Prayer. Of course, it doesn't look at all like a watch.

I trundle downstairs to the bedroom that had once been my

brother's. My parents had moved into the house when I was already away at college, so I never really had my own bedroom here. I lie down on the narrow bed, my body beneath several thin blankets and an afghan made by my mother. I speak to myself in the darkness, telling myself to be calm, to prepare for the unknown of the next day. I say no prayers, waiting instead for sleep to overtake me, and in overtaking, to take me somewhere else, where thoughts of chest masses, large spleens, and surgery are all far away and unimportant.

An eerie half-light filters through the curtains, and I have been awake nearly half an hour as soft padding steps come down the stairs. There is a gentle knock.

"Geoff, are you up? We'd better get going soon."

"I'm up, Dad." I've been hoping that I will not have to get up. "I'll wash up and meet you upstairs. You going to have some breakfast?"

"Yes. I know you can't." His voice turns to go up to the kitchen. "I'll be ready to go when you are. We should be in Rosenow's office by about 7:30." His voice has faded with his footsteps.

My father drives one of his old cars to the Clinic. The arrangement he'd made with Ed Rosenow was for me to be seen briefly as one of the first patients of the day. I'd then be able to go to the laboratory and get any necessary lab tests, after which I'd wait for Ed to get the results and decide on the next move.

My father parks the car at his usual spot in one of the many garages built to accommodate the huge staff and patient load of the clinic. We walk through a series of tunnels that take us to the Mayo Building, one of the large buildings in the heart of the Mayo Clinic. Because of the long and brutal Minnesota winters, tunnels link all of the buildings of the complex. As we walk, I hear the echoing footsteps of others, mostly staff of the clinic, walking quickly to work. For once, I don't feel much like rushing along. But the echoes pull me on, and I silently walk next to my father, who carries his usual load of manuscripts, copies of journal articles, and the notes to himself and his secretary outlining his busy schedule for the day.

Soon, the outlying tunnel from the parking lot joins the main one between the three major clinic buildings, and my father and I are caught up in the early morning rush of physicians and patients alike, all heading to offices, clinics, or laboratories. It is an underground Main Street and civic square, with a drug store, restaurant, barbershop, stores, and connections to hotels. For a moment, I forget it is part of a major medical clinic, until we pass a bookstore with copies of the book *The Brothers Mayo* prominently on display.

We are in the Mayo Building, named for the founding brothers. Above us is an eighteen-story, marble-faced cube occupying nearly a city block. The Clinic is divided into sections for medical and surgical specialties, and most sections have their clinic space on one half of an entire floor of the building. My father and I take an elevator reserved for the staff.

We race upward, stepping out into the Section of Thoracic Medicine on the eighteenth floor. Down one corridor I see a line of doors to a few of the sixteen hundred examination rooms in the Mayo Building. The exam rooms of the Clinic are where physicians see their patients, pass judgments, render opinions, and prescribe therapy. My father goes to the large area of the front desk and speaks a few words to the receptionist, who gives a nod of recognition toward me. A nurse joins my father, and I am ushered by the two of them down the corridor and into a room.

The exam rooms in this, the "new" Clinic building, are almost all identical. Their design is derived directly from that put forth in the early part of this century by Henry Plummer and the Mayo brothers. The empty room into which I am led could be in almost any area of the Clinic. There is a wood examination table with a leather-covered cushion, which is covered in turn with white paper. The paper has the feel of being too stiff to be comfortable and too flimsy to be useful. There is a couch against one wall and a built-in desk. In one corner are a small bench and a curtain that can be pulled around it, permitting a patient to undress in the presence, but not the sight, of the physician.

I don't know what to expect of Ed Rosenow, who he is, what he looks like, what sort of person he is, as I walk into the examining room. But before I really have had time to wait or wonder, Ed Rosenow walks into the room.

My father briefly introduces us, turns to me, and says, "Call me at my office when you're done. Mom or I will get you home. Good luck. Thanks for seeing Geoff, Ed," as he turns back to Rosenow. He then leaves the two of us alone.

Ed begins almost as soon as my father leaves the room. In his early fifties but looking younger, wearing a suit and tie (standard uniform at the Clinic), Ed quickly starts to get my history.

One of the most important of the arts of medicine taught to each generation of physicians is the taking of the history. Of course, most patients aren't trained historians, most of us don't pay much attention to details concerning our health, and most people don't realize the complex relationships between organs of the body and the different symptoms they may produce. For example, someone with a bleeding ulcer may not have pain in his belly, but he may become anemic, leading to decreased exercise tolerance, shortness of breath, or weakness. The bleeding ulcer may also cause changes in the stool pattern. Although these symptoms may seem unrelated, to the trained physician they make perfect sense. The physician, therefore, must guide the patient through his own story, asking the questions that will lead down the right path, that will ultimately show the way to the diagnosis. A famous saying in medicine concerning the importance of taking a good history is "Listen carefully: the patient is telling you the diagnosis."

Ed sits at the desk and smiles at me. "Well, Geoff. Your father told me a bit about why you're here. Why don't you fill in the gaps?"

"Okay. Let me give you my history." My face is fixed, serious. This, I tell myself, is serious business.

"I'm a nearly forty-one-year-old, right-handed pediatric pulmonologist." We both nearly laugh, as if Ed could see a case study from the *New England Journal of Medicine* streaming from my mouth.

"I was in good health until, oh, about two months ago or so when I had a cold and cough that was persistent. I occasionally coughed up some yellow sputum, no blood, and no documented fever. Finally, after about a month, I obtained a sputum culture, which didn't show anything. I took ten days of Bactrim anyway, and the cough got better but took another several weeks to completely resolve. Meanwhile, somewhere during the last two months, coincident with the cough, I felt like I'd pulled a muscle or fractured a rib on the left side of my chest . . . I thought it was from coughing.

"None of this stopped me from running, however, and I ran a fifty-mile race in mid-February; I qualified for a one hundred–mile run next June."

Ed looks at me benevolently, smiling at me as if I was a slightly crazy but nevertheless nonthreatening member of the community.

"Yes," he interrupts, "your father told me that you run a lot. But I didn't know what he meant till now." I rub the top of my head, a habit picked up after watching Kurosawa's *The Seven Samurai* too many times. I gently laugh with him.

"Well, I figured that to keep up with my dad I had to do some things that were a bit on the strange side. Running is sorta what I do when I'm not doing medicine." Ed nods in understanding.

I continue with the history of my running, the pain, and the lack of other symptoms. Every once in a while, Ed interrupts again to clarify some point I've made, to ask questions about various symptoms I might have had: chills, rashes, joint pains, headaches, abdominal pain, nausea, diarrhea. I have negative answers for all of it, except for a brief illness a year before, an illness characterized by fever and pain when I urinated. The workup for that had been negative, but I wound up taking a course of Bactrim for it, and whatever "it" was got better either because of the Bactrim or (as is often the case in medicine) in spite of the Bactrim. Ed asks about foreign travel, and I tell him I'd trekked for a month in Nepal nearly eighteen months before.

After the completion of my history, I am subjected to a rapid yet complete physical exam. My ears, eyes, and mouth are peered into. My lungs and heart are listened to. My large spleen is easily felt, or, as we say in medicine, it is "palpable below the costal (rib cage) margin." I experience my first rectal examination. I dress as Ed writes in my chart, adding to my medical record.

At the Clinic, as at other medical centers, the medical record is the line tracing a patient's progress through the system. In it are the details of patient interviews and physical examinations, laboratory values, operative reports, and other facts that accumulate as a patient is seen, poked, prodded, stuck, X-rayed, operated upon, or autopsied.

Because my father had trained in neurology at the Clinic in the early 1950s, my medical record goes back to my childhood. My record is one of over four million at the Clinic, which, because of the extraordinary vision of its founders, is the repository of one of the most complete and best studied collections of medical records in the world. My father is not only a world-renowned epidemiologist but also the former chairman of epidemiology at the Clinic. As such, he helped to focus many of the important studies from the Clinic using the medical records as a tool to detail aspects of diseases that otherwise would be difficult to study. While not as glamorous as peering into a microscope or growing cells in culture or working with test tubes, the experimental usefulness of a large number of carefully documented records cannot be underestimated. Sifting the medical records of many patients with the same illness may show common traits that reveal new information about that disease, often leading to new theories of the origin of disease or, in some instances, to new treatments. Medical advances come in time for some but too late for many. The many, by having an illness and being cared for at a medical center where teaching and research go on, such as the Mayo Clinic, can lend themselves to the benefit of those who come later.

After finishing his notes in my chart, Ed takes the X rays and looks at them on a view box in the room, examining them carefully, looking at the mass, my ribs, the CT scan. He puts the X rays back in their envelope, sits down, and from a drawer pulls out what looks like a very large laundry list: the laboratory order sheet. He checks off what seems to be a huge number of the possible tests, then turns to me.

"Geoff, I want to get your blood work, an EKG, and chest X ray all this morning. I'll have your X rays sent to our radiologists. I'll call you and tell you the next part of the plan. It should all be done by noon, so I'll call you at home. That's where you'll be, won't you?"

"I suppose so. You can always find me through my dad. I'm really going to be able to get all that stuff done by noon? Back home it would take all day, if I were lucky."

"Well," Ed smiles at me, "you're not back home. I see from your record that you've never had to have a lot of lab work done here, so this should be an interesting experience for you. The Clinic processes a lot of people every day, you know."

"Okay. I'll be at home, and you can call me there."

We shake hands and then walk together to the appointment desk. "Good luck, Geoff. I'll call you soon," Ed says. He turns and walks back to his office, to the rest of his day. I am left with the receptionist who takes the "laundry list" and the X rays from Ed and makes calls and fills out forms for me.

It is still on the early side of 9 A.M.

The receptionist rapidly instructs me as to which test will be done where and in which order. All instructions, slips, and appointments—everything for the next several hours—are contained in a small envelope color-coded for thoracic medicine, my point of origin in the system. I am about to see firsthand that the Mayo Clinic is at the very least a well-oiled machine.

My first stop is to have my blood work done. I retrace many of my steps, down the elevators to the basement/tunnel system, then to a large room seating about 250, which is the central blood-drawing area. Even though it is technically in the tunnel system, the room is airy, two stories high, with clerestory windows and skylights, plants around the perimeter, and huge lithographs by Joan Miró on the walls. Patients are called in groups of fifteen or so into a smaller waiting room, then are called individually into a cubicle where a technician draws their blood into tubes, which are put in a vertical conveyor belt leading directly to the laboratory above. My blood is drawn less than an hour after leaving Ed's office. The most important blood tests will be completed and reported to Rosenow within three hours.

In a similar fashion, I have my EKG and chest X ray. For each, I wait in a large room with many others and am called into a smaller room with a group of five or ten, and finally I am led to a cubicle to change into a paper gown before having the X ray or EKG done. The efficiency of the system is almost frightening. For the EKG, I go into a room that contains an examining table, on which I lie, with the narrow space sufficient for the technician to come in and put the EKG electrodes on me. The electrodes are on small tubes connected to a vacuum system, so they stick to the skin by suction. It takes the technician about twenty seconds to put them on. A voice on an intercom tells me to lie still. About thirty seconds later, the technician reappears, removes the electrodes, and suggests that I should get dressed and go to my next appointment. I feel like a part on an assembly line, being moved inexorably toward my destination, having no control over the process. I tell myself that I should just marvel at the practicality of how the place works, how efficiently it is designed, how many patients can be seen in a day in the system. But I've never enjoyed being a cog in a machine, even if it is a wonderful machine.

I find my way through the tunnels to my father's office on the sixth floor of the building that houses the heart of the medical records system. I walk into his office at about 11:30 in the morning. My father looks up from his work at me, almost surprised that I am back so soon.

"So, how did it go?" he asks.

"Fine, great. Fast, though. I mean, I got all the lab work done in only about two hours or so."

"Well, this is the Clinic, you know. They are efficient," he smiles at the understatement.

"Efficient isn't quite the word I'd use, but I'm not sure what the right word is. Anyway, I'm done. Could I use the phone and call Mom?"

"Sure. Use the one on the desk." I call home, looking out the window at the other buildings as I tell my mother to pick me up.

"The chicken soup is ready for you. I'll be outside the office in five minutes."

I go downstairs to wait and, true to her word, my mother pulls up in five minutes.

"Well, how was the morning? How was Rosenow? What did he say? Did you finish all the lab work?" My mother peppers me with questions. I tell her the basics as we make the short trip home.

When at last I am sitting at the kitchen table, the steaming soup before me, I start to relate the story of my morning.

"Ed was really nice. I felt very comfortable with him, like . . . like I could tell he really knows what he's doing," I say, between spoonfuls of soup.

"He's such a nice man. You know, he lives around the corner, right on the circle."

"Down the street? You're kidding."

"No, really, his house is the second one from the corner. You've probably run past it I don't know how many times. So, how was the Clinic?"

"Impressive. Efficient. Almost too efficient. But, I know that's how they do what they do. I mean, here it is not even 12:30 and I've seen my doc, given my history, had my physical, gotten blood work, an EKG, and X rays done, and made it home for lunch. That's pretty amazing to me. By the way, the soup is great. I think I'll have some more."

My mother gets up from her chair before I can move. She is too accustomed to waiting on the family and is about to take my bowl when the phone rings. She picks it up, says hello, covers the mouthpiece, and turns to me.

"It's for you. It's Dr. Rosenow." She uses the formal term even though he can't hear her. She hands me the phone.

"Hello," I say into the phone.

"Hello, Geoff. Listen, I want you to come back in now. We need to get a sample of your bone marrow."

I am silent for a moment, then can only utter, "Now?"

"Yes. Come to my office, and I'll arrange it from there. We need to do it this afternoon." I hear myself say "okay" and hang up the phone even as I feel myself hurtle toward fear and panic. I know what a "bone marrow" is.

During my residency in pediatrics at Stanford, I spent several months on the hematology-oncology ward, where many children received chemotherapy. I gave a lot of the chemo, either intravenously or intrathecally (into the space around the spinal cord in the lower back). I also learned how to do "marrows," the medical shorthand for sticking a large needle through the thick outer layer of bone into the marrow and aspirating, or sucking out, a sample of cells into a syringe.

Bones have more than one job. A thick, outer layer allows them to physically support us and give our bodies shape and internal strength. The inner, soft marrow is the main source of blood cells for the body, the place where the cells divide, grow, and mature. In some illnesses, like leukemia or lymphoma, abnormal cells can be found in the marrow, often replacing the normal cells with cancerous cells. To diagnose an illness like leukemia, a sample of the bone marrow must be obtained. There are several sites used for bone marrow aspiration. In children, it's relatively easy to get the sample from the anterior iliac crest, at the front of the large bone forming the prominence of the hip.

It was about my second week as an intern on heme-onc when I entered the small treatment room to do my first bone marrow. The nurse and the resident who were there to help me were waiting with Joey, the nine-year-old boy fighting his losing battle with leukemia. He wore his customary knitted wool cap to cover his chemotherapeutically bald head. His usual grin was absent. He was an unwilling veteran of too many bone marrows, too many courses of chemotherapy, and a war he neither chose, desired, nor deserved.

The gurney on which Joey sat took up most of one side of the room. Joey's mother held his thin hand, the one without the IV, and rubbed his shoulder. For some reason, she gently pulled off Joey's hat, and his bald head aged him before me, the veins beneath the skin of his scalp showing a faint blue, his face a mixture of pallor and sallowness atop a fatigue derived from the chronicity of his illness. Joey and I'd quickly become friends soon after my arrival. I had seen him daily on rounds, had traded jokes with him, and had sat during late evenings with his parents, listening to their sorrow amid the dozens of families who each suffered alone and together in the terrible grip of cancer. I now felt that everything about the relationship I had with Joey was on the line.

Joey knew that I'd seen other marrows done, and he knew that I'd never actually done one. As the saying goes in medicine: "See one, do one, teach one." He offered himself, I think now, for my initiation with full understanding and willingness. He hated bone marrows, he told me, but he knew that they had to be done.

As I walked into the room, his gaze passed first to his mother as she said good-bye and went out of the room. She hated the procedure as much as her son did, and she could not stand to be in the room for any part of it. Joey then met my eyes, which tried not to belie my own fear and acknowledged inexperience.

"Dr. K.," he called, "you'll use lots of numbing medicine, won't you?"

"Sure, Joey. I promise I will. And I'll tell you everything I do, before I do it." That was the important part, my resident had said: don't lie. Always say what you're going to do before you do it. And always use enough of the "numbing medicine."

"Okay, Joey, bend your left leg and put it under your right one." I felt with my fingers the bone forming his small right hip. The anterior iliac crest, my target, was broad and easy to feel. The resident, there to supervise and teach, confirmed the location. It was all business now. I opened the bone marrow tray and put on sterile gloves while the nurse poured the Betadine sterilizing solution into a cup. I picked up a gauze square from the tray, dipped it into the Betadine, and turned back to Joey.

"I'm going to clean off your hip, Joey. That's all I'm going to do, first. This'll be a little cold." I hoped he couldn't hear the flutter in my voice or feel the tremulous hand that cleaned his hip with one, then another, then yet a third Betadine-soaked gauze pad. The area was clean. I put a sterile towel with a hole in its center over the site, allowing me access to the bone. I loaded a syringe with nearly a teaspoon and a half of Xylocaine, the wonderful numbing medicine.

"Joey, I'm going to numb the skin. This will be a little bee sting." He said nothing but held his breath.

I put the needle just into the skin, just where I would want to get the marrow. I started to inject the Xylocaine. Joey gave a short gasp and started to cry as the Xylocaine went in with a burning sensation. He held perfectly still, giving me a good target.

"Okay, Joey. I'm sorry. But I want it to be numb. Okay? Joey?"

"Okay," he whimpered. The needle was still in his hip. I angled deeper, injecting the medicine as I went. Joey was still whimpering when my needle hit something hard, the bone. I kept injecting, even as Joey cried out with the sudden extra burn of Xylocaine going into the covering of the bone. I stopped injecting and pulled the needle out.

"I'm done with that, Joey. You're all numb. I'll check and make sure.

Can you feel this?" I asked, touching the skin with the point of the needle.

"No. I don't feel anything there."

"Great," I said, more for myself than for him. I made a small incision with a scalpel, right in the middle of the area, and turned back to the marrow tray. I picked up the large marrow needle, nearly an eighth of an inch in diameter. It looked and felt like an awkward, heavy, outmoded piece of equipment, like a discarded part of an old torture device, with a patina of dull brown, totally unlike the acceptable, shiny, thin, and delicate object a needle should be. If it had been an animal, it would have been an ox. Within its barrel fit a solid metal insert, called a trocar, which gave the entire device the strength to go through solid bone without breaking. I checked the fit of the two, taking the trocar out and replacing it within the needle. With the trocar inside it, the needle was solid.

I silently said a prayer. I wanted the needle to go in straight, not to slide alongside the bone. I wanted the needle to go in just far enough, not all the way through the bone and out the other side, not that that could happen I tried to reassure myself.

"Joey, I'm going to put in the needle. You won't feel much except me pushing on you."

"I know" was the reply. And it was true. He knew far better than I did. And he knew how it really felt far better than I did.

I took the needle-with-trocar assembly and pushed the whole thing into the incision until I felt the bone. Then, with pressure as steady as I could muster, coupled with a slow rotation, I felt it go through the outer layer of bone until I felt a give. The end of the needle was sitting in the marrow. I pulled the trocar out of the needle, which stuck out of Joey's hip like some deadly projectile or a misplaced antenna. I took a large syringe, placed it on the needle, and turned it, locking it in place.

"Okay, Joey, this may hurt," I warned. I was about to aspirate a small amount of the marrow into the syringe. I had been told that it felt like a sucking deep in the bone. I had no idea what that meant, but Joey, who certainly knew, held his breath as I pulled up on the plunger of the syringe as hard as I could, holding the needle in place in the marrow. After what seemed like an eternity but was in actuality only a few seconds, I saw small bits of red tissue and blood, the aspirated marrow, dribble into the syringe. The sample was small, but the technician who took the syringe from my shaking hand told me it was adequate. I put the trocar back into place.

"Joey, I'm taking out the needle . . . now," I said as I pulled out the weapon and covered the wound with a clean piece of gauze. I put special elasticized adhesive tape over the area, to keep pressure on the aspiration site so it wouldn't bleed.

"You okay?" I asked. "We're done," I said, then realized that I was the only one who was done. Joey was the one who still had leukemia.

"Thanks, Dr. K.," Joey said. "You did okay. You gave me enough numbing medicine."

"Thank you, Joey. You were very good. I'll see you later today. After lunch." The gurney was being wheeled out to take Joey back to his bed.

"Okay. See you later."

Joey died less than three months later, his leukemia being stronger, smarter, and far meaner than all the drugs we threw into his tender body. It was to the end unfair: all the pain endured, all those drugs, all that suffering by someone so young, and for what?

Now I hear again Ed's voice as he calls me for my own marrow examination. I swim into the cries of the children like Joey, whose marrow I'd taken in the past. I tell myself that I am feeling the cold Betadine, the hot Xylocaine, even though I've never felt either. The spoon falls from my hand into the soup.

"What was that about?" My mother mimics my own open-mouthed stare. The two of us breathe slowly.

I tell her in two sentences. "Ed said there's something wrong with my blood count. I have to get back and have a bone marrow done this afternoon." I somehow pull myself out of the chair and manage to get my jacket on despite my shaking hands. I am suddenly very cold.

My mother, now silent, drives me back to the Clinic. There are no questions to ask and nothing with which to answer. I say nothing, hearing only the terror within my chest. I shrink in the elevator as it rises to Ed's office. My mother sits in the enormous waiting room, her knitting on her lap. I am quickly ushered into Ed's examining room. He can see at once my agitation as I try to sit, to be calm, not to beg.

"Do we have to do the marrow right now? Couldn't I have the marrow done when the mass is removed, while I'm under anesthesia?" I'd been thinking all the way in the car, trying to find some way out of the procedure.

"I got your lab values, Geoff. Your platelet count is only sixty thousand, your absolute neutrophil count is six hundred. I'm not exactly sure what's going on, but I'm concerned you may have lymphoma. We need a bone marrow biopsy to help with the diagnosis." Ed is, if nothing else, straightforward. There is no point beating around the bush; he is all business and is not going to be swayed.

My blood count is indeed frightening. Platelets are the packages of protoplasm that allow the blood to clot effectively. Their low number increases my risk of bleeding with any injury. In a flash, I remember my easy bleeding when shaving over the last several weeks. The absolute neutrophil count enumerates the white blood cells that are my personal guard against a myriad of potential bacterial invaders. The normal number of these cells is at least three-fold higher than the number right now in my own blood. I have heard stories of cancer patients with counts only a little lower than mine who suddenly developed fever, went into shock, and died all within six hours of their first symptom. Ed is right: something is probably wrong with my bone marrow, and he has to know what it is and he has to know fast.

"Okay . . . okay . . . but could I have something, something for pain."

Ed looks a little surprised, but then I see a glint of recognition on his face: he realizes that I have probably done a lot of marrows on children and heard a lot of crying from them. Perhaps, he thinks, I have reason to fear.

"Sure," he says, "although most of the time it's not needed. But I'll write for some Demerol tablets. Take them and then have the marrow done." He writes out a prescription and hands it to me. I go to the appointment desk for the form and directions, both in the requisite envelope, to take to the bone marrow desk. My mother puts down her knitting, looking up at me with a worried face as I approach her.

"Well, where to now?"

"The pharmacy first. I got a prescription for some Demerol, then I go right to bone marrow." I gaze back at my mother, whose face is drained of color as she stands, saying nothing. I feel, rather suddenly, that I somehow have to be strong, whatever that means, for both of us. I partially turn toward the elevators, telling myself not to be so frightened but not listening to myself at all.

"I'll be all right. I'll take something, then I'll be fine." We are before the elevators, waiting for them.

"All right. I'll be with you." We walk into the elevator and are soon at the pharmacy in the underground subway tunnel under the clinic, and in only a few minutes, I have the two tablets of Demerol, swallowing them down almost immediately.

We walk to the area where the bone marrow will be done. To my surprise, I find myself back where I'd been only hours before, on one end of the large room where I'd waited for my name to be called for my blood tests. It all seems so fitting, after all, the bone marrow being the source of the blood. After delivering my laboratory order form to the desk clerk, my mother and I sit in the waiting area. I desperately want the Demerol to work, willing myself to become sleepy, which is the surest way to stay awake. Nothing happens. I feel no different, and my name isn't called for what seems a long time.

I go to the desk as I begin to feel fatigued. The nurse apologizes for the delay, then offers me a bed to lie down upon in the back area. I accept, and my mother, knitting in hand, waits alone. Led to a bed with curtains pulled around it, I lie down, trying to fall asleep, but only feel more scared. It is as though I were now a patient in an old hospital ward, a room with many beds separated only by curtains. But unlike such a place, I hear no other sounds of any life, of any patients, no footsteps of nurses and physicians, and I feel myself drifting off toward but never into sleep. I am floating totally alone on the sheets, lying there fully clothed, feeling hollow, nearly empty of myself, wanting a sleep that refuses to come quickly enough or soundly enough. I tell myself that I dream softly of other places until I hear a voice jar me awake from a fitful, self-willed rest.

"Dr. Kurland, we're ready now. Would you please come this way?" The voice is attached to a nurse, primly dressed in white.

I have no answer and I slowly arise, following the voice down the short hall and into a room. Just as when I had done the bone marrows on the children, the examining table and small table holding the equipment seem to occupy most of the room. The lights are very bright. I am tired but my fear awakens me to near bursting as the technician, who was, in fact, attached to the voice, introduces herself.

"Hello, Dr. Kurland. I'm Mary. I'll be doing your bone marrow."

"Are . . . are you the doctor?" I ask.

"Oh, heavens no. You don't want one of them to do it, do you? Marrows are all I do, five days a week. I've been doing them for about fifteen years. I could teach a thing or two to the doctors." She chuckles a bit. In my clouded sense of reality, I fight into the present, think hard for a moment (which takes as much concentration as I can muster), and decide that, given the choice, I'd much rather have her do my bone marrow than someone who does them on the side.

One of the ways the Mayo Clinic is able to see so many patients and maintain its high standards is probably traceable in a rambling way to Henry Ford and the idea of the assembly line. The woman who is to do my bone marrow is indeed expert at it. Even though I am a doctor and think a doctor should be the person to do my bone marrow, I realize how lucky I am to have a seasoned pro.

"Take off your shirt, loosen your trousers, and lay down on the bed, please."

I do as instructed and wind up on my back, looking up at her.

"Turn over, Dr. Kurland."

"Don't you do the marrow in the anterior iliac crest?"

"Oh," she laughs, "you're a pediatrician, aren't you?" She looks down, smiling. "No, in big people, we prefer the posterior iliac spine. It's a lot easier. You'll see."

I will? I think to myself.

I turn over and lie facedown on the table, a part of me relaxed, trying to laugh with her. I am, indeed, a "big" person, not a child. I tell myself to try and behave that way. The posterior superior iliac spine is at the back of the pelvic bone, just to the side of the midline. I feel her hand locate the target, just as I had done on Joey and so many children since. And, just as I'd done with Joey, she talks me through the procedure.

"I'm going to clean off the skin back here," her voice says. "This will feel cool." The Betadine goes on. "I'm going to put in the Xylocaine, Dr. Kurland. A little sting here." Calling it a little sting is understating it, I think. I feel the numbing burn of the medicine searing into my skin, then catching the outer covering of the bone, much more sensitive, and suddenly I feel nothing at all.

I hear the sound of metal rubbing on metal as she checks the bone marrow needle and trocar. I force myself to look down at the disturbingly white, clean floor rather than try to turn my head to catch a glimpse of the equipment about to be shoved into me.

"Okay, Dr. Kurland, a little pressure now. This shouldn't hurt at all." I grit my teeth, just the same, for a pain that isn't there. I feel the steady pressure, remembering my own tremulous grasp of the needle as I had bored my way into Joey's hip so long before.

"I'm going to aspirate. You may feel a little something here." Again, my mouth goes taut, and I hold my breath, waiting for the sucking deep in the bone that is the aspiration. There is nothing, mixed with silence. I picture the little droplets of marrow and blood going into the syringe. Still, there is silence from above.

"Dr. Kurland, we're going to get a little biopsy. Just another moment." Before I can say anything more than okay, I hear a light tapping and feel a jarring going through my lower back, reverberating into my bones. Rather than pain, I feel more of a thumping oddity down to my knees and up to my shoulder. It is the needle being hammered, albeit gently, into the substance of my marrow.

"Okay, Dr. Kurland," the voice calls, bringing me into the room again, "I'm going to remove the needle . . . now." And it is out, done, finished. My lower back is numb and feels as if a needle was just tapped into it. Gauze and a large piece of elasticized tape are over the spot of the biopsy. I run my hand over it and recognize it as the same type of tape I'd used on Joey's hip those many years ago.

"Well, how was that? How are you?" she asks.

"I'm . . . I guess I'm okay . . . yes, I'm okay. Can I go? I mean do I have to do anything more or less, or can I just . . . am I done?" I'm standing, trying to get my shirt on. I am shaking, unsteady, my voice cracking with relief, able now to fall apart after gritting my teeth for a time I cannot fully recall. The nurse looks at me knowingly, with a quick smile.

"You had some Demerol, didn't you? Is someone here with you, Dr. Kurland?"

"My mother. Out there." I point in the vague direction of where I think the waiting area might be. My shirt is finally on. I am afraid of falling over, collapsing, but I want only to get out of there and home.

"Well, we're done. Let's take you out."

The corridor has somehow become narrower than I remember it from only a few minutes (or was it longer?) before. We reach the waiting room, and I am turned over to my mother, who puts down her knitting again and looks at me as if I have something strange and organic growing out of my ears.

"Are you all right?"

"Fine, no problem," I lie. "Let's get out of here."

"You don't look so good. Are you sure you can walk to the car?" She stands before me, scrutinizing my face. "I'll get a wheelchair. It'll only take a minute, then I can wheel you to the car."

"I'm fine, just fine," I lie louder. "I don't need a wheelchair. Please, let's just get out of here. I'll take a little nap when I get home, and then I'll be great, ready for some more soup or something."

She grudgingly agrees, and we start to walk back to the car. We first have to negotiate a flight of stairs up to the communicating walkway that will lead us the block or so back to the garage. The stairs have developed high risers and deep treads that were not there when last I walked them. I take each step slowly, deliberately, wondering when they were changed. By the time I reach the top, with the long corridor before us, I am weak and nauseous. I am holding onto my mother's arm as we start down the walkway, but after going only five or six yards, I am suddenly unable to move. My legs are gone, asleep, as if someone has snuck up and poured lead into my shoes. It is as if I'd been rendered useless by the fatiguing effect of gritting my teeth and holding my breath during the marrow, wickedly combined with the drugging effect of the Demerol I'd taken beforehand. In addition, there has been the pressurized choking off of the fear of the marrow itself, which had been bottled inside me and is now suddenly released as I see I am still in one piece after the whole thing is finished. The decompression takes part of my strength, and I lean against the wall, then try to sit, then find myself suddenly helpless on the floor. I have no idea exactly how I have gotten there.

My mother, who had been at my side as I crumpled into a ball at her feet, now kneels with me, looking again into my face. Her own face now reflects back an oxymoronic combination of calm panic mixed with sadness: watching her first son now helpless before her and knowing that she must get me up and to the car, then home to rest, she has to place panic behind her in order to help me.

"Geoff, are you okay? What's the matter?" She asks in a rather matter-of-fact voice. Her nursing training, even so many years ago, tells her now that she shouldn't be upset lest I become upset.

"I . . . I don't know . . . I'm just so tired . . . I . . . I'll be all right . . . I'll just sleep here for a minute," I mumble, closing my eyes and feeling the coolness of the wall and floor against my back and legs. My eyes close. I start to drift away.

I look up to see my mother, as calmly as possible under the circumstances, stand up and turn back down the corridor, back toward the waiting area we'd left minutes before.

"You wait here. I'll get a wheelchair," she says, then adds the totally unnecessary, "don't move." Her voice precedes her down the corridor far away. I can give no argument or complaint. The corridor is very quiet, and while I sit or lie there, no one passes.

After five, fifteen, or thirty minutes, she returns with the promised wheelchair, and together we both manage to heave my carcass into the seat. She rolls me down the corridor toward the car, telling me that we should have gotten a wheelchair as soon as my marrow was done, that I shouldn't push myself so hard, that I should take it easy. In other words, I should admit that I'm sick. I hate being wheeled around; I hate being unable to move on my own power. But I am so exhausted that I cannot complain anymore. Mysteriously, I find myself back in the car without a clue as to how I got in. The wheelchair disappears, and I am suddenly inside the house, transported through time, space, and feeling. For some reason, I have a desperate sense that it will not be the last time I'll be in a wheelchair.

Dinner following Demerol is a quiet affair without my participation. My father asks the perfunctory questions that require short answers: yes, no, or maybe. I find my way to bed and nearly immediately into a deep sleep. It is peaceful but will not last long, I know.

The next morning, now much more awake and somehow refreshed, I walk into Ed Rosenow's examining room. I sit again on the brown leather couch. After a brief wait, there is a gentle knock on the door. Ed strides in and sits squarely before me in a chair that he has deliberately picked up and placed between the couch and the examining table. He leans forward a bit and looks at me intently. He hesitates for a moment, as if he were weighing his words, what to say and how to say it. He looks at me, straight on, as if to say: "Listen, I want to only say this once." As if I feel the weight of the words he holds loosely in his mouth, I lean back slightly and gaze at him, intent on his face. His mouth moves, and I hear the only words I am to hear and remember for a while:

"Geoff, you have hairy cell leukemia."

He may be saying more. In fact, I know he is saying more. But I sit there with a locked expression on my face, hearing almost nothing except the sound in my head telling me that I hear nothing, that I am not there, that I am dying, that I am not dying, that I don't know what is happening to me. And somehow part of me sees Ed Rosenow and feels in some way sorry for him, for being the messenger of such terrifying news. And after what seems hours, during which I have left the room, talked with my parents, tried to comfort Karin, watched myself die, then start to live again, I find myself with the same locked expression, sitting on the couch, with Ed calmly speaking to me:

". . . you to meet Tom Habermann, who is a hematologist and knows a lot about hairy cell leukemia. We'll go to his office now; it's down on West Fifteen."

And I will myself to get up and follow Ed to the elevator. As we ride in the otherwise empty elevator, Ed tells me of the oracular meeting he'd had with this Tom Habermann just after I'd gone off to get my bone marrow the previous day. "I was in the staff elevator and there was Tom Habermann, and I told him I was seeing this forty-year-old physician (that's you) with a mediastinal mass and a big spleen. And I told him I thought he might have lymphoma. Tom looked right back and said, 'He's probably got hairy cell leukemia and a thymoma. I just took care of another guy who had that.' And wouldn't you know, you've got hairy cell leukemia."

By that time we are at Tom's office, only three floors down. Ed introduces us as he might introduce fellow physicians to each other. But I know (and Tom knows) who is the doctor and who is the patient. Tom had been filled in earlier by Ed, who soon excuses himself to get back to work. I am reminded of the time, seemingly long ago, when I'd been on my college track team, receiving, then passing the baton in a relay race. Now, I am the baton, and Tom Habermann has me for the next mile or two, or perhaps, if things go well or if they don't go well, longer. I only hope he's ready to run.

3

"Well, how are you? I suppose that's not a great question right now."
It is a youthful Midwestern voice. "Ed's already filled me in a fair
amount, so I don't have to ask you too many questions. Amazing story,
though."

I look at Tom Habermann, who is in his midthirties with the look of
fresh-faced youth behind his glasses and beneath his short, brown hair.
He is half smiling in a serious way, but his face is telling me to relax.

"Yeah. Some story. I don't think I like being a story. I think I'd rather
just go home and forget the whole thing." I look down at my hands,
which are on the brown leather of the couch of Tom's examination
room. Each exam room, I am convinced, has just such a couch, as if the
Clinic got a fantastic deal on couches by ordering a trainload of them.

"Listen, let's go and look at your slides. We'll talk as we go, okay?"

I pull myself up from the couch. I am a bit taller and thinner than
Habermann. His face is round and open, and he smiles again as he leads
me to the hallway. He looks as if he'd played sports back in high school,
baseball perhaps, but discovered he wouldn't be a star and found himself a better niche in medicine. Like Ed, he wears a suit and tie.

"Okay. I guess it'll be an introspective experience," I say. Tom laughs out loud, and I find myself laughing with him. We walk down the corridor and into the staff elevator. In a few minutes, we are walking and talking more as colleagues than as physician and patient.

"You really haven't had much in the way of symptoms, have you? I mean, except for the chest pain, whatever that was, right?" Tom asks.

"Yeah. I had a cough that wouldn't quit for a while last January and February, but I kept running."

"Oh, right, Ed was telling me about that, the running, I mean. You did a what, a fifty-mile run?" He looks at me a bit sideways, his eyes telling me he thinks I'm nuts.

"Well, it was something to do. Actually, it was to qualify for the big time, a hundred-mile run."

"A hundred miles? I don't like to drive a hundred miles! Where do you do something like that? Better yet, why would anyone want to do something like that?"

"As they say: 'If you have to ask why, then you'll never be able to understand.' I've been running a long time." I slow down a bit, as if the words I am about to say have more tangible weight. "I probably have been running nearly as long as you've been alive. That's a guess, at least."

We are going down a ramp in the subway, heading back toward the gigantic room in which I'd sat only yesterday, waiting to have my blood drawn, waiting for my name to be called for the bone marrow. We pass the framed lithographs on the walls, cases displaying pre-Columbian artwork, and occasional sculptures, all of which are there to brighten the place and distract the patients from the real reason they are here. People rush down and through the ramp without stopping, though; it is an unseen museum.

"Anyway," I continue, "this particular race is over the Sierra Nevada Mountains in California."

"Over mountains?" Tom is shaking his head a bit.

"Yeah. It's almost all on trails . . . you know, rocks, snakes, trees . . . and there's a lot of hills . . . about seventeen thousand feet of cumulative uphill and about twenty-one thousand feet of cumulative downhill in the thing . . ."

"You are nuts. But . . ."

"You are right, I am. And proud of it . . ." I turn toward him as we approach the large waiting room. "I figure you should know the kind of person you're dealing with . . . someone who's not necessarily playing with a full deck . . ."

"Fair enough." He shakes his head in agreement, laughing softly as he does.

"And you?" It's my turn for the questions. "How'd you get here?"

"The Clinic? I'm originally from the Midwest, mostly Wisconsin. My father's a pharmacist, so I guess I had a head start to medicine, sorta like you. I went to med school in Omaha, came here for my residency, and really liked it. I stayed in hematology here . . . and I'm still here. My folks are in Missouri. My dad retired a while back. I get to see them pretty often, take the kids to see the grandparents . . . that's nice for all of them. You're not married . . . never were?"

"No . . . no . . . well, I'm not . . . but that's another story . . . if you thought the running stuff was strange, I'd better save it for later." We've gone past the cavernous waiting room containing the communal blood test crowd, have gone up a flight of stairs (were these the stairs I dazed up after my bone marrow?), and are walking down another corridor.

"You know, Ed ran into me in the elevator and told me about your case before I saw your blood smear," Tom says as we step into a large, bright room with a series of tables upon which sits a herd of microscopes. Here laboratory technicians examine blood smears by the hundreds and bone marrow specimens by the dozens each day. A blood smear is nothing more than a glass slide on which a drop of blood has been placed, then spread over the surface of the slide, one cell thick. The smear is then stained with chemicals that bind to substances in the different cells. Because the chemicals are of varying colors, the cells can be seen more easily under the microscope. Cells with different structures take up staining materials in characteristic ways, allowing cells to be differentiated under the microscope. My blood smear had caught the attention of the technician, whose trained eye recognized the unusual cells when she (or he) saw them. Habermann, after seeing the slide, had found my other laboratory work and called Rosenow, who then called me.

Tom retrieves my marrow slides and places one on the microscope. Looking into the eyepiece, he adjusts the focus as he moves the slide beneath the thick lens of the microscope. He turns the microscope partially in my direction.

"You want a look?"

"Well, I'm better with chest X rays." I hesitate, wondering if I want to return to being a physician for a few minutes. "It's been a while since I've looked at a marrow. But I'll give it a shot." I think now of Joey and his marrow as well as the other bone marrows I'd gotten from my little patients with leukemia. That was years before, during my residency, and I'd not looked at a marrow since. It is ironic that my reintroduction to "Bone Marrow Examination 101" is to be with my own marrow. I peer into the eyepiece of the microscope and get my first look at the enemy.

Normally, the bone marrow contains some fat as well as the myriad of what are known as precursor cells, those cells that are developing in an ordered dance into the mature cells that will finally escape from the marrow and make their way into the circulating blood. Red blood cells that carry oxygen to our tissues, the different types of white cells that fight infections, and the tiny platelets necessary for blood to clot, all have their parentage and infancy in the marrow. A normal marrow thus has a wide variety of cells, cells of different sizes, cells that stain darker or lighter.

I don't have to be a card-carrying hematologist to see that my marrow is definitely not normal. The slide of my bone marrow is boring: most of the cells are of one type, relentlessly alike, clones of each other. The other normal cells have been pushed aside and crowded out by these cellular Xerox copies, bullying cells, unruly, ill-mannered, and overly fecund intruders.

Hairy cell leukemia was appropriately named: the cells, rather than being nice and round, the way we drew them in junior high school science courses, are, well, *hairy*: they have many tiny projections from their walls. The "hairs" are actually an unevenness and exuberance of the cell membrane, leading to undulating ruffles. Bertha Bouroncle first described what was to be called hairy cell leukemia in 1958. The name she chose to describe it, leukemic reticuloendotheliosis, proved not to be a best-seller. Because of the characteristic appearance of the cells under the microscope, the name hairy cell leukemia became the moniker.

Tom puts another slide on the microscope. "This is the TRAP stain we did on your marrow," he says.

I give him a blank look.

"*TRAP* stands for Tartrate-Resistant Acid Phosphatase, not for how you feel. It's a stain that is more or less specific for hairy cell leukemia. You'll see that almost all of the cells in the marrow take up the stain and are dark on this slide."

I look into the microscope at the TRAP slide. Tom's right; the cells filling my marrow have dark granules in them, the mark of the hairy cell. My diagnosis is confirmed beyond question.

In my practice, I often see children who are sent to me by other pediatricians seeking my opinion. For most of those children, a chest X ray is needed, and in many cases, the child has already had many X rays. I try to show the X ray to the child and the parents, to explain the findings that are on the X ray, to help the family (and the child) understand what is going on in the child's lungs. I always think that if the family comprehends an illness and how it works, there is a better chance that they will be able to help with treatment. Although this seems to make intuitive sense, I find it remarkable that I am usually the first doctor who shows and explains the X rays to the patient and parents.

Now, in this laboratory at the Mayo Clinic, the tables are turned. I am being shown my own diagnosis, allowed to view a previously hidden part of myself, to understand what I shall be fighting. I now realize that for several months my body had been giving me warnings I had chosen to ignore, warnings that something was not right with me. And I remember all the excuses I'd come up with to explain them. In December, for example, I'd had an ingrown toenail. I'd figured it was a nuisance from my running, tight shoes, or cutting my nails wrong, but it took more than a week to heal. In January and February during my training for the fifty-mile run I'd had a cold and cough. The symptoms refused to abate and finally after weeks of what should have been a benign, self-limited illness, I took an antibiotic, something I almost never do. My chest started to hurt; I ignored it thinking it was a pulled muscle or cracked rib. The persistent pain eventually led me to get the X ray revealing the mass in my chest.

In January, I had taken aspirin for the chest pain and began having excessive bleeding when I cut myself shaving. Aspirin interferes with blood clotting, but this side effect is usually minor, especially with the small dose of aspirin I'd been taking. Yet I stupidly assured myself that the bloody face staring back at me from the mirror could be explained simply by the use of aspirin. Normally, platelets number some 150,000 to 300,000 per cubic milliliter of blood. The hairy cells had overrun my bone marrow, and the cells that produce platelets were in short supply. As a result, my platelet count was down to 60,000. This lowered platelet count, in combination with the amount of aspirin I had taken, explained my bleeding.

I had participated in my own deception, and the truth stands revealed in the microscope. As I peer into the microscope, I see the multitude of small cells taking up the stain, the multiplying reasons for my chronic cold, my bleeding, my fatigue; and I know that all of those mysterious symptoms are now explained. In the long run, recognizing the truth makes many things easier, or at least easier to deal with.

I move back from the microscope, then look in once more. The cells I see have only one true purpose: which is to kill me. No, it's not intentional, but their continued survival will result in my death, which in turn will lead to their death. A more perfect parasite would have planned better: survival after the host is killed is preferable to death coupled with a form of suicide. The obverse of the situation is blazingly simple: the hairy cell leukemia cells must all be killed.

My life is at a discernable crossroads, and I must choose which path I will follow. The direction I go is to be my choice, but my fate, no matter what I choose, is to be dictated in part by my illness. And the two main choices before me are vastly different. I can give in to the enemy, concede defeat, and simply wait for the disease to kill me; or I can take on my adversary on whatever terms it dictates. The leukemia has, at least for now, the upper hand. It will not stop and give me time to consider any other options: it's swept away most of my alternatives just as it's dislocated most of the normal cells in my bone marrow.

The realization of my predicament jolts me awake, and I just as suddenly find myself ready, even eager, to begin to fight for my own life. More importantly, I suddenly feel stronger. I know I am the patient, but I have seen my own hairy cells; they are mine, a part of me, carrying my own genetic code within them. I remember little of what Ed Rosenow told me, and I haven't had a real talk with Tom Habermann. Yet as I look into the microscope, I am newly armed against my enemy. Somehow, I foolishly tell myself, I am going to win the fight because I know what and who the enemy is, what they look like. At the same time, I realize I have absolutely no idea of how the fighting and winning will be done.

Tom puts the slides away, and we head back to his office. My mind is filled with myriad questions, each competing to be asked and confusing me as we walk. I can tell that Tom senses my confusion.

"It's probably hard to look at your own marrow like that," he says as we walk down the steps.

"That's nothing. You should have seen my face when I looked at my chest X ray and saw that big mass. I don't know how to say it. I just don't have the right word . . . and this may sound strange, but I'm glad I saw it . . . my marrow, I mean. I mean I'm glad I saw what I'm up against. Although I'm still not sure what I'm up against."

The shock of the words *hairy cell leukemia* is being replaced by the acceptance of the truth that I have leukemia. And even though I am a physician, my understanding of what the diagnosis actually means to me is almost nil. Am I going to die? Is there any treatment? Will I need other tests? Is the mass in my chest a form of leukemia . . . or something else? Will I still need an operation?

"Well, let's get back to the office and talk." Tom is leading the way back. "There's a lot to decide, and we should do it as soon as we can."

"Yes, let's decide. I mean I've got . . ."

"A million questions," Tom finishes my sentence for me. "We'll talk in the office."

Thinking all the way through the corridors and elevators to the hematology floor, I mentally put my questions into some semblance of order. But who am I to suggest that the "let's decide" implies that I know enough to help make any decisions? I have to tell myself to be patient and to be the patient. It would be easier on me to be the doctor. I wouldn't experience the same fear, confront the emotions, face my parents, friends, and especially Karin with the overwhelming truth of my own vulnerability. The illness seeks to destroy that feeling that I had as a child and never lost, that I would never die, the lie I always carry with me. As the physician, I can look at my disease as a disease, a curious medical problem, not really my problem, rather than a life-threatening part of myself. I can hide from the reality of the situation within the white-coated persona of myself as the doctor. I have a feeling that it will not be the last time I catch myself wanting to be the physician.

"What now? I mean what happens now?" I ask as we settle back in Tom's office.

"That's not exactly clear. The mass in your chest, it could be something related to the leukemia, like a lymphoma, or it could be another relatively benign process, like a thymoma. We need to know what it is. It might change your therapy."

I look back at Tom. "Great," I tell myself, "he doesn't know what this thing in my chest is. Great." But I know that there's no way that he can know what it is. And the list of things it could be is a wide spectrum from something really bad to something sorta not so bad. Now I know how my patient's feel when I tell them, "I don't know." And I'm not sure I like it.

"Biopsy? Mediastinoscopy?" I suggest as a way to find out what's pushing my trachea to the side. Mediastinoscopy is a technique for looking into that small area behind my sternum where the mass is located, using a very small tube placed thorough an incision at the base of the neck. Mediastinoscopy avoids a large incision, and the sternum doesn't have to be sawed vertically in two. I am hoping to miss out on the experience of major chest surgery, now that I know I have leukemia. But my hope is too soon dashed.

"No. Too dangerous. Your platelet count is way too low, and bleeding could be a problem . . . well, let's just say we don't want that problem, especially during mediastinoscopy. Trying to stop major mediastinal bleeding through a mediastinoscope is like trying to turn off a faucet through a peashooter."

The number of platelets in my blood is very low, and platelets are essential to stop bleeding, to allow the blood to clot. Unfortunately, there are other important structures in the area of the mass, structures including the aorta and other large blood vessels. A false move taking a biopsy through a mediastinoscope could prove fatal if the mass the surgeon biopsies turns out to be a large blood vessel. If the mass itself has a lot of blood vessels, then taking a biopsy of it through the mediastinoscope might also lead to a lot of uncontrolled bleeding. Tom's right: it is too risky. Any bleeding at all might just lead to an emergency sternotomy, an operation cutting through the sternum, just the one I'm hoping to avoid. And any operation preceded by the word *emergency* always carries a higher risk.

"Actually," Tom says, "I've talked that over with some other specialists around the country already. Everyone agrees that attacking the mass now is just not the way to go. We need to improve your blood counts first."

Tom has done his homework. He's spoken to other physicians, put his own thoughts out there, and gotten some ideas. Some patients might think that this is a sign of weakness by a physician who is in over his head. In reality, all of us physicians are in over our heads at times. Or at least, all physicians who take care of sick people wind up in over their heads at times. It's just that few of us admit it out loud, and we get used to treading water for periods of time. The really smart physician is the one who knows when things are getting out of hand and gets the right help fast. Even better, the gifted physician can get help and make it seem a natural part of the practice of medicine. I feel I'm lucky enough to have a doc smart enough to call the cavalry in when it's needed.

During my training, one of my mentors often reminded me that the majority of medical decisions are based on insufficient data. This is especially true in complicated cases, as I am proving to be. *Clinical judgment* is a term applied to making medical decisions in the face of limited facts, of knowing which illness or problem is most likely, of making the right move, calling the right shots. And clinical judgment can be taught, but only up to a point. Much of it is learned by watching other physicians go through the thought process involved in making decisions. But some part of clinical judgment is realized only by walking the lonely tightrope between right and wrong plans, the difference perhaps being paid in a steep price by the patient. Clinical judgment must sometimes be the result of learning gained from seeing the negative result of well-intentioned, often well thought out, unfortunately incorrect plans.

An adage I tell my residents summarizes one (somewhat cynical) explanation of how clinical judgment is attained:

How do you get good clinical judgment?
Experience.
How do you get experience?
Bad judgment.

In other words, clinical medicine with real patients is different from typical patients as they are presented in textbooks. Making the right decision for each patient requires thought, and the physician must weigh the possibilities, understand extenuating circumstances, and interpret the meaning (or potential meaning) of the data available. Many times, a decision must be made as to whether more information, in the form of lab tests or X rays, is needed before a final decision can be made. In some instances, there are no easy answers, and clinical judgment is relied upon. In some instances, it helps to talk with other physicians, describe the situation, and see what they say. Among other things, that is what Tom had done by talking with other hematologist-oncologists. He looks back at me now.

"A lot is changing in the treatment of hairy cell leukemia. There is much better treatment than there was only five or ten years ago. But we have to know what your chest mass is, although I'm not sure we have to find that out today. A quick biopsy might not give us enough tissue, and the risk of bleeding is too high. I think we need to do a splenectomy first. That will almost certainly improve your counts; then, after you've recovered from the splenectomy, we can have your chest mass removed entirely."

I sit there, looking back at him, dumbfounded. We've traveled a circuitous and speedy route that has swerved suddenly from the presence of a mass in my chest to a diagnosis of leukemia to having my spleen removed. We haven't even passed "go" and gotten the two hundred dollars.

"Splenectomy? Now?"

"Well, actually, yes. Before any of the recent medical treatments for hairy cell leukemia, splenectomy was almost standard therapy. Like I said, it will almost certainly improve your blood counts and allow for a safe sternotomy to get at the mass."

The answer as to the next step, then, lies in my spleen, or rather in its removal. There are actually two reasons that my blood cells, and particularly my platelets, are low. The first reason I've seen with all too much clarity through the microscope. My bone marrow is almost completely overridden with hairy cells, cramping the normal production of my platelets. The second reason is that my spleen is also congested with leukemia cells.

Normally, the spleen filters the blood, removing damaged or old cells. A spleen that is congested with leukemic cells, however, filters too well, like the thin, fiberglass filter in my furnace that becomes more efficient as it gets more clogged with filtered dust. Now, my spleen is culling out not just abnormal cells, but too many normal cells as well, leading to low platelets, red blood cells, and white blood cells. As Tom has said, one of the treatments for patients with hairy cell leukemia has been splenectomy, and in those patients, blood counts, including platelet counts, often markedly improved. A splenectomy probably won't cure my leukemia, but it'll help, buying me some platelets and some time to allow the surgeons to find out what's hiding in my chest.

Medicine isn't immune from infighting between its specialists, and throughout my training, I'd heard the various jibes directed from one branch of medicine toward another. Several of the more well known (and derogatory) are directed at surgeons and include such phrases as "Heal with steel" and "When in doubt, cut it out." But one of my favorite surgery-related phrases was said to me by a surgeon, who pointed out that pediatricians and internists spent a lot of time wringing their collective hands about the patient while the surgeons washed their hands so they could "Separate the patient from his disease." I am now the universal patient, about to be separated from my spleen, which, although not the complete disease, is certainly a place to start the disease-ridding process.

The last several days distill into this moment, the instant I must answer the first real question: am I ready to start back on the road to whatever health I am to be left with? Do I refuse treatment; do I ask for more time to think over my options (what options?); do I search out a second (hopefully more benign) second opinion somewhere? Or do I pull in my breath, look into the eyes of my recognized enemy, and tell the gathered troops that the battle will be joined? For me, the choice is easy and overwhelmingly obvious.

"Okay, I think I understand. Let's get going. I'm ready." But I can't help still feeling like a physician. "I've got one question. Is there anything I can read? I mean about hairy cell leukemia. I don't know much about it . . . maybe I could learn something."

Sure, I'm still a physician, and I somehow want to learn about illness. But this is my illness. Am I really interested in learning for myself the physician or for myself the patient? My professional interest in disease isn't quashed by the fact that I have the disease. I also believe that it is good for any patient to know more than just the name of their disease.

"I'll give you some references. You know where the library is?"

"Sure. All I want is a few. I don't need everything ever written about it. I just want to know . . . to know what I'm up against."

"Well, as I said, a lot is changing in treatment of hairy cell." Tom leaves off the "leukemia," as if it were a silent letter in a word. "Interferon is effective in a lot of cases. There is at least one new drug, called Pentostatin, which looks even better. There's a lot of talk about it working in nonsplenectomized patients, but your chest mass makes it difficult to avoid the splenectomy. So let's arrange for the surgery, then you can get to the library."

I look at my watch while Tom jots down some articles for me. It has only been a few hours since Ed told me my diagnosis, but it seems like I'd passed through Forever.

Tom calls Ed Rosenow, who soon is in Tom's office. They discuss my case in front of me. I sit on the couch for part of the discussion, stand up near them, sit back down, and stand up. They speak a little to me, acknowledging my presence, but mainly they speak to each other. I eavesdrop on the conversation, as I used to do by silently picking up the telephone extension while my parents talked with friends or relatives, back when I was a child.

"Who's operating tomorrow?" Ed asks.

Tomorrow?! I silently think. They're talking about operating that soon?

"I think van Heerden should do it. He's really slick. The schedule's right here." Tom reaches into the desk drawer and pulls out a flat calendar with weekdays colored blue or orange. "Hmm . . . van Heerden is on for Thursday. I'd go for that. Only two days away . . ."

Two days?

"You want to call him?" Ed suggests.

Tom picks up the phone. He gets through to van Heerden right away, as if van Heerden were sitting around waiting for the call. It's never this efficient back home. I hear one end of the conversation.

". . . a forty-year-old physician with an anterior mediastinal mass, splenomegaly, and his marrow shows he's got hairy cell leukemia . . . actually, it's Len Kurland's son . . . isn't that the truth . . . yeah, wouldn't you know it has to be a staff guy's family member . . . anyway, Ed and I feel that he should have a splenectomy first . . . his platelets are only sixty K . . . yeah, and do the sternotomy later . . . he's in my office now . . . okay . . . Tomorrow? . . . Okay, I'll set it up. Thanks . . . yeah, see you soon."

Tom nods at Ed and turns to me.

"You'll see Jon van Heerden tomorrow. Surgery will be on Thursday morning. We'll set it up now."

"And now?" I ask.

They look back and forth to each other, but after a moment, Tom softly smiles.

"You've probably had enough of this for one day. Why don't you get some lunch or something? I suppose you'd like to tell your folks, unless you think I should."

"No, no . . . I'll tell them. And yes, I've had enough for at least one day and probably a few more."

We all shake hands, as if we're striking a deal, and, as if I were a somnambulist, Tom gently leads me out to the front desk, where once more the phone calls are made, the schedule finalized, forms filled out and put in the standard envelope, and instructions given to me as to where to be at what time tomorrow. I take my package of instructions, ride the elevator down, wend my way into the tunnel and, my feet directing themselves seemingly without any help from me, find myself back in my father's building. It is about noon.

I go up to the sixth floor and past the rows of cubicles with desks, each piled with charts, IBM cards, computer paper. There is the quiet clicking of the electric typewriters and the background hum of the word processors. I approach the area of my father's secretary, surrounded by file cabinets and shelves containing numerous cardboard boxes, book sized and numbered, each one corresponding to one or two of the papers written by my father and his many collaborators over the years. The numbers on the boxes run to well over the two hundred mark.

"Hi, Linda," I say to the dark-haired woman peering at the computer screen.

"Oh, Geoff. Your father's in his office. He told me to send you in when you got here. Let's see . . . yes, he's off the phone for the moment . . . better get him now."

I walk around a corner and into the office. It is only about ten feet long and perhaps five or six feet wide but is on the corner of the building and offers a view over some of the lesser Clinic buildings to the prairie beyond the city. A couch with tired upholstery upon which sit some books and papers is set against the wall opposite the door through which I enter. There are model airplanes, copies of those flown by my brother Keith when he'd been in the Marines, on the windowsill. A mobile of small prop planes flutters above the end of the couch. On the wall above the couch and on the short wall to my left are framed diplomas and photographs. The diplomas are far from the usual medical or graduate school diplomas. These are, instead, unusual papers of recognition: charter membership in the Western Pacific Neurological Society, diplomas and awards written in Japanese. Most of the photographs were taken in the tropics: sunset in the Marianas, groups of scientists wearing tropical suits in the western Pacific. There is my father's photograph of my sister, the youngest of the siblings, taken some ten or so years earlier, when she was approaching adolescence with the speed of a freight train without a brake on the downhill side of the Rockies. The first time I'd seen it, I didn't recognize it as my sister, thinking instead that the young woman whose face was framed by leaves, looking to the side of the camera, must have been a professional model. Finally, there is a photograph of my father with Albert Schweitzer, each of them wearing a similar white hat, my father smiling at Schweitzer and at the camera. Schweitzer's thick mustache makes it almost impossible to tell if he is smiling or scowling. Schweitzer had given my father the hat he is wearing in the photograph, sort of a necessary piece of clothing and a welcoming badge on arrival at Lambaréné, Schweitzer's hospital in the Congo. Since that day, my father has worn a white cotton brimmed hat wherever he goes, partly in homage to Schweitzer and partly in deference to his sunburn-prone balding pate. The hat now sits on the couch, and my father is standing rather than sitting at his desk at the not-so-far end of the room.

"Well, what's up?" he asks.

I tell him the diagnosis. He looks about as blank as I must have when Ed Rosenow had said it to me.

"What? Hairy cell leukemia? What does Ed want to do?" He doesn't look scared or panicked. He seems skeptical, as if he's turning the diagnosis over in his mind.

"I think Tom Habermann is taking over. He's the hematologist . . . seems to know a lot about hairy cell." I, like Habermann, now leave "leukemia" off.

"I don't think I've met Habermann, but I've heard about him. Actually, now that I think about it, he had wanted to put together the Clinic experience with hairy cell leukemia . . . I seem to recall that. So what now? What's with this mediastinal mass? How does that fit in?"

"They're not sure what that is, but they think I've got to have a splenectomy first, because my blood counts are pretty bad. My spleen is huge and my platelets are only sixty thousand. They're pretty sure a splenectomy should raise my counts enough to make it safe to remove the mass. I'm supposed to meet a Jon van Heerden tomorrow, and the splenectomy is on Thursday. After I'm healed up in six weeks or so, I get my chest cracked," I say with a wry smile.

My father seems stunned by it all but recovers quickly. "I know van Heerden. I've heard he's a terrific surgeon." He appears a bit relieved with his own news.

"Listen," he says, "let's get a quick bite of lunch, then you can go home. We'll just go down to the cafeteria here."

"Sure. But I'm going to the library after lunch and home a bit later. Habermann gave me a few references, so I thought I'd read up a bit on hairy cell, see what I can learn." He nods and gives me his best version of a knowing look but still isn't ready to take it all in.

We start toward the elevator, walking past the desks, files, and word processors again. On the way down and then over a rapid-fire lunch of soup, I again summarize the morning, trying to answer my father's questions, which are all too often ones I realized I should have asked: What are the risks of doing the splenectomy with my platelet count so low? When will I have the mass in my chest removed, and who's going to do that surgery? What is the likelihood that the chest mass is another malignancy like a lymphoma? Although not an expert on hairy cell leukemia, my father certainly can think better as a physician than I can at that moment.

"I tell you what, Dad. I'll see what I can find in the library. What I can't figure out, I'll ask Habermann as soon as I see him. Fair enough?"

"Sure. Sure. But do you really want to go to the library? Do you really want to read up on this? I mean, you're the patient, not the doctor."

"Yeah. But . . . I don't know; maybe I can learn something from this."

"Oh, I'm sure you'll learn from this." He doesn't weigh the import of the words just spoken. "Do you want me to tell Mom? It might be best to let her in on it somewhat gently. I'll call if you want."

"Um . . . okay. Okay. Then I'll call her when I'm done in the library and get a ride home."

"Why don't you go home with me, instead? I won't have to work too much longer. Want a quick swim before dinner?"

"No . . . no thanks. I think I'd better see what I can learn. Assuming I can concentrate enough to learn anything at all. Maybe I'll run later."

"You sure? I mean are you sure you want to run? I mean . . ." His voice trails off.

"Don't worry, Dad. I won't be running too far. And I doubt that I'll be in the library all that long, anyway. I'll call Mom when I'm done."

I appreciate how my father is a more well-rounded physician-scientist than he might appear at times since he doesn't spend a lot of time with patients. One might think that he's more interested in laboratory results, physical findings, those reproducible marks of disease, rather than the fluid and plastic feelings and personal histories of the patients whose real lives, lived through time, form the basis of and the reason for the medical record in the first place.

My father seeks the truth about disease by distilling medical records into their essence, searching there for the common traits of illness, the thread that binds together the differing histories, laboratory tests, and physical findings derived from the lives of the sufferers, in order to solve the mystery lying deep within the records, hidden within the patients themselves. By delving so deeply into his subject, he sometimes might seem to be pursuing an arcane and rather abstract triumph, but for my father, the work is of everyday importance, exquisitely relevant to modern medicine. He is so at home in his job that he probably can see himself doing nothing else. And, as he often reminds me, his position at the Clinic allows him to utilize its vast medical record system, which some have called a national medical treasure, in his continuing studies of a whole variety of diseases. The almost commonplace way he approaches his job coupled with the fact that he still finds time every day for a swim, confirm his total immersion in work and play. He'd honed his epidemiological skills at Harvard, Johns Hopkins, the Clinic, and the National Institutes of Health before returning to the Mayo Clinic in 1964. His major interest had always been the epidemiology of neurologic diseases, and he's already spent over thirty years of his career investigating amyotrophic lateral sclerosis, better known as Lou Gehrig's disease, on the island of Guam in the western Pacific.

I always secretly thought that one of the reasons he so liked to study the disease on Guam was the fact that the snorkeling and swimming were so good. After one of those early trips, he brought my brothers and me presents of masks and snorkels, making us the envy of our friends at the local pool. The ability to just stay underwater watching everyone else seemed to me, a mere nine-year-old, as much of an advance as, say, the discovery of electricity. The other presents from the mysterious islands of the western Pacific—the Palauan storyboards, the tiki love sticks, the war masks—all paled by comparison. Back then, in the mid-1950s, swimming was for all of us, including my father, the main obsession encouraged outside of work or, for my brothers and me, school.

Like my father, I know what it is to become obsessed with one's work, although I doubt that I'll ever be as successful as he. To some extent, the major way I've been able to match my father has not been in work, but in play. As he was and still is a determined swimmer, I am a determined runner. On trips, my father packs his bathing suit; I take my shorts, shirt, running shoes, and socks. When he checks into a motel, my father first tests the temperature in the swimming pool (if it's too cold, he's been known to immediately check out and go somewhere else). When I arrive at a hotel, I first inquire as to where I can safely run in the neighborhood.

But here, after lunch, I have my own job to do, my own task, to discover what I can about hairy cell leukemia. My father steps into the elevator, wishes me luck, and is carried back up to his office. I go across the street to the Plummer Building, in whose upper floors is contained the vast holdings of the medical library of the Mayo Clinic. Preparing to go to the library, on a new assignment for myself, I know that if I choose to do so, I can probably learn all that I need to know about hairy cell leukemia and do a pretty good job of it. The question my father had asked a few minutes before was the right one. Even though we both know I could learn about it, the question remains: should I learn about it? I am faced with a dilemma: Am I the physician, or at least one of the physicians, or am I the patient? How far can I allow myself to be both? Can I relinquish control over my life to some disease?

I am used to being in charge of my life (not to mention the lives of my patients). But I know that I can't possibly direct my own care, at least not completely since I know next to nothing about hairy cell leukemia. And energy spent in trying to read as much as I can about the disease may rob me of my ability to think clearly as a patient, to be able to do the other things so necessary to maintain my life, my sanity. Anyway, I ask myself, why would I want to be directly responsible for the major decisions about my illness? Sir William Osler, one of the great physicians of the early twentieth century, said: "The physician who treats himself has a fool for a patient."

But giving up being a doc is difficult, and my feet find their way to the medical library, where I sign in not as a patient, but as an assistant professor of pediatrics, University of California, Davis. I wander into the holdings and pull several of the references Tom had given me, along with a recent textbook of hematology. Finding a quiet carrel at the end of one of the stacks of books, I start to read.

The brief chapter on hairy cell leukemia in the hematology text-book is depressing enough for a start, suggesting that interferon may be helpful but not commonly associated with complete remission from the disease. I am hoping it is out of date, at least according to what Tom had been saying. I look over several of the articles Tom had suggested. Generally, they are discussions of long-term results of various treatments in a relatively large number of patients. I look at survival curves, the representation of percentages of patients who remained alive over time after their diagnosis. Without therapy, the curves show that about 40 percent of the patients survived five or more years; the newer treatments improved survival, but nothing gave a survival rate of 100 percent. There is Death, staring back at me from the curves, as if it is choosing to mock those of us who refer to the graphs as *survival* curves. I read case reports: descriptions of individual patients, their histories, findings, courses. Too many of these hit close to home, sounding very much like me. With a mixture of morbid fas-cination, scientific curiosity, and personal trepidation, I read of the complications suffered by many of my predecessors with hairy cell leukemia, those who went before me and paid the deeply personal price on behalf of a medical establishment that was still learning about the disease itself. Overwhelming fatal infections, failures of various drugs to stem the growth of the leukemic cells, enlarged spleens rupturing within debilitated bodies . . . and occasional successes of therapies that were, and remained, experimental.

Repeatedly, I find myself gazing out the window, looking at the flat Minnesota land surrounding Rochester, the prairie with its distant horizon, the cumulus clouds floating against the deep blue sky. Each time I try to return to the reading, I first must force my mind back from its wandering, perhaps to avoid my turning inward once more to self-destruct in depressed response to the grim literature before me. Finally, after taking some limited notes and copying some of the main articles, I take my leave of the library, realizing that my inability to concentrate fully on this task is actually my own message telling myself that it's okay to accept my disease, accept its risks, accept my physicians, and accept their knowledge, even given that hairy cell leukemia has only recently been described and is still in the process of being explored. Many things are imperfect, and medicine, I know, is certainly one of them. I have always said that people should never expect total perfection from their physicians: perfect physicians are the product of television and movies, not reality. I am facing eyeball to eyeball the reality of that imperfection and with it the possibility that the imperfection of a young science and the imperfection based on the best of intentions might cost me my own life.

My mother drives slowly up to the curb where I wait. I slip into the car with as much of a smile as I can muster. My mother returns my look with a bleak stare.

"Hey, lady, thanks for the ride."

"Very funny. Dad told me. I . . ." She is not looking at me as she drives out onto the unbusy street that characterizes the quiet that is Rochester in midafternoon before the Clinic closes. "I . . . I don't know what to say. Are you okay? Did you find out anything at the library?"

"Not too much . . . some stuff but not everything. I can't learn everything, at least not right now."

"Anything in particular? What is hairy cell leukemia, anyway? I've never even heard of it." We're already approaching the house: the advantage and disadvantage of living in a small town.

"First of all, it's rare. Only about 2 percent of all adult leukemia cases are hairy cell. I'm not sure if that's good or bad. It's a chronic type of leukemia, even without treatment there's a 40 percent long-term survival."

"Forty percent doesn't sound like much to me." She had turned toward me but now quickly looks away. "But I suppose it's not zero, either."

"I don't particularly like the odds myself. I suppose I always tell patients that if it's a 1 percent chance of something happening, either good or bad, and it happens to you, then your odds are 100 percent."

"And you meet Jon van Heerden tomorrow? I've heard very good things about him. Oh, what'll you do this afternoon. Swim with Dad?"

"No. I think I'll go for a run and then relax. I may not be able to run for a while, you know."

"Yes," she sighs, "you may not be able to . . . for a while . . ."

I change into my running stuff and come to the kitchen to stretch before going outside. Soup is heating, my mother tending it as I lie on the floor pulling my legs from one difficult position to another.

"You know, I'm glad you're going for a run." She only half turns toward me, instead choosing to peer into the soup kettle. The kettle is an old elliptical pan, inherited from her mother, more appropriate for baking a brisket of beef than making soup.

"So am I. I'm tougher than I look."

"Oh, really?" She slowly stirs the soup.

I run, only a few miles, but I run, and manage for a few of the minutes to forget my diagnosis, the prospect of surgery, the survival curves for hairy cell leukemia, and the Clinic. The rest of the afternoon I dutifully ignore anything to do with medicine. I watch television, the news, the weather channel, anything in the vast wasteland that is American TV. I don't have a television at home, and I haven't had one for a long time; I am an anomaly, for I try to read before I fall asleep instead of watching Johnny Carson. The only time I ever actually watch TV, it seems, are those times when I visit home. It now seems rather backward: the time I should be visiting, talking with my folks, I choose to watch the box that provides easy answers to all our problems, instant winners, capsule comments, and circumscribed worldviews.

Soon it is evening, and I eat what dinner I can, hearing the repetitive questions within myself: What will happen next? What will I do next? And always the answer returns: I don't know. I palpably feel the control over my life slipping inexorably from my grasp. I even tell myself that part of its loss is my own choice, as if that makes it all right. Only by convincing myself that I am giving it up willingly do I stand any chance of being able to reclaim it. Later in the night, I have one more assignment.

The phone line sounds hollow as I speak into it. "Hi, Karin. How are things out there?"

"Fine, fine. Well," the cheery voice says, "what's up?" She perhaps expects an equally cheery answer, but she can only get the answer I can give, and I must give it to her. The line is silent, first for a moment, then another.

"What? What . . . leukemia?"

"Hairy cell. It's called hairy cell leukemia."

She sees me dying on the other end of the line. "Are you okay? No, that's not what I mean. Are . . . what are . . . what . . ." Her voice trails off. I see her eyes watering, her jaw shaking just a little. I want to reach through the line to her.

"Listen. I have to get my spleen out, probably in a couple of days. I see the surgeon tomorrow. That should help my blood counts. I'll have to come back here in about a month and a half to have this thing in my chest removed. They haven't told me much more."

"Oh, God . . ."

"Listen. I actually feel okay. I'm going to be fine . . . really."

"Should I come out there? You know I'll come out there."

"No. The kids need you. Right now things here are okay enough. Surgery will be over and I should be back in Sacramento in maybe a week or so. I know you'd come out, but believe me, you don't have to, not right now. Is that okay?"

"Yes . . . no . . . I don't know. I suppose so. Is there anything I can do? Anything you need? Do people at the hospital know?"

"I'll let Ruth know, and I'm sure she can spread the word. No, I don't need anything right now, except to get my spleen out, to start to get better. There is something, actually . . ."

"Yes?"

"Think about me."

"Honey, I think about you all the time."

"That's all I need and all I need to know. I'll be back soon, I promise. And I'll call as much as I can. My folks'll let you know what's going on, too. Listen, I better get to sleep. I'm meeting my surgeon in the morning, and I want to look my best."

"Very funny. But you always look your best."

"Actually, I look my best when I'm with you."

"Don't overdo it. But you will be careful, won't you?"

"Careful? Of course, but I suppose it's more important to tell that to the surgeon."

"Well, tell him for me, please."

"It's a deal. Now, I've got to get some sleep. Say hi to the kids. I love you."

"I love you, too. Call me."

I reluctantly hang up the phone. The house is silent, and I fall into bed.

After a quick breakfast, my mother drives me to the Clinic to meet Jon van Heerden. She accompanies me up the elevator and sits with me in the cavernous waiting room. She knits; I try to read. Unlike her, I get little accomplished and cannot concentrate on the lines in front of me. I am ushered into van Heerden's examination room, yet another copy of the other exam rooms I've been in before. After only a few minutes, I hear a rustling of paper outside the closed door, as someone peruses my chart. A moment later, van Heerden nearly bursts through the door. A thin, almost gaunt, short man in his late forties, van Heerden's South African Dutch accent, a mixture of not-quite British and not-quite Dutch, is evident as he introduces himself. Sparkling eyes that return my look offset his very short hair and thin face.

"Interesting story," he says. "Tom Habermann told me about you. I was reading your chart. You run a lot, it seems."

I rub the back of my head and look down, smiling, "Yes, you could say I do."

"Well, we'll just have to see about getting you back to that as soon as is reasonable, right?"

I brighten, looking up. "Absolutely, absolutely."

"Let me just take a quick look at you. Could you take off your shirt and hop up on the table, please?"

He briefly examines my belly, gently palpating my enormous spleen, then listens to my chest, my heart. He sits down at the desk in the room as I put my shirt back on.

"Let's see," he says as he looks at his schedule book. He calls his secretary to schedule my case and turns back to me. The entire process—discussion, examination, arranging for the surgery—has taken only about fifteen or twenty minutes.

"I'll have you come in to hospital early tomorrow, say 6:30. Nothing to eat or drink after midnight. All you have to do now is go and pre-register. And don't worry, it should go just fine. I'm going to send you back to Ed and have him give the final okay. I think you should have a Pneumovax shot."

In only a few minutes, I am back with Ed, my mother again in the waiting room. Ed had by then arranged to give me the Pneumococcal vaccine, which will hopefully offer some protection against an overwhelming infection that can suddenly strike people without spleens. Ed tells me that while not 100 percent effective, it's worth getting and has to be given before my spleen is removed. He sends me off to register for surgery.

My mother and I wait patiently in the registration area on the first floor of the Mayo Building. There is little except the centrally placed bank of elevators to obstruct the nearly half-square-block expanse of white marble, reflecting the glow of the light all around us. My mother, sitting beside me, knits quietly.

"What are you knitting now, Mom?"

"Caps for the premature babies at St. Mary's. I can do one of these in about ten minutes. Their little heads are so tiny . . . but you probably know that. You took care of preemies, didn't you?"

"Yeah, plenty during residency." I glance down at the knitted wool that doesn't look like much of anything in her hands. "I guess you got quite a few done today, with the waiting and all, eh?"

"Well, no . . . it's been a tough day. I've had trouble working on them. It's been a tough day for both of us, I suppose."

"For both of us," I agree.

I expect to wait for hours in the lobby but hear my name called after only a few minutes. Going up to the large registration desk, I'm soon directed into a cubicle. The admissions clerk, smiling, asks the usual information: date of birth, address, insurance, next-of-kin . . . the perfunctory and premonitory types of questions asked by any self-respecting medical center. The usual answers suffice. I am then asked my religious preference. When I'm asked that question in almost any other context, I tell people that I'm a physician who runs a lot, and leave it at that. But it somehow doesn't seem like quite the right answer when asked the day before my surgery. I give a blank look.

"Religious preference?" The clerk asks once more.

"Oh. Uh . . . how about Unitarian? Sure," I say quietly, almost to myself. "Unitarian . . ."

Even though their ancestry (and thus mine) and that of almost all of our relatives is Jewish, my parents raised me and my siblings without any strict religion in mind, unless one considers Unitarian Sunday school as an example of a strict religion. To me, Unitarian Sunday school seems closer to a kind of oxymoron. I remember spending much of the time in Sunday school exploring the world around me. It was in Sunday school, not in my father's office, that I first gazed into a microscope at a suspended drop of pond water, surprised by the host of moving cells more like apparitions of another world. If anything, I learned more about other religions by going to their services as a part of my Unitarian Sunday school experience: Baptist, Catholic, Buddhist faiths were all subjects of study there. Incredibly, I later found out from one of my uncles that my father had been fervently religious earlier in his life, so much so that he'd been nicknamed "Kosh" for his attention to the strict Jewish dietary laws. But later, sometime during his college days at Hopkins, he felt that any dogmatism, be it Jewish, Catholic, or Hindu, was not for him. Now, the closest my father comes to being religious is in his love of exercise: still swimming his half a mile a day, wearing a newer version of the mask and snorkel he brought back with him from Guam so many years ago. Like father, like son: running for me is a quasi-religious event. But that won't do, I guess, for St. Mary's. I wonder, might it make a difference if I tell them that I'm Catholic? They'd probably find out and punish me; perhaps I have it in me to follow some strict religion after all.

"Okay. Unitarian." The clerk puts the finishing touches on the registration form. I sign in the areas marked with Xs. My presurgery instructions from her are brief: St. Mary's Hospital Admissions, 6:30 the following morning. Nothing to eat or drink tonight after midnight.

We go home, my mother and I, wrapped in silence, except for some brief planning for tomorrow. We agree that she'll take me to St. Mary's in the morning. It is not yet late afternoon, but I choose not to run today, as if my strength can be hoarded somehow to get me through tomorrow a bit more efficiently. Or, perhaps, I am silently bargaining for something, some respite, some greater hope, some reward of cure if I make the gesture of giving up this, my own version of religion, as a way of allowing myself into a different one.

A few hours later, we sit at the table over a dinner initially far too quiet for its own good. Throughout my life, I've always had trouble talking about my feelings, hopes, and fears with my parents, indeed, with most people. My parents themselves have also been quiet about innermost feelings, at least with their children. I've never had the experience of revealing myself to others, and I've been slow to learn how difficult my life was as a result. My tendency to hide myself from others hadn't helped my relationships in the past. I've always been uncomfortable talking about things that really mattered: trust, love, fear. So I've always taken the supposed easy way out: I simply didn't talk much about it at all. Bragging to myself that I was being self-sufficient, in reality, I was just alone. And now, even with my parents here, I am alone. Karin, my closest, my dearest, my most beloved, is some thousand miles away. It is ironic, as my aloneness at this very moment is in the midst of what I feel is a relationship. All my other relationships were at heart too much of a sham on my part, a result of my own fear of intimacy. I had been too afraid to trust myself with someone else's needs and had just as strongly resisted relinquishing my own needs to another. I had kept my soul apart from Ann, ultimately driving her away, ironically into the life of my former partner. I've only recently begun to awaken to the realization that I have to be willing to give up myself to gain myself in the person and life of another. My hope with Karin, I repeatedly tell myself, rests on my treating her differently: I must have her as a part of my life, not as an accessory to it. If this is to work, I must be open, truthful, and allow her into my own feelings, reciprocating by being there for her.

But tonight, before surgery, it's hard to talk about the swirlings within me; since I'm unable to speak about them, the thoughts and fears are hard for me to pin down, to examine. To their credit, my parents try their best to get me to talk as much as I am willing. In a pattern so typical of my own life as a scientist and physician, it seems easier to approach the whole problem from the facts I've learned in only the last few days from the reading I'd done about hairy cell leukemia. The scientific aspects of my illness, rather than the metaphysical and personal perspective gained by actually having the illness, are less threatening to me. It is easier to talk about how a gun works than to explain the feeling of staring into a loaded barrel.

"Well, what did you learn about the leukemia?" my father asks as we try to eat.

I lean back in the chair, away from the table, and look up at the ceiling, rather than at my father. My mother quietly puts down her fork. The ceiling light is bright, shining in my eyes, burning into the room, now so quiet.

"Well, like I told Mom earlier, it's not common."

"How common?" my father asks. He is, after all, a physician who deals with numbers all the time. I look over at my mother's worried face.

"It's only about 1 or 2 percent of all adult leukemias. What's weird is that, up until very recently, there was no really good treatment for it.

I mean, the usual chemotherapy used for leukemia didn't work very well." My voice trails off into the air, into the ceiling light, as I ask myself silently, What will happen next? What will I do?

"Chemotherapy? Didn't work? Why?" My mother's face is lined and worried, for I had told her only part of what I'd learned earlier in the day. The kitchen has the silence of the moon, the murmuring quiet of the trail alongside the American River in Sacramento on which I was running only a few weeks before. I wish the radio or even the TV were on, a diversion to insinuate itself between me and the truth.

"Most chemotherapy is designed to kill rapidly dividing cells. You know, like tumor cells. Anyway, the main side effect is that they kill too many cells that are supposed to be dividing quickly, like blood cells and cells lining the gut."

"So the chemotherapy kills the normal cells? I thought it was supposed to kill tumor cells. I mean, even if it kills normal cells, won't it kill more of the tumor cells?"

"Well . . . it isn't that selective. Most chemotherapy is still relatively crude, what we'd call nonspecific. It's something like using a shotgun instead of a pistol, a machete instead of pruning shears. It's like the chemotherapy kills the innocent bystanders along with the intended target and hopes there are enough innocent bystanders left standing around when the chemotheraphy is done." Silence, for the moment, faces me down. My mother slowly nods.

"Let me give you an example, Mom." I do some quick calculating in my head. "The average red blood cell survives about 120 days. In other words, to stay even with the number of red blood cells we have, a little less than 1 percent have to be replaced every day. And there are probably well over a hundred million red blood cells in a teaspoonful of blood. And we have, literally, several quarts of blood. So if you're just talking about red blood cells, the numbers we have to produce each day are enormous. Add in all the white blood cells, cells lining the gut, platelets . . . well, the numbers of cells we have to make are huge. So with chemotherapy, even when it works, patients still become anemic, have increased risk for infections, tend to bleed. Anyway, the stuff I read suggested that the chemotherapies they tried didn't kill hairy cells all that much better than they killed normal cells. So the patients got sick, anemic, developed infections, and often died from the side effects of the chemotherapy, without the leukemia being cured. It's a version of the old story about the cure being worse than the disease."

I have a wry smile on my face, but I'm remembering how I'd seen the workings of chemotherapy from the vantage point of a resident in pediatrics. Even though a lot of the chemotherapy "worked" for child-hood leukemia, it seemed back then that much of my time was spent taking care of patients suffering from the side effects of the supposedly life-saving drugs I'd pushed into their veins. Most of them were bald headed, thin, anemic, vomiting, and frightened after they got their chemotherapy. They were always at risk of invasion by hordes of bac-teria ready to sweep through their bodies as soon as the thin barriers of skin or mucous membrane were breached.

Just giving them their chemotherapy had been harrowing at times. Virtually all of it back then required brand new intravenous lines with each infusion, and several of the drugs were highly toxic. I remem-bered that when I arrived on the oncology ward to start as the intern, I was introduced to one of my patients, a beautiful fourteen-year-old girl. When her chemotherapy had been given just a few days before, the needle had slipped out of the vein, allowing the medicine to go into her arm, beneath the skin. The entire area became inflamed, burned. It took weeks to heal and eventually required plastic surgery to close the scar. I sit now at the dinner table, trying to put the thought of chemotherapy out of my mind, trying to forget about side effects like nausea and vomiting, infections, bleeding.

I think about the baldness common to most of the patients I'd taken care of. I've always been proud of my full head of hair and wore it especially long during the sixties. As a medical student at Stanford, I'd gone into San Francisco many times to the shows at the Fillmore. Rock and roll was an influence on my life, as it was on most others of my generation. Like many, I played at playing the guitar and had been in a (not very good) band in college. Long hair had been "in," and it would have been hard to pick me out as being a medical student during those times. I certainly don't want to lose my hair. But, then again, I don't want to have hairy cell leukemia. And I don't want to lose my life to save my head of hair, which I know will grow back after the chemotherapy is done. That is, if I survive.

My mother is looking intently at me, not knowing what to say or ask. She starts to get up, but slumps back down, her face pale now, and her gaze drops to her plate.

"You know," I say to her, "it was tough going to the library, trying to read about this stuff. It was just too close to home. The case reports sounded too familiar, too much like me. Part of me doesn't want to know anything at all, just be a patient, just go along with whatever happens. Maybe that's best for me, I don't know . . . I don't know how I should be with all this."

"How can anyone know how they're supposed to be with this?" my mother asks. I look back at her.

"Yeah, you're right." None of us at the table really knows how we're supposed to behave in the situation we find ourselves in. "But I did learn some things about the disease. And I think that it's good that I did . . . that I went to the library . . . that I tried. I'm used to being in control of my life, you know. It's a way of holding on to some of that . . . to hold on to some of myself . . . I'd be lying if I said I weren't scared, but I didn't finish telling you some of the other stuff I learned."

"Like what?" My father looks up from his cup of tea.

"Well, interferon works on hairy cell leukemia. Can you believe that? I mean, this was the stuff that made the cover of *Time* magazine, and I almost laughed when I saw it back then. It was supposed to be the next wonder drug, able to cure everything, but was something of a flop, at least that's what I'd always thought. Anyway, I never used it treating kids. But it's effective in hairy cell. It doesn't always lead to a cure, but a lot of people get better with it. Actually, another weird thing about hairy cell is that it has a fairly high rate of spontaneous remission."

"What do you mean, spontaneous?" my mother asks.

"I mean it just goes into remission sometimes. Who knows, maybe it'll happen to me . . . maybe after my splenectomy . . ."

"Is it linked with any viruses . . . like AIDS?" It is my father the epidemiologist and scientist.

"Gee, I don't remember seeing anything like that mentioned. But with it just going away like that makes you wonder if there might be some infection causing it. The infection goes, and sooner or later so does the leukemia."

"Could you have gotten anything in Nepal during your trip there?"

"Tom didn't make much of the fact that'd I'd been there, Dad. I remember mentioning my trip to Rosenow . . . I'm sure he told Tom. Neither said anything more about it."

"Well, they should know, I guess." He looks at his watch and starts to get up. "It's getting late; you've got to get up early."

"Yeah, so they can put me to sleep."

"I'm going to drive you to St. Marys in the morning," my mother says. "We should all try to get some sleep."

"Okay. I'll see you in the morning, Mom. I'll see you when I'm out of surgery, Dad." I get up from the table to help clear the dishes.

"Sit down," my mother says. "Relax. I'll do it."

"No, I'll help. After all, I may not be able to help out for the next few nights."

My father stays in his chair for a moment, reading the paper, then, as if suddenly awakened, snatches up his own plate to take it to the sink. I smile at my mother, who smiles back; we both know my father almost never helps to clear the table; he is used to being served by my mother. Indeed, my mother has been accustomed to waiting on all of us, my father, my brothers, sister, and me, all during our childhood years. She'd always answered our clamorings for her to sit down and eat with a quiet, "In a minute . . . let me bring you some more brisket."

After the table is cleared and the dishes stowed in the dishwasher, I sit down again. My father is washing up for bed. My mother brings over a last cup of tea for her and me. The rest of the house is dark and quiet, and it is just the two of us in the kitchen, sitting across from each other at the table.

"How do you feel? I mean, really?" she asks.

"Under the circumstances, okay, I guess. I know it won't be easy, but there's just something I feel that tells me I'm going to be okay."

"I know you'll be okay," my mother says, not very convincingly. "You've always been tough."

"Thanks. I take that as a compliment. Thanks."

"I meant it as a compliment. You know, your father is worried about your running, but I think you know what's best for you. You always have."

"I'm not sure if 'always' is the right word, but I've tried to do what I think is right. I can understand how Dad feels. Anyway, if I do well with all of this, my running has to get some of the credit, along with you and Dad . . . and probably Karin. That reminds me, I've got to call her; I promised I would tonight."

"Yes, you better. Give her our love when you talk with her."

We finish our tea, hug, and say good night. I tiptoe down the stairs, even though I'm the only one down there. I pull the phone into the bedroom, my brother Steve's bedroom. I flop onto the old swaybacked bed and dial.

"Hello." Karin's bright voice reflects the fact that it is two hours earlier in Sacramento.

"Hi." There is a moment of silence on the other end of the phone, a few seconds for Karin to swallow hard. Her tone drops a few notches, and her voice softens into syrup.

"Hi, hon. Are you all right? Surgery is tomorrow, right?"

"Right." Silence. "Early morning. I'll be . . . I'll be okay. I miss you . . . I . . ."

"I miss you too. I love you . . . the kids told me to tell you to get better soon. I'm telling you to get better soon . . . and come back soon. You will come back soon, won't you?"

"As soon as I can. You know that. I really do miss you, you know. How is everything back there?"

"Oh, about the same." And she tells me of the hospital, the latest pharmacy gossip, her neighbors at home, the beautiful local weather.

"Geoff, you will be all right, won't you?" Her voice is now not the same, shaking inside. I feel the same fear but hope my voice doesn't betray me. It is enough for one of us to be afraid more or less in the open.

"I'll be all right. I promise. My folks say hi, and they promised me they'd call you as soon as things were settled down."

"Okay, but I'll want to talk to you."

"Sure," I laugh, "but they may be able to call you sooner than I will."

"Well, all right. Now get a good night's sleep. Remember, I love you. I mean it. I want to you to get well. Soon."

"I will. I love you, too. You know that."

"Yes."

"Yes. Wish me luck again, then good night."

"Good night. Good luck. I love you."

"I love you, too. Good night, Karin." The line clicks. My parents are asleep, and it is as if I am now alone in the house.

A few minutes later, I try to read a soon-to-be-forgotten novel, the words on the page foreign scribblings, meaningless to me as my mind wanders off to the other reading I'd done earlier today and to the much more distant time when I had been a resident on the pediatric oncology ward. Just as they had at dinner, those memories now force their way into my consciousness, even as I try to fight them off.

I am suddenly there again, working on that ward, walking the corridors at night, checking on the patients, hoping that disaster won't appear. Some of the parents, banding together for support, sit in the alcove between the two ward areas. They are smoking (this before hospitals saw the wisdom of being smoke free) and talking in quiet voices, comparing each child's progress or side effects or tumor or new hope. The morning will soon come, with the hours of rounds, where decisions about treatment will be made by the attending physicians.

After rounds, the nurses organize the medication schedule. My first patient for chemotherapy is already in the treatment room, the same room where bone marrows were done. He looks up as I enter, and I see him sitting on the gurney, bald headed, thin, with the sallow complexion that results from anemia, chronic illness, and borderline malnutrition. I sit on the small stool before him, my fingertips joining my eyes in the search for veins on the back of his hand and his lower arm. A tourniquet above his elbow is tightened in the hope that what veins he has will appear. Today I am lucky, for I can see a few, fragile and blue beneath skin as dry and thin as yellowed parchment. I feel my hands shaking beneath my attempts to appear calm. The child cries softly as he tries to hold still, knowing that an imperfect IV means another stick with another needle. I look up at his face, quiet tears beneath his eyes, his gaunt expression belied by his long and beautiful eyelashes, a common finding in leukemic children I was once told.

"Okay, Danny, hold on," I say as I take the small needle in my fingers and pierce the dry skin, guiding the thin, hollow steel into a minute vein. I watch the blood flow into my syringe, and a nurse takes off Danny's tourniquet as I tape the needle securely, periodically flushing salt water solution through the needle into the vein to make sure the vein stays okay, that the medicine to come will not burn the skin. The nurse is talking to Danny, caressing him gently with her hand and her voice: "It's okay, Danny. You're doing fine. It's in, now, Danny." There is a stifled sigh of relief from Danny and me.

And I take the proffered syringe filled with the chosen poison. It is a red liquid, a solution of Daunorubicin, another experimental treatment being tried for Danny, whose leukemia has outsmarted all the previously tried regimens. Although designed to selectively kill those leukemic cells, the toxic effects of Daunorubicin led to its nickname as "The Red Death." I hook the syringe into the lock on the end of the tubing from the IV needle and slowly infuse the drug into the vein, the heart, the marrow, the body of the desperate child now so still before me. I follow the drug with a short infusion of saline, remove the IV, and place a fresh bandage on the site of entry.

"Okay Danny. All done." I lift him off the gurney like a feather. He is twelve years old and weighs perhaps thirty pounds.

"Thank you, Dr. K." He walks out of the room with the nurse. His parents are waiting by his bed, where they will help him through the next day or two of emesis and IV fluids. Danny always thanks me: after I push poison into him, after I steal marrow from him, after I examine him, after I explain that the chemotherapy is not working that well.

I vainly try to sleep now even as I remember and am with those ravaged feverish bodies, fighting the toxic effects of their chemotherapy, the devastating aftereffects of the loss of normal as well as leukemic cells. All of us working on the oncology ward look upon the side effects of chemotherapy as one of the costs to be borne if the poisons given to cure the diseases are to succeed. For many of the children, it is a ragged three-way race between the potentially fatal toxic effects of the chemotherapy, the regenerative powers of the normal cell lines trying to restore body defenses, and the killing leukemia. Even now, even after all those years, I still remember many of the children who died despite my best efforts at keeping them alive. Danny was only one of many who lost the race to leukemia; is my race to turn out any differently?

And now, lying in bed, I want only to be granted sleep, to not have to think about the next day, the next week, the next jolt of the next unknown. And as I lie there in the dark so soon after receiving my own diagnosis of leukemia, so soon after reading the case histories that sound too much like my own, case histories of patients succumbing to their disease despite the private agonies of chemotherapy, I suddenly feel myself being hijacked, cast in a small craft on a voyage in just the same way those children I'd cared for had been. I see myself as a lone man now adrift on that same broad ocean, higher than all around, watching the storm gather, with lightning striking suddenly, with a flash of heat bursting over the sea, in an instant of light that is the end.

4

It is early morning, seemingly hours before my alarm is to sound, and against my will, I am awake. The sun won't be up for more than an hour and the ceiling above me is a formless white gray reflecting what little light emerges from beneath the door back down into my eyes. I feel my blood, carrying my personal intruders, those unwanted cells, coursing through me, finding its way to my arms, legs, brain. It seems to roil within my soon-to-be-removed spleen. I lie alone, feeling the air enter my lungs, the hairs on my arms and legs recoil against the covers of the bed. I turn and look at the clock and see that in reality only a few minutes remain before I am due to get up.

Deep within me is a heightened awareness of my own life, of my being alive. It is the same feeling before the gun sounds starting the race, when every pulled muscle and small sprain are magnified, even as I prepare to run, daring my injuries to stop me.

There is a quiet padding down the steps before the halting knock on the door.

"Geoff, it's time to get up."

"I'm up already, Dad."

"Did you sleep okay?"

"Actually, once I got to sleep, it was fine. I'll be ready to go in a few minutes."

"Your mother's upstairs. I'll tell her you'll be up soon."

His tentative steps retreat up the stairs as I pull myself out of bed and to the bathroom where I quickly wash and shave, wanting to look good for the surgical team, although they probably couldn't care less. Last night, I packed the few things I'll take with me: toothbrush, glasses instead of my usual contact lenses, a book. I trudge up the stairs with my small packet and find the light on in the kitchen and my mother sitting, as if she'd been there all night, awaiting me. She knows I'm not allowed to eat or drink before the surgery, so that part of her mothering has been taken away from her. I approach the table, silent, with nothing to say. My mother looks up. We momentarily stare at one another. This is no time to be speaking of the world outside the door.

"Did you sleep okay?" She asks in a sleep-deprived voice.

"Actually, Mom, not too bad."

"That's good, even though you're just going to be put back to sleep."

"That's true . . . the anesthesiologist will put me to sleep. But that's not why we pay them, you know."

"It's not? And why do we pay them?" My mother's look is serious, as if I'm hiding something important from her.

"We pay them to wake us up, Mom." She looks worried; her mouth drops. "Mom, relax. It's a joke. It's a joke."

"Well, I forgot to laugh." Her face, however, breaks into a smile. If my sense of humor is intact, it can't be that bad.

"You know, I just wish we could relax, sit here, have some breakfast . . ."

"And forget all about this stuff," I finish the sentence for her.

"Yes. Well, you have your things. Let's get to the hospital."

"The sooner we get there . . . the sooner we get there. Although I'm not sure we need to rush. You know the old story about the man who was on his way to be hanged."

My mother stares at me.

"So this guy is on his way to be hanged, and there's this huge crowd of people wanting to watch his execution. There are so many people that they block the road to the gallows, slowing the wagon he's riding in." Her mouth is partly opened, as if she were stifling some word of warning in her throat.

"And so the guy leans out of the wagon, sees all the folks rushing toward the gallows, and yells out at them 'Hey, don't be in such a hurry. Nothing'll happen till I get there.' " I cackle, and after a moment, so does my mother.

We walk together to the car and drive in the loosening darkness the half mile to St. Mary's, the enormous facility that for over a hundred years has been the main hospital for Mayo Clinic patients. The eastern sky is graying as we walk into the vast lobby and registration area. The scene is reminiscent of a gathering of college freshmen on the first day of orientation, except that we all look much too old to be college freshmen. And, rather than excited anticipation, none of us looks very happy to be here. We wait in the large room; we avoid acknowledging each other, trying to appear outwardly calm. We size each other up, trying to guess each other's malady without appearing to be interested in finding it out. Conversations are soft, short, with voices falling away sometimes before sentences are fully ended. Many of us are pale, suffering from the effects of the disease that is to be surgically attacked. Our clothes are workmanlike and not too fancy, as if we all chose garments that are somehow disposable, to be discarded after surgery, as if that outward change will magically effect an inward transformation to health. And we probably have each individually reasoned that there was, after all, no need to dress up for an event that will focus on our naked bodies.

"Geoff," my mother says, "let me hold your valuables."

"What?"

"You know, your wallet, your watch . . . you know you won't need them." She scrutinizes my face. "Don't worry," she laughs, "I won't spend your money, and I'll give them all back to you when you're out of surgery, promise. It's better than having the hospital folks hold them for you."

"What money?" I say as I reach in my pocket and quietly hand over my wallet, then my watch. I save for last the bracelet on my right wrist, which I'd bartered for while trekking in Nepal in 1985. Made of cheap silver and small bits of turquoise, it has the phrase "Om Mani Padme Om" in raised Nepali letters. It translates to "Behold, the jewel in the lotus flower." The phrase celebrates contemplation and tells us that each of us can, if we work at it, achieve the peace of mind, the equanimity that comes through understanding. I am not a Buddhist, but from the very day I purchased it, I have worn the bracelet because of the message it gives and the hope it represents. I look down at the inscription one more time, deliberately remove it, and place it in my mother's hand.

"Hold on to this, Mom. You know where I got it."

"And you'll be able to go back there, you know."

"I hope so." I set my jaw as I turn toward her.

After only a few minutes, a woman who is our guide and greeter appears. Our group of patients says its collective good-byes. I try to be nonchalant and ready for surgery but realize how much I fail as I turn once more to my mother. Suddenly she looks older. I feel lost and alone. "I'll . . . I'll see you soon. Will you know where to wait for me?"

"Don't worry. They'll show me where to wait for you. You'll be fine. I'll see you soon. I'll be there when you wake up."

The guide leads us from the large reception area through otherwise hidden areas of the hospital, and after the first few twists and turns of the early morning forced march, I am totally lost. Perhaps, I tell myself, they make the path difficult to discourage any last-minute breaks for freedom.

After what seems like fifteen or twenty minutes, we arrive at an area that has the appearance of a part of the hospital only recently rediscovered after years of disuse. The room to which I am led is unadorned save for two beds with taut, ironed sheets. A crucifix hangs on one wall. Curtains attached via metal hooks to the ceiling separate the beds, offering the only privacy. After consulting a paper on a clipboard, my guide indicates that the bed closest to the door is mine. She leaves me there, my own papers in a box at the door, as I sit alone in the room on the edge of my assigned bed, waiting in the midst of the silence.

The wait is brief, for a nurse soon bustles in, her lilting voice and smile suggest that she's been up for hours already and is one of those who gather more energy as they work.

"Dr. Kurland?"

I nod. "That's me, last time I checked."

"Good. Well, I'm . . . ," she introduces herself. I self-consciously put out my hand to shake hers. "I see you're here for a splenectomy. By Dr. van Heerden, right?"

"Right. What do I do?"

She laughs softly as she hands me a plastic bag and what looks like a green cotton rag. "Put your valuables in here, if you have any," she says, indicating the bag, "and please put on this gown. You can hang up your clothes in the closet there." She points to a narrow door in the wall across from the foot of the bed. "I'll be back to talk with you and get your vitals in a few minutes." She turns and is gone.

I remove my clothes and put on the ill-becoming gown. The nurse returns just as I finish changing, as if she's watched from a hidden camera placed by some sadistic psychologist doing research on people under stress. She carries a clipboard with yet another form to fill out. I answer the questions put to me: my name, my address, my expected surgery, allergies to medicines, medicines I am taking. She takes my vitals or, as they are officially known, vital signs: my pulse rate, temperature, respiratory rate, blood pressure, weight, height.

I hold out my arm, and she clips the identiband bracelet around my wrist where my Nepal bracelet had been. This is now my talisman, the thin, transparent plastic encasing a paper tab on which are imprinted the name, medical record number, and hospital ward of the patient. In case I become lost or "something happens" to me, they'll know who I am, where I belong.

The nurse thanks me (I'm not sure what I've done to deserve her thanks) and turns to go. I thank her in turn and find myself alone. I lie down on the bed, suddenly feeling exhausted, but I am unable to sleep and too afraid to move. The edges of the corridor visible through the door are dim and the walls of my room a tannish brown that absorbs light and sound, leaving this semidarkness resonant with the silence of the echoing hall outside the door. Once again, I feel my heart beating, my blood coursing, my breath rising and falling. I want so much to be with someone, with Karin, away from all this. And yet I want, at the same time, to be alone facing my illness. I have been a prisoner of this self-administered fear of giving up part of myself to anyone, the fear of losing control over any part of my life. Karin is in California, and I am alone in a room somewhere in the heart of St. Mary's Hospital. I tell myself: I'm a big boy. I can take care of myself. What that truly means is: I'm afraid to not be a big boy. I've got to show that I can take care of myself.

I push the world away and face the walls of the room. My eyes become heavy as I see my body move closer to the wall, away from the door, away from the outside corridor where others walk slowly, the echoes of their steps fading away. The sheets, once cold and taut, now feel warm and soft as I fall deeper and deeper into the bed.

"Dr. Kurland . . . it's time."

Startled awake, I turn to my right and see a gurney, the ship of the hospital. An orderly, standing on the other side, is smiling like the Cheshire cat at my taut lips and widened eyes, leftovers from an unre-membered dream.

"Could you slide over and get aboard, please?" He's the captain of this ship, and he wears a white uniform that bespeaks his command. He only lacks the hat with scrambled eggs. The gurney is the same height as the bed, and he maneuvers it alongside. I do as I am asked. As I lie down again, I am strapped in for the ride, watching as the orderly puts up the side rails. I had done the same action so many times before for children whom I had wheeled to bronchoscopies. The orderly checks my bracelet and pushes the gurney into the corridor. I am on my back, watching the ceiling tiles and lights fly by. Like the walk ear-lier in the morning, the fleeting glimpses of walls, doors, and intersec-tions gives me no clue as to which direction I am being taken. Far more frightening, however, is the lack of any way to truly judge the distance I've traveled as I see only the blur of repetitive white squares. Nor is there a sense of time. I may have been pushed for a few hundred yards or a third of a mile through the corridors of St. Mary's. I tell myself that it doesn't matter: I know my journey will end up somewhere in the operating room.

The term *operating room* is a misnomer: the name implies a single room devoted to surgery. In fact, when most physicians use the term *operating room*, or OR, they are referring to a large area of a hospital, only part of which is devoted to rooms where operations take place. There is also a preoperative area, sometimes called a holding area, where patients are prepared for surgery. And there is a postoperative or recovery area, where patients can be watched (*monitored* is the medical term) as they emerge from anesthesia and from which they can be safely sent to a regular nursing floor or an intensive care unit. In addition, the OR contains the charting areas for the physicians and nurses as well as changing rooms, where OR scrub suits are exchanged for normal clothes. There are storage rooms for the machines, instruments, drugs, and dressings that make the operations possible. There are facilities to sterilize everything that might touch a patient. The OR is a beehive of activity within the hospital and a world unto itself.

The day-to-day activities of the OR are usually presided over by nurses rather than physicians, and OR nurses have a reputation for being tough. This is particularly true for those who really run the place by organizing the schedules, setting policy, or doing any of a dozen other tasks. When I was a medical student, it was well known that one should stay out of the way of, and on the good side of, the OR head nurse. People who think that physicians have all the power in hospitals are wrong. Much of the true power in an institution such as a hospital rests with administrators and people who run certain areas of the hospital. Head nurses, particularly the OR head nurse, wield a lot of that power.

My gurney is rolled into the fluorescent brightness of the large holding room, and another orderly takes over the driving, finally stashing me between two gurneys. I partially sit up and take a look around, seeing that both sides of the room are divided into narrow, curtained cubicles to accommodate the two-foot-wide, six-and-a-half-foot-long carts. The room looks like a patient parking garage, with each of us face up on our gurneys. The major difference between the room and a parking garage is the sound, or rather, the lack of it. Talk, what there is of it, is in low tones, broken minimally by the determined step of orderlies, physicians, and nurses amid the parked vehicles.

I wait, hearing snippets of conversations around the room, trying to figure out the illnesses of the other patients. I catch myself holding the perverse hope that the other patients are worse off than I am. Perhaps it is not so much a perversity as a means of preservation—others much sicker than me are still alive. I am saved from this fairy tale of self-interest by the arrival of two scrub-suited men at my side.

"Dr. Kurland, I'm Dr. . . . and this is Dr. . . . ," the first one introduces himself and his companion as my staff anesthesiologist and the resident who will be handling my case. Anesthesiology, like any other part of medicine, is taught by book and by supervised hands-on experience. St. Mary's Hospital is, like the Mayo Clinic and almost all hospitals affiliated with a medical school, a teaching hospital. My anesthesia will be administered by the resident, learning anesthesia under the direction of the staff anesthesiologist. Some might think that it is less safe to get medical care in this way, from someone learning the ins and outs of the technique. I, on the other hand, feel it is probably safer: two people have to decide what is best, so mistakes are less likely, and the teacher, in order to teach well, must be especially competent and up to date in the latest advances in the field.

So, I tell myself, I don't have one bit of trepidation about my anesthesia. Yet I now realize how bizarre my situation is. I'm about to undergo surgery and am meeting my anesthesiology team for the first time. After all, these are the people responsible not only for putting me to sleep but also for making sure I wake up mentally competent. Whenever I've been asked my advice concerning surgery, I always tell people that the anesthesiologist is very nearly as important as the surgeon. After all, it doesn't matter if the surgery goes well if you're not awake to appreciate it afterward.

They quickly confirm who I am (identiband time), what operation I expect, and who will do it. Then they hypnotize me.

"Dr. Kurland," intones the staff physician, "we're going to take you into the room, and we'll start an IV. Then we'll give you some medicine that will make you very sleepy . . . everything is going to be just fine . . . everything is going to be just fine. . . ."

The anesthesiologist will probably disagree with me when I say that he is hypnotizing me, but that's what he's doing. I should know: I partially hypnotize each child I bronchoscope, even though there's no watch on a chain. People under stress, whether children about to be bronchoscoped or a physician about to have his spleen removed, are very susceptible to hypnotic suggestion. Now, more than anything, I want to be comfortable, to have someone take care of me. And here are two complete strangers (but such nice reassuring strangers, I think) offering all that to me. Like the children I've taken care of, I am ready to succumb to that chance to escape the stress of surgery.

Only a few minutes later, I again watch the ceiling as I am smoothly rolled along into the operating room. The OR lights are like giant silver bowls suspended above me; they leave no shadows. A blood pressure cuff is placed around my left arm and inflates. My hand feels away, apart from me. A masked Dr. van Heerden appears, looks down, smiles behind his mask, and says something I don't quite catch. His eyes reassure. I smile back, feeling more relaxed, yet still with a small twinge of nervousness. A plastic mask with cool gas fits gently over my mouth and nose. A voice tells me that I will feel a little stick, as the IV is placed into the back of my wrist. Another blue surgical mask looks down, and now a distant voice says that they will be starting. Just who, I wonder, are "they"? The surgical light above my head doubles in brightness, then begins to grow dim, graying as the medication in my veins takes hold. I feel suddenly very calm, overwhelmingly unafraid, and somehow wonderfully happy as the surgical light fades into nothingness in a distance that seems to stretch into forever, a distance calling back to me with voices quietly reading off a series of numbers: someone's heart rate, blood pressure, respiratory rate, temperature, the vital signs telling all of us that the patient is actually alive despite the appearance of death. It must be someone else, I think.

"Dr. Kurland, time to get back into bed."

I don't recognize the voice, but in the fading fog of the anesthetic, now lifting, I know that I am no longer in the operating room. The lights, once so bright in my eyes, are gone, replaced by a tan, clouded light reflecting off unfamiliar walls. I look at my side, covered with a thin sheet, and see that I am back on yet another gurney next to another hospital bed in another unfamiliar room. The nurse picks up the plastic bag holding my IV solution. I trace the tubing back to my left wrist, then see my mother at the foot of the gurney, there to help me with the move to what will be my bed. The distance I have to traverse is perhaps two feet but feels more like half a mile or half a marathon as I roll onto my right side and crawl on hands and knees from the gurney onto the bed. As I move I feel the entire left side of my abdomen rebel; the incision, there beneath the dressing, screams back at me for disturbing it, threatening to rend itself apart. I am halfway between the gurney and the safety of the bed when I stop, like the comedic once-a-year fisherman caught with one foot on the dock and the other on the rowboat moving away. My abdomen is about to open, I'm convinced. I freeze, unable or unwilling to move.

"Come on, Geoff. I'll help you over."

I look at my mother, who most certainly should not be lifting any weight at all, then look down at the bed, the gurney, my abdomen, and, for the first time since I was six or seven years old, call out for my mommy. My mother is caught completely off guard, but somehow has the wherewithal to answer my plea as any mother of a six- or seven-year-old in trouble. Her hands join those of the nurse, over my shoulders now trembling. She guides me across the short but infinite space to the bed, those last few precious inches to my destination. We look at each other, both realizing what I'd said. I laugh inwardly, at myself, and for a moment feel sheepish about calling for her. She just looks back with a mixture of deep concern and a little embarrassment. The nurse has the good sense to keep quiet for a moment.

My incision is not about to burst apart. The pain I have is real but survivable. My mother, being "mommy" once more for a moment, sits down in a chair at the foot of the bed and takes out her knitting. As the nurse settles me in, checks my IV, and takes my temperature, my heart and respiratory rate, my blood pressure, my mother has begun her own vigil, waiting for her son to heal.

5

"Are you okay? Do you need anything? Bed pan? Anything?" She asks as she feels me stir. My mother's voice is far away, down a tunnel, out in a hallway. I slip in and out of the room. I float above myself. When I return, I try not to move too much, try not to feel the rippling seams of nausea rising slowly into my consciousness.

Something within pulls me back to the room, gently urging me to try to awaken. There is a half groan that emerges as I try to sit up and turn over simultaneously, a postoperative, dry land version of a very awkward dive. The skein of wool, the nearly finished cap, the needles are placed upon the chair as my mother pulls herself up to the bed. A nurse appears in the doorway on the other side of my bed, as if she'd been called, although I have no idea who could have called her. There are two faces looking intently into mine, then at each other, and then quickly, together, the women place a tan, plastic emesis basin in my hands, which are held before my abdomen.

"Here," one of the voices calls. "You look sick. Do you have to vomit?"

My mother had completed most of her nursing training by the

time she married my father. Some parts of the training must be analogous to riding a bicycle: after doing it once, you never forget how to do it. In addition, she is my mother and has observed my childhood illnesses and those of my brothers and sister. Just by looking at me, she knows the likely answer to the question she—or the nurse, I'm not sure—just put to me, before the question was even asked. My face must look green; it sure feels that way to me. All in the room know I'm going to puke.

"Oh, God. I'm afraid to . . . but I feel so . . ."

One of the strangely wonderful things about the combination of nausea and vomiting is that, despite the odiousness that is the predisposing nausea, the immediate result of vomiting usually is the resolution, even if only temporary, of the horrible feeling that is nausea. But it is one thing to simply vomit and quite another to vomit just after abdominal surgery, with the belly held closed with only a few thin nylon stitches. In the midst of my nausea, I remind myself that abdominal wounds can break open after surgery. The technical term for a surgical wound that separates is *dehiscence*, and it is never good for that to happen. But this is lost on me as the sweat pours from my forehead, chest, and neck as the overwhelming nausea wins out and I lean desperately toward and almost into the tiny emesis basin.

For now, I am focused only on emptying the contents of my gut into the basin and don't much care about possibly finding part of my guts beside me on the bed. So I let go and allow myself the freedom to surrender to the power of the small area in my brain that controls the reflex that is vomiting. And I remain in one piece afterward. I immediately feel better (especially when I see that I haven't "spilled my guts") and hope that there will be no more vomiting.

Over the next several hours, I sleep, or try to sleep, as the last vestiges of the general anesthetics I'd received are metabolized. Often, surgeons put some long-acting local anesthetic into the skin edges of a wound as they close it, but I'm not sure if van Heerden did that. Within the next few hours, however, I feel the pain of the incision itself along with the combined effect of having the skin and muscles of the wall of my abdomen forcibly pulled apart (retracted) to allow van Heerden and his resident to work inside my belly. I'm not especially big: five feet, nine and a half inches tall, 155 pounds, and my belly is not too big, either. My mind now reels at the thought of one or two human hands, together with instruments like scalpels, scissors, forceps, clamps, all working within that small space. In addition, there was my spleen, which, I was told by all who saw my CT scan, was huge. No wonder I feel as if someone had played racquetball inside me.

As a medical student, I was involved in several abdominal operations, mostly to hold a retractor that pulled apart those muscle layers, enabling the surgeon to work in the confining space of a body cavity. I never wondered how my retracting those muscles affected the post-operative pain a patient might have. Patients usually do fine after the healing of the skin, for the skin has more nerve endings than many internal organs. But my skin was sliced apart and spliced together less than half a day ago and is the main source of my pain right now.

Most physicians, before they were physicians, sat with varying degrees of discomfort before some dean or professor or medical student and tried to answer in some original or novel way the same basic question: "Why do you want to go into medicine?" As trite as it sounds, many of us, myself included, entered the field of medicine from a heartfelt desire to alleviate suffering, to "help people." (I also believe that some of us mistakenly thought—but never said aloud—that medicine is a good way to make money, only later to discover the truth that it may be a good way, but it most certainly isn't an easy way.)

One of the paradoxes of modern medicine is that a lot of the pain is brought on by physicians as part of their efforts to alleviate suffering. If we forget about the pain wrought by "bleeding" patients or amputations without anesthesia in the "old days" of medicine (say, before the late 1800s), physicians in the past didn't or couldn't do too many things that actually caused patients to have more pain on their road to survival. That wasn't because the patients survived without pain. It was usually because they didn't survive at all. Even as recently as when my father was an intern, there wasn't as much that could be done to (not just for) patients. Only fifty years ago, antibiotics were a novelty, routine cardiac bypass surgery was a half decade away, and cancer chemotherapy was in its infancy. Now, medicine and surgery can truly do wonders, but often at enormous costs (physical, emotional, and, yes, financial) to patients. Yet antedating all of modern medicine is the means to prevent pain. Even if an old saying is "Pain is nature's way of telling you to slow down," pain, or at least overwhelming pain, isn't necessarily inevitable, even following surgery. The medical establishment has at its disposal a veritable cornucopia of medications to help the patient handle pain. And as in so many aspects of medicine and life, sometimes the oldest (or at least one of the oldest) is still the best. "Morphine," another saying goes, "is here for a reason."

Morphine, like its congeners, is truly a wonder drug, lifesaving to the patient with real pain. Morphine is related to opium, which has been used since before recorded history. Opium is obtained from the juice of poppy capsules (the word *opium* is itself derived from the Greek word for juice). Its effects on the psyche were probably known to ancient Sumerians, whose ideogram for the poppy means "joy" and "plants." In 1680, the great English physician Sydenham, who described, among other things, some of the symptoms of rheumatic fever, wrote, "Among the remedies which it has pleased Almighty God to give to man to relieve his sufferings, none is so universal and so efficacious as opium." Morphine was the first alkaloid isolated from opium, and its discovery by a young German pharmacist in 1803 led to the isolation of another well-known opium alkaloid, codeine, less than thirty years later. Now, there are numerous other synthetic agents with similar properties to morphine, but they owe their ultimate parentage to morphine, opium, and the poppy.

They say that morphine takes away pain, but that isn't true, for it does not remove pain. Instead, it removes the patient from the pain, to a place more associated with sleep, rest, and dreams. (The name *morphine* is derived from Morpheus, the Greek god of dreams.) The pain is there, whether from an abdominal incision, a broken bone, or a burn, but the patient, the full psyche of the patient, isn't there to worry about the pain.

But for now, I feel my incision, and I care. The instruments are again retracting the skin and muscles of my abdomen, opening wide the split in my belly. They make room for the many hands and scalpels and clamps and sponges, freeing my spleen and delivering it as a child from the womb of my own abdomen. I feel the sutures set into the layers of tissue and muscle and skin, holding the edges together against the threatened rupture from my vomiting. My belly hurts, and I am frozen with fear, afraid to move because of the pain, afraid that I will look down to see my viscera beside me staining my sheets with my blood and the torn-open landscape of my abdomen mocking me and my surgeon with his meager sutures.

"Are you hurting, Dr. Kurland?" the nurse asks. Like my mother, who probably had been the one who asked me if I had to vomit, my nurse knows the answer just by looking at me. "You have morphine ordered," she says quietly.

I have never had morphine, even though I've given it to some of my patients. For many of those patients, the morphine I prescribed was to ease the pain as they healed from surgery. That had been back when I worked in general pediatrics, as an intern and resident, caring for those children who'd been through difficult surgery or were recovering from severe trauma. But more recently, my experience with morphine has been different, for I've used it to ease the final hours of my young patients with cystic fibrosis whose lungs were failing and whose suffocation and slow strangulation caused an agonizing death. I'd had to watch, helpless and frustrated, at the bedside of too many of my patients as they struggled to breathe their last. I knew there had to be a way to ease their passage into eternity. The perception of not having enough air, of not being able to breathe, is by all accounts horrific. Morphine rids the mind of some of that sensation, allowing the patient peace. It usually took only a little of the drug to work its wonders, leaving patients comfortable, families grateful, and my conscience clear as I felt I lived up to my oath pledging to try my best to prevent suffering, even as I admitted defeat by a more powerful enemy.

"Great," I say in a half moan, half whisper to the nurse. "Something . . . anything . . . my belly just hurts . . ."

"Fine. Which arm do you want it in?"

"Arm? In? You mean I can't get it IV?" I've almost always given it intravenously to my patients, because, I'd been taught, it hurts when given into a muscle. Maybe, I tell myself, I don't really want this.

"Oh, no," the nurse assures me. "It's ordered IM." She knows I'm a doctor, so she uses the shorthand for intramuscular.

Being right-handed, I offer my left shoulder to the nurse, and the needle goes into the muscle without any pain at all. "No problem," I whisper to myself. Then I realize that my teachers had been correct: intravenous morphine is not especially painful, but intramuscular morphine is quite a different matter. I not only feel the morphine, I experience it: a nearly indescribable burning, so deep and so overwhelming that I am sure the needle has somehow slipped and entered my marrow and I am being injected with some fiery liquid, something other than a medicine to soothe. For the first seconds during and immediately after the injection, I hold my breath, lips pressed together, teeth clenched, my voice screaming silently within my chest as I see dim yellow stars circling against the black background of my tightly closed eyes.

"God . . . that was as bad or worse than my belly pain. Can't I get that stuff IV?"

"Well, I can talk to your doctor . . . I can't guarantee anything . . . but you know, that's why they call it a 'pain shot.'" She gives me a little smile, as if to tell me: your patients sometimes get it this way, so now you know how it feels, doctor.

I can't return her smile. I try again to think of a way to ask for a different form of the injection. Some medical centers have so-called patient controlled analgesia, or PCA, where the patient has a special computerized IV pump that contains a limited amount of narcotic to be used as needed. When he has pain, the patient activates the pump with a button that delivers a preset dose of medication. Although it might seem easy to abuse such a system, it has built-in safeguards, for it can be programmed to limit the amount of narcotic given over any period of time. In addition, the fact that the patient has a sense of control over his pain management usually leads to less, rather than more, narcotic use in the postoperative period. But such a device seems not to be in vogue at the Mayo Clinic, or at least it isn't used by the van Heerden surgical team. Meanwhile, my left shoulder burns with the morphine given deep into the muscle.

I am trying to think, to remind myself to ask the resident or van Heerden or the nurse if there might be a way for me to get my morphine intravenously instead of intramuscularly. But somehow, time has slowed down, my thoughts come in gauzy waves, then drift slowly about the room before landing in my brain. And suddenly I don't care. I don't really have to think. Everything is now so quiet, so peaceful. Even my shoulder no longer hurts. My abdomen, so recently operated upon, is fine, without much feeling. Even if there is some feeling, I tell myself, it isn't really a bad feeling, just an empty one. It's still the late morning or the early afternoon, for my operation, after all, had only taken a few hours, so it must be the same day, I guess. The light at the window in my room dims progressively, and I sink farther and farther into the bed. My mother has taken her seat by the window. Has she been talking to me? Was I answering? The questions no longer enter my brain. They remain only partially formed in the air above my bed. The words of the '60s rock group Procul Harum become real before me "as the ceiling flew away . . ." The clicking of my mother's knitting needles recedes into a great distance, echoing around me. The light from the window has now focused into a small point, just as the surgical lights had earlier this very morning. My abdomen, with its fresh incision, has lost its insistent cry. It is now in the next room or down the hall. Or perhaps I am the one who has moved, now above the bed, now out the door, now down the corridor, finally outside the hospital and somewhere far away.

I'm not sure how long I've been away from my room, but I am awake with darkness outside my window. My brother Robert, finished with his orthopedic rounds for the day, stands next to my bed. Every once in a while he speaks, but I'm not sure if he's talking to me. It seems a one-sided conversation as I waver into and out of drowsiness. It's probably a good thing that I'm so out of it; he's probably at a loss for something to say. I mean, what kind of conversation would we have, anyway? I'm newly diagnosed, fresh from surgery, with a future that is as out of focus as my own vision.

In reality, the five of us, four brothers and one sister, have never been especially close to each other. Even back when Robert and I were both at Stanford, he as an undergraduate and I as a medical student, we rarely did things together, almost never spent long hours talking into the night, mutually trying to solve the questions and problems of our separate lives. Having no experience in dealing with my siblings about those issues of life before, how am I supposed to start now? Will I ever be able to talk with them about my fear, my confusion over the swerving turn my life has just taken? The oldest of the five of us, am I to be the first to die? My entire life, devoted to being whole, strong, and healthy, now seeks to turn on me and prevent me from reaching out to some of those who perhaps can help me: my family.

My brother pats my hand gently. I look up at him from the pillow, my eyes now starting to sharpen, focusing on him.

"Listen," he says, "I want you to hang in there. We need you."

Need me for what, I wonder. "Okay. I'll hang in there, wherever 'there' is." I close my eyes as he picks up his jacket and leaves.

I need morphine again tonight and again see the stars pinpointed in my closed eyes even as the electric burn in my arm leads me back into sleep. Just before I fall asleep, I see my father, a shape, shimmering beside the bed, then realize that he'd actually been here earlier today. I remember almost nothing of the conversation, if we had any. The clicking of the needles accompanies me into the evening, along with one or perhaps two more injections of morphine, with the nurse reminding me where I'd gotten the last injection so I can try a different spot ("Maybe it won't hurt so much," but it always does) and then feeling myself fade away into a forced sleep, the stars, once clear in the blackness seen through the window, are now whirling beside and within me as I wander into an impenetrable distance.

Despite my drug-induced travels of the night, the morning brings a new light. I can tell somehow that I am on the mend. I know I won't be allowed to eat for another day or so, because my gut is still recovering from the surgery. When the gut is disturbed or manipulated during surgery, it goes on strike and doesn't move. This is known as *ileus*, a term derived from the Greek word for colic. Certain drugs can also cause ileus, and morphine is one of them. I try to avoid any more of the pain shots, and discover that my belly is tolerable without them. I tell myself that things aren't so bad, after all. My healing comes from more than my gut and abdomen; it comes from within my own psyche.

But healing from what? I am healing from the surgery I've just had, the removal of my spleen. But the surgery really didn't touch my marrow, to rid it of the hairy cells that are growing there, pushing the

normal cells out of their way. I am only at the beginning, the start of
the war I am sure lies before me. It is as if I've been participating in one
of the Pyrrhic battles of the war, a battle that has taken its toll on me but
hasn't done much to the enemy. The realization of the long road ahead
and the uncertainty of treatment now comes to me full bore. I remember that only a couple of days ago Tom Habermann had talked about
the use of interferon and had mentioned another drug that looked
promising. But surgery had to come first, and now, as I lie in bed, I lack
any grasp of what is going to happen to me or where I am going next.

My leukemia (I call it "my leukemia" as if it were some pet) now
dictates my life to me. I am no longer the captain of my own ship;
instead, I am relegated to the position of passenger in steerage. I seek
some ways to make up for this lack of control and power. Even as my
belly hurts and burns, I decide not to take morphine at all and ask
instead for things to read to take my mind off the pain.

And I learn once again to walk first in order to run later. It happens
less than thirty-six hours after my surgery. It is afternoon, and my
mother is in the room knitting as I slowly sit up in bed. She can tell that
I am regaining strength, and she looks up at the nurse coming through
the door with a set look on her face and determination in her step.

"Dr. Kurland," the nurse says, "how about a little walk?"

"Great," my mother answers for me.

I first think to myself, "How about shooting myself or perhaps doing
my own root canal?" I'm not sure I feel *that* strong. But my mother and
the nurse seem to be colluding on this. I don't have a choice.

"Now?" I ask, trying to jockey for time.

"Well, it's afternoon. You've been up for a while. Let's give it a try."

Let's? I think again: Who is this "us" when it's going to be me? I half
smile then, for I know that it really would be good for me to get up
and about. "Fine. I'll give it a try."

"I'll help him," my mother offers. Now I know she's colluding in this.

"Great. While you're doing that, Dr. Kurland, I can change the
sheets on your bed. They could use it." She's definitely right on that.

"How long will that take? I mean I'm not sure I can go too far."

"Don't worry," my mother chimes in. "I'll help you walk, and you'll come back to nice, clean sheets." The nurse disappears into the hall for a moment and returns pushing a wheelchair.

"I thought I was going to walk," I say.

"You are, Dr. Kurland. The wheelchair is something to lean on, to push. Believe me, it'll be a lot easier this way."

My mother is at my side. "I'll help you up. We'll walk a bit together. Here are some slippers." Her knitting lies on the chair by the foot of the bed. My mother's hair is up in a bun, and she has a loose silk blouse on under her sweater. She helps me into some disposable terry cloth slippers with rubber soles, the type handed out to hospitalized patients who don't own slippers, people like me. I laboriously grimace my way into a bathrobe, unfamiliar because it is my father's and because I don't own a bathrobe. I've never seen the need for one, walking around my house in blue jeans and a T-shirt, the bathrobe of my generation. Anyway, I've already found that jeans have to be coaxed on when you're on a bed, and I'd be worried about straining my incision.

"Okay," I say at last, sitting on the side of the bed, bathrobe and slippers on, ready to start, gauging the distance to the floor and thence to the wheelchair. It seems like a long way for both, though it is measured in inches and a few feet. You would think I'm preparing to leap into space on a bungee cord. "Here goes."

And with that I slowly straighten out, rising as I inch my way off the bed until my slippered feet caress the floor. My body, partially bent from holding my abdomen closed for a day and a half, elongates with the slow speed of a young butterfly emerging from its cocoon, waiting for the sun's warmth to dry its wings and harden its chitinous thorax. I grasp at the handles of the wheelchair, gripping them as if they would save me from drowning or breaking apart should I slip and fall. My belly tenses, the incision under its bandage crying to me to be careful. My IV line pulls taut against the pole that will accompany the wheelchair, my mother, and me on the excursion du jour. I rise farther and finally stand at the back of the wheelchair, looking down at my feet, then up at my mother. It has taken me several minutes to accomplish this simple feat of standing up on my own two feet.

"Well, lady, where do you want to go? The store? The car?"

"All right, wise guy," my mother laughs back, "how about just out and down the hall a little bit?"

"Well, okay, this time . . . but next time . . . just you wait . . ."

"Oh, I can wait, all right."

I push off slowly and step by step make it the eight feet to the door, taking another couple of minutes in the process, waiting between paces to make sure I am still in one piece. I continue out into the corridor and turn down the hall.

"Listen, Geoff. I said just go a little bit. Don't overdo it."

"Don't worry, Mom. This is one time I probably won't overdo it." We are now several yards down the hallway. I realize I will be able to keep going yet feel almost drained of strength. Perhaps five or ten yards down the hall are all I'll be able to muster.

"I think I should go back. This is so weird." I laboriously turn the wheelchair around and start an agonizingly slow trudge to my room. "I mean, six week ago I ran fifty miles. Fifty miles! Now, I have trouble going a few yards. God, I'm so wiped out." We are nearly back at the room. I see my bed, now with clean sheets and fresh pillowcases, and suddenly can think of nothing other than getting back in and falling asleep.

I get the chair into the room and maneuver it sideways to the bed. With help, I traverse the two open feet of floor, sit on the bed and watch my mother pull off my slippers. She and the nurse help me wiggle out of my bathrobe, then lift my legs, allowing me back onto the sheets, now taut and clean and white and smelling for the first time in many hours like something other than a sweating body that had recently been operated upon.

I gaze at the nurse and my mother. "You know, I do feel better. Thanks for the walk."

"Anytime," my mother replies. "It's probably the only chance I have of keeping up with you. You'll go farther tomorrow."

"I know." This, I tell myself, is going to be just like getting back into running shape, only on a micro scale. This is how I will have to get better: yard by yard at first, then quarter mile by quarter mile later, and finally mile by mile. It is fitting that I am a long-distance runner with a great deal of patience, for I am in this for the long run. And I will need patience by the barrel, the truckful, the trainload. I've had lots of injuries that I've had to recover from in the past. I know that for each of those injuries, I had to hold myself in check until I was whole and ready to run hard. This time, there is no question of trying to push myself, at least not yet. The few yards I've just walked felt like miles of trail under my feet. And I feel just as tired as if I'd run many miles, and the clicking of my mother's knitting needles fades once more into the distance.

I awake later in the afternoon. The light through the window is more muted and the knitting quieter. My mother looks up as I stir.

"Geoff . . . are you awake?"

"Um . . . yeah . . ."

"How do you feel? How is your incision?"

"I feel okay. I feel better. I'm hungry. I hope I can start to eat soon. What time is it?"

"It's afternoon. Dad said he'd be over after his swim. He should be here soon."

"Okay. Did he say anything? About me, I mean."

"No, just that he'd be over after his swim. He asked how you were doing. I told him you'd walked." It was probably different some forty years before, when I took my first tentative steps back there in Baltimore (or perhaps it had been in New Orleans or maybe Boston). Then, I suppose my parents would have been waiting eagerly for their firstborn to try his legs, so wobbly, so young, and so full of presumed promise. Now, my tentative steps are a slogging attempt at reestablishing my life. I lie back and peer at the ceiling. I try to read. I slide in and out of sleep but progressively feel myself awakening.

The darkness is gathering but night has not fallen when my father strides into the room. He has his white cotton hat on. His jacket is open and his white shirt tieless. His briefcase is in his left hand and in his right are what seem to be some loose papers.

"Hi, Geoff. How are you feeling? Mom said you guys went for a little walk. That sounds great."

"Not too bad, Dad. Yeah, we toured the hallway for a few minutes. Not much, but a start."

"Well, I brought you something you will probably be interested in. Take a look at this."

He holds out the white and unmistakable magazine: *The New England Journal of Medicine*. The medical establishment has nicknames or shorthand for the major journals: The Green Journal instead of *The American Journal of Medicine*, JCI for *The Journal of Clinical Investigation*, and the NEJM for *The New England Journal of Medicine*. The NEJM looks like no other publication: thin, with only seventy-five to a hundred pages, with a white cover on which is printed the table of contents. Its outward appearance has changed but little over the last one hundred plus years, and it remains one of the major journals in terms of its importance and readership. I've never had a paper in the NEJM and may never at my current rate, but it is one of my favorites to read.

I take the copy from my father's hand. It is the latest edition, literally, as they say, hot off the press. I notice that the actual press date is April 2, 1987, still several days away. At first, I think that my father is bringing me something to keep my mind occupied or to take it off my illness. But that isn't the reason at all. The first article in the edition I hold is entitled "Remissions in Hairy-cell leukemia with Pentostatin (2'-deoxycoformycin)."

Pentostatin. This is the new drug, the protocol-only drug mentioned by Habermann a few days before when I'd first met him. My memory of that meeting is still swirling in bits and pieces through my mind, but the strange name Pentostatin, sounding like a potential name for some rock band, now suddenly clangs like a large bell.

I quickly read the abstract—the summary of the findings of the study that is placed at the beginning of the article—and let out a breath. The success of Pentostatin in treating the small number of patients in the study is nothing short of remarkable: 96 percent of the patients showed a clinical response; 59 percent went into complete remission. In other words, almost all patients improved, and in over half of the patients, the leukemic cells were destroyed to the point where they weren't seen in the bone marrow anymore. Even more amazing to me was that there was no continued therapy after patients went into remission, and yet they stayed in remission, for at least a year in one case.

"Pretty interesting, eh?" says my father. I look up slowly from the abstract.

"Wow . . . interesting isn't quite the word I'd use . . . more like amazing. And what a coincidence . . . amazing . . . amazing . . ."

"I didn't read the entire article, but it sure looks good to me."

"I'll say . . . but I'm going to read it. Now I remember that Habermann told me about this stuff, but I didn't think there'd be an article out on it just now. He was telling me that Pentostatin is a protocol drug. I wonder if I'll be a candidate for it."

"Well, why don't you take some time and read this and then talk with Habermann about it when you're out of here. First things first, though. How was your walk?"

"Short, but not especially sweet," I say. "But I'm feeling better overall. And now with this," I pick up the journal, "I somehow feel even stronger."

"You look better. Apparently your blood counts are better, too."

"I didn't know that. That's great. That's great." I almost laugh. The room seems brighter, lighter. The splenectomy had done what it was supposed to do; my low platelet count and white blood count are already starting to correct toward normal.

My father, however, can't stay too long, and soon he and then my mother leave for home and dinner. I read the article on Pentostatin. It looks to me like a good clinical study, even describing a positive response in some patients who didn't get better after splenectomy or interferon treatment. I lie back in the bed, willing the light outside to continue, even as darkness descends. I feel a light filling my room, and I tell myself that I will indeed be all right.

In the morning, van Heerden arrives to see me with his entire retinue: medical students, specialty nurses, residents (who in the Mayo Clinic tradition are known as fellows). Van Heerden is briefed about my condition while outside my door, and I can hear the murmuring comments, the questions to the medical students, the halting answers, the words of van Heerden summarizing the plan before the entry.

They all then march in and arrange themselves around the foot of the bed. Van Heerden himself removes the dressing and looks at my incision, pokes, prods gently, and listens to my abdomen with his stethoscope before replacing the tapes over the gauze. He stands up and gazes at me. He gently leans down, looking me straight in the eyes.

"Dr. Kurland, you have remarkably little subcutaneous tissue," he smiles.

"Thank you," I reply to the compliment. "That's the result of years of running."

"Well, you made our job much easier then, and it looks as though you're bouncing back quite well. By the way, you did have some oozing during surgery, so we had to give you several units of platelets. But overall it went quite nicely. Now, fluids today, hopefully something more substantial tomorrow." We shake hands as if this is a business deal. The fellow in charge dutifully writes the order to advance my diet from nothing to a little something. The team marches out.

Of course, I had made it easier for the team, I was sure. I remember again those surgical cases as a medical student, operating on obese abdomens, with incisions into thicknesses of fat overlying poorly toned muscles, with me at one end of a retractor pulling "gently, but firmly" to spread the incision. An operating room is seldom a quiet place, and surgeons talk about many things, including the attributes of the patients on whom they operate. I could hear van Heerden saying how easy it was to operate on someone with only a few percent body fat, with good muscle tone, someone who would heal quickly.

The thought that I'd been given platelets doesn't bother me too much. It points up how difficult, or even disastrous, a biopsy of my chest mass might have been. Any bleeding probably wouldn't have responded to platelets because my spleen would have continued to trap them. But this is the age of AIDS, and anyone who gets blood products hopes they are not tainted. Fortunately, the risk of AIDS, or any other blood-borne illness, from the supply at St. Mary's is about the lowest in the country: most of the blood is donated locally, by the people at the Clinic or in the community. I rapidly put the thought of any problem like that out of my mind. I think instead about trying to drink some fluids.

I am weak, but I force myself to read, or at least skim, once more through the Pentostatin article. After the first few pages, I find myself so fatigued that I can barely stay awake, and I cannot focus on the tables of small print floating on the white pages fluttering in my hands. I am suddenly asleep but awaken some hours later feeling a new strength, a determination to win, to beat this disease rising within me. I call for the nurse and to our combined surprise find myself behind the wheelchair alone, pushing my way down the hall, one foot in front of the other, farther than I'd walked only a few hours ago. I pull myself, with my own power, back into bed, and drink some of the fluids I am now allowed. The sky is now black outside my window; the sun will be erupting in the east in a little while, and I know that soon I will be allowed to have food, real food. I shall come back: to running, to work, to Karin, to my life. And it will be somehow fitting for me to start solid food tomorrow or the following day, to start out afresh, healing from my operation. For in only a few days, it will be my forty-first birthday, the start of my new year and, in a way, my renewed life before me. It will be, I tell myself, one of a series of renewals, of rebirths, of discoveries that will lead me out of the relative darkness of my illness into the light of true recovery and well-being.

6

ᴐ March 1987 ᴐ

It is less than a week after my splenectomy, a Sunday night, and, still weak and unsteady, I celebrate my forty-first birthday.

My celebratory day is totally different from that of a year ago, when I hit the "Big 4-0." Then, the house staff conspired to have my afternoon clinic run overtime by secretly adding a "new" patient named Harry Hare, with a convoluted history (dutifully retold to me by one of the conspiratory residents). The resident went on and on about the mother's numerous problems with her son: his unusual skin color (described by his mother as bluish), his unusual diet (only leafy green vegetables according to his mother), his unusual gait (more hopping than walking).

"What the hell does all that have to do with his lung problem? I mean, this is a pulmonary clinic, isn't it? Why don't we have any outside records on this kid? How did he get scheduled? And why was he scheduled at the end of clinic?"

"Well, apparently he has rapid, shallow breathing and the clinic docs weren't sure what it meant. They must have scheduled it through your secretary; guess she forgot to let you know, Dr. K. The mother brought up all that other stuff," the resident assured me. I made a mental note to have a little talk with my secretary.

I made the resident go through the entire history, the family history ("What? He was one of quintuplets?? He has how many brothers and sisters??? Are you sure?"), and the laborious physical exam, detailing a cyanosis totally unfamiliar to me, large ears, unusual hands and feet. I was not looking forward to examining this patient.

"Well, from what you've told me, I don't have a clue as to what this kid has. Nothing rings any bells with me. No X rays?"

"Sorry, Dr. K., they didn't bring any with them."

"Okay, guess we better take a look and see what's going on." I got up and started down the corridor, a retinue of house staff, students, and nurses, all appropriately straight-faced, in my wake. I walked into the examining room and was confronted by Harry Hare, who was none other than the nearly six-foot-tall chief pediatric resident in a purple-blue rabbit suit and mask. The whole clinic yelled "Happy Birthday" (or was it "Hoppy Birthday"?). I was silent and embarrassed, especially after all the grief I'd given the resident. I took out my stethoscope and listened to the "patient" while they took our picture. And then about twenty of us, students, residents, and nurses, went out for Chinese food. I paid the bill; it was one of the best birthdays I'd had.

Today my abdominal incision still pulls against the stitches, and my walk is slow and careful. I am allowed the first solid food since my splenectomy: a bite of potatoes mashed into submission, a few morsels of meatlike substance, and the obligatory cup of bouillon soup (still the culinary mainstay of the ward). No Chinese food for me, at least not for a few days.

Two of the nurses come into my room where I've propped myself up on two pillows. Having slept on and off for much of the day, I'm now stuck with nothing to do but read or watch TV. I've unwisely chosen the latter and find myself dubiously entertained by another late primetime sitcom with an uneasy ensemble cast, an unlikely spoof on Hollywood's interpretation of the real world, and an augmented laugh track. It's a little after 9 P.M.

"Dr. Kurland, could you come with us for a moment, please?"

"Sure, if you don't want me to get anywhere too fast. Anything's gotta be better than this stuff. Well, maybe not anything," I say, feeling the pull of my stitches as I slowly swing myself to the edge of the bed. "Why?"

"We want to show you something and ask your opinion," one of them says.

"My opinion? How about 'Buy low, sell high'? Sure, let's go."

I ease onto the floor, shaking into my slippers, snailing my way into the corridor. Compared to a couple of days ago, I'm now a slightly faster snail. They lead me into the small kitchen on the ward, waiting patiently for the several minutes it takes me to traverse the five or ten yards. The pantry is lit as brightly as an interrogation room for captured terrorists. Entering, I hold my hand up to shade my eyes from the glare. Then I hear the nurses quietly say, rather than yell, for this is a hospital and it is nearly ten at night, "Surprise! Happy Birthday!"

I look on the white Formica-topped table and see a white frosted cupcake with a single lit candle. I am speechless as I sit down on a high, backless stool at the table, wearing ill-fitting pajamas and my father's old robe. After blowing out the candle, which sits somewhat precariously in the cupcake, I join in a softly sung and somewhat out of tune version of "Happy Birthday." Slowly savoring the overly sweet icing, I eat my birthday cupcake as I thank the nurses for their kindness. They can see that in my weak state I won't last long, so they lead me back up the corridor to my room, helping me gently to return to bed. I am feeling incapacitated and certainly far older than my years. At my age, after all, birthdays are something to be ignored, in the vain hope that they will just go away and not count.

For that matter, I'd been brought up to downplay the importance of my birthday. When I was a kid, birthdays were usually celebrated with a small family breakfast "party" with cake along with scrambled eggs and toast before we trooped off to school. Presents were usually zany, things like Hershey's Kisses, hair tonic (when I used the stuff), or extra socks. Often, a "present" that someone else needed was thrown in with the gifts. If my brother needed new underwear, I might get it on my birthday and discover that it was his size, not mine. I don't think any of us really minded the crazy way we did birthdays. My father and mother told us that things we truly needed were provided when we actually needed them, instead of waiting for a birthday or other holiday. In a way, they did it to minimize the importance of a birthday, emphasizing instead that every day is potentially special.

Now, years later, I appreciate this even more. But, following the first of what Habermann has told me will be at least two surgeries, I carry a dichotomous view of the days I am to spend in the hospital. On one hand, they are days given back to me, to start to recoup my losses to leukemia, a new chance to fight back, to not give in to my disease, to focus my attention squarely on the foe and defeat it once and for all. On the other hand, these days are somehow lost or perhaps borrowed ones to merely survive rather than savor. They represent a time to get through and then forget about in order to be able to live undistracted in the weeks, months, and perhaps years that I hope will be given to me after my leukemia is gone.

It is hard to learn to relax and to accept while still conserving a portion of will and strength for a future time. Every patient with a chronic illness must do this or learn to do this. Every patient must realize that not every single moment is the turning point of his illness. It is this appreciation of what is and what is not important that is so very hard to learn. I have already found myself learning to let go of some of the little aspects of my illness, even this early in my course.

When first diagnosed, only a week ago, I tried to read articles about hairy cell leukemia in the medical library. I asked about my lab results, placing equal emphasis on all of them, wanting to see the result of every single blood test, every bit of data about my case even though some were clearly more important than others. In some ways, this only distracted me. I enveloped myself in information as if it were some mystic insulation against reality. I found myself worrying about small remarks from Habermann or minute parts of an article that I vainly tried to read. Are they really important? Do they pertain to me? Should I be worried? It will, I am sure, take months for me to get a solid feel for my illness, into which I have fallen as into a sudden trap. And I am a physician, someone who can understand a fair amount about the labs, the X rays, the bodily changes wrought by my illness that we in medicine refer to as pathophysiology. Now, for once, I see clearly what my patients and their parents must be going through, especially soon after I hand them a diagnosis like cystic fibrosis. How can I expect them to let go of the minutiae, to live their lives and let me worry about the details of their care?

The initial pain of my incision is diminished, and it is clear that I will heal satisfactorily. I find myself settling into a quiet, almost mindless routine. I'm not acutely ill; I'm being kept in the hospital long enough to recover from the surgery. My gut's already starting to work, and I've learned that my platelet count has returned to the normal range. The few days of my hospitalization are boring yet exhausting, and I am too tired to do much except sleep. It is as if all of the interrupted sleep from those nights on call has caught up with me at last. Or perhaps it is the aftereffect of the anesthesia. Or possibly the weakness I experience is secondary to the leukemia itself. I drift uneasily to sleep for hours during the afternoons, only to have trouble falling asleep at night. I stay up reading or watching television. After watching TV for a while here, I'm more convinced that it is good that I don't have one. I've grown accustomed to spending most of my time running or working, since my working hours at the hospital often number ten to twelve per day and my run usually takes another one to two. There is little enough time for other useful stuff, like eating, sleeping, or being with friends. There's been little enough time to be with Karin.

Another part of my hospital life has been taken up by the inevitable phone calls and cards. Within a day of my diagnosis, most of my friends and relatives knew what I had, and the word had spread out to my colleagues around the country. I let David Orenstein in Pittsburgh know that I wouldn't be able to get back there for my second visit in early April, as we'd scheduled. Spike Miller, my chairman at Davis, calls to cheer me up and tell me that my illness, he's sure, will be a temporary setback. Aunts, uncles, and cousins all asking the same questions, getting the same answers: I am going to be all right; yes, I am tired, but I am getting stronger; yes, I will "hang in there."

I speak several more times with Karin, each time missing her more, each time hearing the fear in both of our voices, each time feeling an added distance from my bed in Minnesota to hers in California. She still offers to come out to be with me; I tell her I'll be okay, that she should stay and take care of her children. I want her here with me but also have to face my disease, at least in its early stages, alone. It's been much the same when I speak with my relatives, my colleagues in Sacramento, my friends. I somehow feel that much of what I am to go through will have to be done alone.

It is the fifth day after my splenectomy, a week after my diagnosis, the day after my birthday. I am discharged from St. Mary's, taken to the hospital entrance in a wheelchair (hospital rules, I'm told). I enter the car carefully under my own limited power, and my mother and I drive the few blocks home in a warming afternoon. I look out the window at passing trees as if seeing them for the first time.

"Guess what I made for you for dinner," my mother says.

"Chicken soup, I hope."

"You got it. Are you hungry?"

"Yes. No. Not really. I don't know. I don't know . . . well, I do know what I want to do before I eat."

"What? Take a shower? Rest? Call Karin?"

"Actually . . . and don't get mad, Mom . . . I think I want to sorta walk a bit. I want to put on my stuff and walk . . . just a little bit."

Her mouth tightens as she turns slightly toward me in the car.

"Do you really think that's a good idea? Don't you think you should take it a little easy?"

"Van Heerden said it was okay, as long as I didn't go hard . . . or very far . . . and believe me, I couldn't even if I had to. I just want to put my stuff on and get out there . . . even if it'll only be a few yards. It's important to me, you know what I mean?"

For a moment, she says nothing. But then she nods. "I think I understand. I'll have soup ready for you when you get back. You won't go very far . . . and you'll stop if it hurts, won't you?"

"Promise. It'll take me longer to get ready to do it than it will to do it."

We're home. I cautiously negotiate the steps to the downstairs bedroom. I pull open the gym bag with my running stuff, my shoes, stretch tights, shirt, and the bicycling hat I always wear. I slowly put on my clothes and climb the stairs into the kitchen. While my mother watches, I tentatively stretch, avoiding any tugging of my incision, for a few minutes, then stand up.

"Back in a minute or two. How far is it around the circle?" My parents live in "Pill Hill," the area where nearly every house is owned by a physician at the Clinic.

"I think a third or a half mile or so. You're not going to . . ."

"No, I'm not going all the way around. But I need to know the goal. It makes it easier for me." I smile, and she smiles back.

I step outside and walk down the short driveway to the street and face left, then walk on the street to the next telephone pole. When I reach it, I break into a slow jog, almost as slow as a walk. When I reach the next telephone pole, perhaps fifteen yards away, I walk again, until the next pole, and alternately walk and jog by about four houses, maybe a hundred yards, maybe less. I turn around and come home the same way, walking to one telephone pole, jogging to the next. My whole "workout" takes only about five minutes, and I'm back in the kitchen.

My mother could say something about how short my "run" has been. But she doesn't, instead asking, "How was it?"

"Under the circumstances, okay. Not very far. Not very fast, that's for sure."

"You'll go farther tomorrow. Wash up, and I'll have your soup ready for you."

"Great. I'll be up in a couple of minutes."

I know that I will go farther tomorrow, and the next day, and the next. That is how it will have to be, each day taken with increasing distance or speed, until I'm back. It will take time, but the only way to do it is one day at a time, one telephone pole farther at a time, one quarter mile more at a time, until the miles add up, until my feet and legs are back into the strength they had once known, and I'm able once more to go for the distances I'd done so recently. I will keep it to myself that I'm still planning some day to run Western States, all one hundred miles of it.

Two days later, only about nine days after being handed my diagnosis, I enter Tom Habermann's examining room. I again sit on the brown leather couch, trying to read whatever magazine was left by the previous patient. I hear the shuffle of papers outside the door as my chart is removed from the rack and quickly surveyed, followed by the opening of the door.

"You look great. How do you feel?" Tom sits at his desk, smiling a soft cat grin at me.

"Okay, I guess, for having my abdomen opened a week ago. I started to walk around the block. Well, actually, more like walk-jog." I see his smile freeze, then drop a bit. "Real slow. Van Heerden had said it would be okay, as long as I don't overdo it," I offer.

"Just don't overdo it," Tom warns, and he looks out the window, then back at me. "I suppose it is good that you're getting back to your running. Hop up on the exam table; let me take a look."

"I'll have trouble hopping, but I can jog up there if you want." I pull myself up, take off my shirt, and I am subjected to a quick look and listen by Tom. He feels under my arms, along my neck, in my belly, and in my groin, as he searches for any lymph nodes enlarged by leukemia. I gingerly slide off the table and slowly reenter my shirt as he sits down at the desk, writes a bit in my chart, and turns to me, smiling broadly.

"Your father called me. He asked me if one of the factors contributing to your getting hairy cell leukemia is that you might be run down with too much work and too much running. He seems more worried about the running. I told him he shouldn't worry, but you know your dad."

"I figured he would ask you about that. My dad worries about that a lot. He should talk, with all the work and swimming he does. But he's always talked to me about not overdoing it, ever since I was running in college, during med school, during residency . . . whatever. Don't worry; I think I'm finally learning to listen to my body. But now what? I mean, what's next? Interferon? Pentostatin?"

"Well, your counts are fine. Actually, the response of your counts, just from the splenectomy, has been dramatic. Your platelet count has nearly tripled, and your neutrophils are normal. I called around and spoke to some other hematologists with an interest in hairy cell. I think we should give you a rest, take out the chest mass, and then wait and see. We may not need to give you any chemotherapy for a while, and I think we shouldn't give you any unless we really have to."

"What? No chemotherapy? What'll happen to the leukemia? Won't it just get worse?"

"Not necessarily. Remember, this is a chronic leukemia. And before we had any effective chemotherapy, 40 percent of the patients with it had long-term survival. Everybody I talked to agrees that we should hold off on chemotherapy as long as your counts stay up. They could stay up for only a few months, but they might stay up for years. I don't know. I can't tell you how long. But if your counts do drop and you need to receive chemotherapy, then I think you should get Pentostatin. I just want to make sure you can get it if you need it."

"What does that mean, 'to make sure I can get it?' Can't I get it?"

"It's a study drug. You have to be in a clinical study, on protocol."

The words sink in. A "study drug" means that Pentostatin is experimental. You can't go down to the drugstore and get this stuff. If I am going to get Pentostatin, I will have to be a research subject, or, as some patients or their parents sometimes say to me, a "guinea pig." Not only am I on the other side of the hospital bed from my usual place, I'm even on the other side of the research bench. Uncertainty bores into me, along with the feeling of being out of control of yet another aspect of this, my life as a patient.

I've grown up amid research from my childhood through my own career in medicine. My father had always been involved in research, but his work had seemed nebulous and strangely romanticized to me. His research involved traveling to the exotic western Pacific and seeing patients who, in the films and photographs I saw, showed the signs of mysterious neurological diseases as they attempted haltingly to walk on dirt roads in front of crude houses with galvanized tin roofs. Pigs and dogs seemed always to be wandering about in those pictures, moments of lives from a different era and realm of the earth. I always wondered at the good fortune that allowed my father to see such places, meet so many people (some of whom visited our home), write or give lectures about all of it, and get paid in the process.

When I was a high school student and in need of a research project for the science fair, my father arranged for me to work in a laboratory at the National Institutes of Health. I remember the marvel of designing the experiment, using the seemingly wondrous equipment, which, in retrospect, was rather simplistic stuff. In a way, it was my first exposure to what could be called a hypothesis-driven experiment, one that I designed, rather than one that I reproduced from a laboratory manual.

Majoring in biology at Amherst, I spent a lot of my undergraduate time in the chemistry and biology laboratories. I sought them out for refuge from the rest of the campus as places for quiet study, places to think and write. I'd often find myself arriving in my dorm after studying late on a Saturday night to find the others partying. It wasn't that I was antisocial (far from it); rather, I was inefficient and needed to study and work a lot just to keep up. Most others I knew at school did their work in their dorm rooms, but I used my dorm as a place to sleep and relax. Even as I carried out my honors project in biology, I found myself falling far short of the goal I'd set for experiments to complete. I learned that research, any research, always takes more time than expected, and that Murphy's Law, which says, "Anything that can go wrong, will go wrong, and at the worst possible moment," is an understatement.

In medical school, I was lucky enough to be selected to participate in a program, sponsored by the National Institutes of Health, to train physician-scientists. The program paid my tuition, no small amount at Stanford, even back in the late sixties, and actually paid me a small stipend throughout the school year. As a result, I was one of the few graduates in my year without an overwhelming debt to pay back to the government, to banks, or to parents. It took me six years to finish medical school because I took time off in order to complete the experiments and write a scientific paper, which was my first medical publication. The time factor involved in that research wore me out, but did not kill my interest in research, even as I realized that I was not going to be a major star. I told myself then, even as I tell myself now, that one doesn't do research to be a star, one does it for the excitement, challenge, and fun that comes with that particular territory.

That first medical research territory of mine, ironically enough, had been the study of an experimental cancer in mice. Basic experiments using single molecules in test tubes or identical cells in dishes are difficult enough. Requiring exacting conditions and expensive equipment, they can at least provide answers to simple, direct questions. Using animals sometimes allows scientists to ask more involved questions, but animals are much more intricate than single cells or molecules. In an effort to minimize the complexities of animals, science has turned to inbred species: mice or rats that are absolutely identical to one another. But sooner or later, scientists and the society they are part of want answers to questions that relate to people. Does a drug work? How can we prevent a disease like measles? Is too much cholesterol really bad for you, and if so, why? It's hard to get the exact answer by studying molecules, cells, or experimental animals, although scientists can get a good idea of where to look for the answers. So people, all of us different from one another, must be the final "experimental animal." All my adult life I have firmly believed that the steps leading forward to this end are worthwhile.

But as I look now at Tom Habermann and realize that Pentostatin will be available to me only if I am one of those experimental animals known as a subject in a clinical study, I feel scared and alone. But I also understand that Pentostatin, like any other drug, ultimately must be tested on patients like me in order to determine its safety and effectiveness. I know that being a research subject carries some degree of risk while offering new hope not just for me, but for other patients yet to come. And I also know that I have a choice of sorts. I could, after all, just say no to Pentostatin, since it is experimental. The *New England Journal of Medicine* article, however, is much too tantalizing for me. I see Pentostatin as my best hope for a cure, for getting rid of the leukemia, for getting my life back into my own hands. For me, the choice is made in the blink of an eye. There will be no long nights agonizing over my decision, and I hope there will be no periods of self-doubt, of asking myself "what if . . ." My lot, my future, all my chips are immediately placed on Habermann's plan and on Habermann himself. All I need now is to learn of the future, at least as much as he is willing or able to tell me.

"Okay, so what's the protocol?" I ask. "Is it comparing interferon against Pentostatin, or interferon with Pentostatin, or Pentostatin alone, or . . ." My mind runs out of combinations.

"Actually, I'm finishing up writing a protocol for ECOG, and it should go through soon," Tom replies.

"ECOG?"

"Eastern Cooperative Oncology Group. Your dad mentioned that you'd looked at a job in Pittsburgh. Some of the investigators in ECOG are there at the university. There's a similar study through the Western group, and Davis is in it, so you could be on that if you decided to stay in Sacramento."

Oncology is the study of cancer. ECOG is a group of physicians, virtually all at teaching centers, who have joined together to do clinical trials of cancer treatments. In ECOG, as in the other collective groups, each cancer is treated under an agreed-upon protocol that determines which patients can (and cannot) receive the treatment being studied, how the treatment is given, how complications are treated, and how patients are followed for their care during treatment. The group can compare different treatments more effectively and much more quickly than any single center because in a collective, many more patients can be studied simultaneously. While there are shortcomings of such collective efforts, they may be the only effective way to study relatively rare cancers like hairy cell leukemia.

"The ECOG protocol I'm writing up will use a course of interferon, followed by a course of Pentostatin in hairy cell patients," Tom says.

"Would I be eligible? Will it be open to patients who've had a splenectomy?"

"The way it's written, yes. As long as you don't get a big-league infection or something, you'd be eligible. But right now you don't need to be on chemotherapy. Right now we need to set up your chest surgery and arrange for your follow-up in Sacramento."

He turns back to his desk and reaches for the phone. "I'm going to call Jim Pluth. I'd like him to take out the mass in your chest." Tom quickly looks up and then dials the number. While waiting, Tom writes some notes in my chart, the phone cradled against his neck.

"Hi, Jim." Tom looks at me as he sells my case to Pluth. "I'd like to send someone over to you . . . you know Len Kurland? . . . yeah, well, his son, Geoff, is here . . . here in my office . . . he's a pediatric pulmonologist in California and has hairy cell leukemia . . . van Heerden just did his splenectomy . . . yeah, his counts were pretty low . . . they're fine now . . . anyway, he actually presented with an anterior mediastinal mass and we're not . . . yeah, some story, huh? . . . lymphoma?

thymoma? . . . well, we're not sure either, and I wanted to have you take a look . . . yeah, sternotomy . . . yes, sure . . . well . . . about a month I thought . . . let him recover from the splenectomy . . . oh, he'll do fine; he's a runner, actually just ran a fifty-mile race . . . no fifty, not fifteen . . . yeah, fifty miles . . . yeah, that's what I thought." Habermann seems to be enjoying this part of the conversation, and he flashes a smirky smile at me. "Anyway, I can send him over and get his films to you . . . preferably now . . . what day are you in the O.R.?" Habermann pulls an operating room schedule down from the bulletin board on the wall behind the desk and peers at it while he listens to Pluth on the other end. "Okay, that would be Monday . . . May eleventh? Is that okay with you?" He asks the phone but looks over at me, asking me the same. I nod. "Sounds fine . . . it looks like it's okay with Geoff . . . Okay, I'll send him over this afternoon." Habermann smiles into the phone as he talks, leaning back slightly in his chair. His self-confidence fills the room and the phone. I sit, watching the performance.

"Okay," he says as he returns the phone to its cradle, "you'll go over and meet Jim Pluth this afternoon. I'll make sure he has your films. His operating day is Monday, so we've scheduled your sternotomy for May eleventh, the second Monday in the month. I'll want to see you on Friday the eighth, get your blood work, and make sure everything is set. You sure that's okay?"

"Uh . . . sure . . . sure. I'll just make sure I'm off service in May."

Habermann looks back, smiling gently at me, as if to say, "*Of course* you'll be off service in May. What's more important, being on service or taking care of your life?" There have been lots of times I'm sure my priorities have been backward. But I know I'll have to rearrange my call schedule to allow for my surgery. It's a mirror image, as it were, to my past, when I'd always had to rearrange my life to fulfill the overwhelming needs at the hospital. For once, the hospital will have to take a backseat. It seems unfortunate that it takes leukemia to stop the abuse to which I've been a willing subject.

"Now," Tom says, "who's your physician in Sacramento?"

"I don't know . . . I mean I really don't have one . . . at least not a hematologist, anyway." I give a blank look.

"I figured you probably wouldn't. Well, I've already checked with some people in the Western Oncology Group. They gave me the name of Fred Meyers at UC Davis."

"Fred Meyers . . . I've heard of him . . . supposed to be pretty sharp . . . I think he just joined the faculty. I don't know him personally, but I'll make the arrangements to see him as soon as I get back."

"I'll write him, give him a summary. I'll want you to get your counts done once every couple of weeks."

"That should be no problem. I'll make sure you get copies of all the results."

"Let's make that appointment for May eighth, and then you can get to Pluth's office and make the other arrangements. That should do it." We walk down the hall to the main desk, where the appointment is made. "Okay," Tom turns to me, "you call me if there are any problems or questions. I'll send a summary to Meyers. See you in about a month. Keep the faith." He holds his outstretched hand to me. We shake on it (another business deal?), and I walk out to the waiting room.

My mother, who'd accompanied me, is in her chair where I'd left her, knitting another cap. She didn't want to go back into the examination room, preferring to sit, knitting or reading, in the waiting room. It was quite the opposite of my hospital stay, when she made every effort to be in my room most of the day, even while I was too sick or too weak to do anything.

"Where to now?" she asks, looking up. The clicking continues. "Are you all done with Habermann?"

"Or is he all done with me?" She looks at me seriously after stifling a short laugh. I tell her the plan. The clicking stops and knitting is gathered.

"We know Jim Pluth . . . I'm pretty sure we do. I've heard he's very nice. Say, since you don't have to go right over, why don't we get some lunch first? You can tell me what Habermann said over lunch. How about it?"

We take the elevator down to the subterranean corridors of the Clinic, find a cafeteria, get our little meals, and sit down. There is a fountain in the hall, whose splashing susurration seeks to soothe the collective fears and miseries in the subway.

"Well?" she starts.

"Well, what?"

"What next, what is the next step? What did Habermann say?"

"Habermann wants the mass removed on Monday, May eleventh. He wants Jim Pluth to do it. Tom'll see me the Friday before and get my blood work done. I'll arrange to come back in early May." I speak between quick bites, as if I'm trying to instantly recover the weight I'd lost following my surgery.

"That sounds fine," my mother lies, hardly touching her food. "Like I said, Jim Pluth is a very nice man. I think Dad and I met him at one of the Clinic functions . . . I'm not sure which one . . . but he's supposed to be very good."

"If Habermann says he's okay, that's good enough for me." I take a few more bites. "But no chemotherapy for now. Tom says my counts are good and we should wait."

"No chemotherapy? He doesn't think that's dangerous, does he?"

"That what's dangerous?"

"Not getting chemotherapy. I mean, shouldn't you get something to get rid of the leukemia?"

"Well, the way he explained it, no . . . at least not right now. He says my counts are okay, and he wants to wait. I mean, I'm not especially eager to get chemotherapy, but at the same time, I'm not sure I want to walk around waiting until I need it. It makes me feel sorta like a time bomb, like I might go off someday. But Tom said I'll probably be able to get this new drug, Pentostatin, if I need it. He told me it'll be on a protocol that I could be on."

"Protocol?"

"Experimental. I get to be a subject in a research project."

"Experimental drug? Does it work? I mean, I'm sure it . . . I'm sure it works . . . but . . . do you have to be an experimental subject . . . ?"

". . . to get the drug?" I finish the sentence for her. "Yeah. That's the way it is."

She has taken only a few bites of the small salad serving as her lunch.

"Is there an alternative? To the protocol, I mean."

"Sure. I could say no. Sounds like Nancy Reagan . . . Just Say No." I laugh. "But actually, the choice seems pretty obvious to me. It won't be my first time as an experimental subject."

"What? You've been in an experiment?"

"Come on, Mom, you make it sound like I was working with Frankenstein or something. No, when I was a first year med student I volunteered to be in a research project near Stanford. I had to pedal a bike at a set rate, lying down, which isn't that easy. But the hard part was that they were studying body temperature during exercise . . . core body temperature. So I had to pedal this bike thing, lying flat on my back, with all sorts of electrodes plastered on me, and with a special temperature probe stuck up my butt." Her mouth is gaping at me as I start the description, but the last image of me with a rectal probe and pedaling a bicycle opens the flood gates, and we are suddenly laughing hysterically there in the cafeteria. My mother has a marvelous laugh, but what makes it special is the fact that she laughs to the point of tears when something really funny happens. And she is nearly there now.

"I can . . . just . . . see . . . you." She has to stop and catch her breath.

"Yeah, there I was, pedaling like crazy with the wire thing up there. Oh, it was weird, let me tell you." My mother is shaking, crying, and laughing.

"But actually, Mom," and now I am serious, "this will be different. I mean, this time, the experiment has a bit more personal importance."

She stops laughing and looks across the table at me. I can hear again the splash of the fountain combining with the voices of the other diners into a whisper of mixed words of hope and fear.

"There's interferon alone, which has a good chance of helping me, but a relatively small chance of curing me, putting me into remission. Pentostatin offers me my only good chance of complete remission, at least as far as I see it. I'm ready to accept the risks involved with being in a study for the chance at getting rid of my leukemia, once and for all. It's just not me to want to take something that will maybe keep me hanging around half cured. I want it all or nothing. And you know something?"

"What?"

"It's gonna work."

"I hope you're right." She takes a small bite of her salad.

A few minutes later, we sit beside each other on one of dozens of chairs trying to be couches in another waiting room that could double for the train station serving a small community. Listening for my name to be called, I walk over to the side of the room to look more closely at the enormous mural painted on the wall. Almost every floor of the Clinic building has a mural occupying one wall of the waiting area. Each mural had been commissioned by the Clinic to portray some aspect of medicine or science as seen through the unique vision of the artist. I'm just starting to read the plaque describing the artist and the meaning of the mural (Art Appreciation 101?) when my name is called. I walk over to my mother before I head up to the desk.

"Back soon, Mom. Sure you don't want to come in with me?"

"No . . . no, I'll wait here." She's already hard at work on her knitting.

I'm shown into yet another seemingly identical examination room and sit on yet another brown couch, awaiting Pluth. I have only a few minutes to myself, as he soon strides into the room. He looks every inch the surgeon. Better still, he looks every inch the cardiac surgeon. Jim Pluth is tall and solid looking with stylishly gray hair. He sticks out his right hand and enfolds my own within it. His left hand holds my chart and X rays.

"Hi, Geoff. I spoke with Tom. He told me about you. This," and here he holds the X ray up over our heads a bit, allowing the fluorescent light to illuminate the film, "should be easy. Median sternotomy, take a few days to recover. We probably can stay out of the pleural space."

"I hope so."

The pleural space he's talking about staying out of is the actual space enfolding and enclosing the lungs. The term *space* is somewhat of a misnomer, for it is vanishingly thin, one side a membrane actually covering the lungs and the other side a second membrane on the inner wall of the chest and the structures between the lungs. Normally, the space holds only a few teaspoonfuls of thin fluid, which lubricates the membranes and allows the lungs to easily expand and contract with each breath. If Pluth enters that space, either inadvertently or because the mass in my chest extends into it, then air will get in, and my lung might not inflate properly. I would then need a chest tube, a plastic tube as big around as a little finger, going through my skin and chest wall and into the space. The tube, hooked up to a suction line, would keep my lung expanded until the hole in the pleura healed.

"You on any medications?" Pluth asks.

"No. Actually, wait a minute, yes . . . I take a nasal spray, a steroid for my hay fever." I realize I'd forgotten about that medication entirely until that moment. "Will that be a problem?" I tell him the dose.

"No problem at all," is the confident reply. "Say, do those steroids work? I mean, I've got some hay fever, too. What do you think."

I am taken aback for a moment. Pluth is asking my medical opinion? I think for an instant, then become a medical colleague for a moment. "Yeah, they work. They're stronger than . . . ," I name an alternative, "but they aren't as comfortable. I mean, they burn a bit. But they work better."

"Kinda like 'No pain, no gain,' huh?"

"Yeah, sorta."

"May eleventh still okay with you?"

"Sure . . . sure. I'll make it work."

"Fine. May eleventh. You'll see Habermann on the eighth; he'll get the lab work, then get you admitted. You'll have to come in the night before, on Sunday the tenth, because there is a lot to do, some stuff to get you ready. So it's easier that way. Okay?"

"Okay."

He sticks out his hand again, and we shake on it. We walk down to the reception desk, he makes the arrangements with the nurse/receptionist, and we part. I walk out to my mother, who looks up with a startled face.

"That was quick. Are you all set already?"

"All set. Let's go home. I've got a little run to do."

"Yes, sir!" she says, as she gathers up her knitting yet again.

We drive home, and again, my stretching takes more time than the "run." I go only a telephone pole or two farther than yesterday. But I do the entire short distance without any walking. It is my first true run since the splenectomy. And once again, the chicken soup is ready when I am finished, showered, and dressed.

I see my life divided into parts, some of which must take on a new role for my preservation. One of the parts is that played by my healthy persona, itself responsible for carrying on a version of normal life. The rest of me is stuck firmly in the midst of this illness, which I've paradoxically carried within me as if it were an evil stowaway on a ship, intent upon destroying the invaded vessel. In any case, my body is being taken over by this usurper, and it holds me hostage to its will. I have heard of people held captive, hostages, who perform small, seemingly insignificant, tasks repetitively and with great care on a regular basis, for they embody the sanity and the control their captors seek to destroy. I am like one of those captives held against my will, and I will amplify some part of my life to a level of fanaticism as a way of maintaining control. Running is one way I can prevent my illness from totally dominating my life. But it is not the only way.

Soon after my discharge from the hospital, my father helps me with my show, my charade of well-being. We are at the dinner table, finishing up another of my mother's great meals. My strength is slowly but visibly returning, and I sit there with my second cup of tea, wolfing cookies for dessert.

"Geoff, I just got this and thought you should take a look at it." He passes over an open, slick magazine, all bright graphics, drawings, and colored tables, not at all the dull, boring look of a medical journal. I look at the cover and then the article he's opened for me. It is a financial mag, like *Forbes*. The article outlines the best individual retirement accounts for long-term investors.

"Do you have an IRA?" my father asks.

"Uh, no, I don't think so." Personal economics is not my strong suit. Chalk that up to having gone to college and medical school during the sixties, when peace and love didn't mix well with money, capitalism, and the military-industrial complex.

"Well, you probably should. You know, plan for your retirement and all. Anyway, it looks like one of these funds is pretty good. I have some money in it, and it's doing well. Do you have any extra money lying around?"

"I've got a few bucks. Not many, I suppose. I'm in academic medicine, you know. But I'm not especially good at that sort of stuff. The money stuff, I mean."

"It was hard for me to learn, too. I did okay, as you probably know."

For a physician who spent most of his time in the public health service rather than in private practice, on a salary that was good but not great, my father, in fact, has done quite well. He is shrewd with money, has invested wisely, and now, near retirement, makes more than I do and has the pensions and annuities to insure that he'll continue to do so for quite a while. And I know he's not asking about my lack of plans in the IRA area for fun. It's just easier for him and for me to deal with things in the concrete mold of money, instead of the tricky plasticity of emotional things like death.

"Well," I agree, "it looks pretty good, at least according to this article." I'm concentrating on the main table on the first page. "But can I put the money in now and get it off my taxes?"

"That's the whole point. Put it in before April 15 and it comes right off the top, up to two thousand. In your tax bracket it's like getting about 30 percent of the investment free." My father knows more about my tax bracket than I do.

"Okay, I'll do it, soon as I get back. Actually, I'll call these guys tomorrow and have them send the forms to me." Part of my future is in the planning stage already, and I still have at least one surgery and perhaps chemotherapy to get through.

"Now," my father says, having gotten through that bit of business, "let's go over the plan for when you get back here. I'll get your ticket for you."

"Dad, I can do that."

"I know you can. But I've got all these frequent flier miles, and you don't know exactly when you'll be able to get back to Sacramento. I can take care of all that from this end. Trust me, it'll be easier."

He is, as usual, right. He's traveled all over the place. His frequent flier printouts probably look like classified documents from some secret government agency, several pages long. We agree that he'll get the ticket. I brief him on the plans I'd made with Habermann and Pluth for my return in early May. I tell him of Fred Meyers, who'll be following me in Sacramento.

"Sounds like things are all set," he says. "I've already gotten you a ticket back to Sacramento in a couple of days, not that we want to get rid of you. You can spend that time resting up here and getting strong on your mother's cooking. Unless you want to come over to the office and do some work."

"I think I'll pass up the work part. But how about some conferences here? Can you get me the schedule? I might as well learn something before I head back." I stop myself and stare at my parents. "As if I haven't learned anything over the last week and a half."

My mother, standing at the end of the room, had been silent for the exchange between my father and me. But now she can't resist the obvious.

"As if none of us has learned anything over the last week and a half," she says. I turn to look at her, but she is looking away, up at the ceiling.

7

The bed with its recently changed sheets is cool and the room still dark as I feel the fluttering of my eyelids, awakening me again into my nightmare. Memories of last night filter into my brain. Soon they'll be bringing my breakfast or perhaps the scale to document my continuing weight loss, or one of the interns will come in and ask me how I had slept. "Badly," I will tell him or her, reviewing again the same symptoms that the Pittsburgh house staff and Dr. Ellis have become accustomed to over the last three weeks or so. They are probably tired of and frustrated by my persistent nightly fevers and chills. The days, fencing in the fevers, have run into each other, melting into each other even as I seem to melt before the medical minds here.

Larry Ellis always tries to look upbeat even as he admits a lack of new leads to explain my symptoms. He reminds me of my brother a little over a year ago when he told me to "Hang in there." I'm alone with my illness. No one has told me that they know how I feel. My friends can see from my face that they can't even come close to knowing what I know.

I'm marginally lucky today, as breakfast arrives first. When asked where to get a good meal, most folks don't think first of their local hospital. Hospital breakfasts are the worst of the bad. I look at the cold cereal and the once-warm egg and maybe-bacon. I drink some tepid tea; perhaps that will whet my dwindling appetite. No such luck. I pick at the food until the tray is removed. I try to read and fail. Finally, I pull myself slowly from the bed and wander down the hall to the ward station. I peer into the medication room, where one of the nurses is gathering together some intravenous tubing and a bottle of yellow liquid destined for the body of another patient with cancer.

"Hi, Dr. Kurland. Feeling any better?"

"To be honest, no . . . no. But I thought I'd . . ." She looks at me as first I stare into the small medication room, then at the tubing, then at nothing. She turns fully toward me, trying to smile.

"Are you all right? Dr. Kurland? Are you all right?"

"Yes . . . no . . . I don't know . . . maybe I . . ." I find I can't ask for help. All the weeks I've been there I've tried to keep a happy face, if not for myself, then for the others around me. It has been a dissolving game, a facade, a fabrication. And here I stand, before the nurse, unable to show what I feel, trying to hide the despair that is overtaking me. It is as if I've hit "The Wall," that legendary point twenty miles into the marathon where it seems someone sneaks up and pours lead into your shoes. The major difference between the marathon and my current life is that if you decide to quit after you hit The Wall in the marathon, you can rest up and run again. The race I'm in right now doesn't allow that luxury.

"Would you like to wash up?" The nurse's voice returns me to the reality of the medication room.

"Huh?" I grunt.

"Wash up . . . take a shower . . . shave. I don't think you have any tests this morning, at least as far as I know. How about it? Here's the shaver." She hands me an electric razor. Because of the chemotherapy and low platelet counts shared by most of the patients here, using a regular razor is forbidden.

"Well, maybe that would be a good idea." I feel a bit brighter. "Sure . . . I'll come back after I shave and get set for a shower."

"It's a deal. I'll tape over your IV so it won't get wet."

I slowly walk back down the hall, clutching the razor as if it is some holy talisman destined to heal me. I wash my face. I look into the mirror at the stranger peering back at me. Someone thin, with a two-day-old smattering of black-and-gray beard on his otherwise pale face, eyes deep blue. I shake my head, then shave as best I can. A little later after a turn in the communal ward shower, I put on new hospital-issue pajamas and feel better, or at least cleaner.

I return the razor and continue down the hall to the patient lounge, which houses the communal TV. I have not succumbed to renting a TV for my bed: that truly would be the last straw, closing off the last possibility of staying active enough to keep my blood from totally stagnating, to keep myself alive enough to fight off the demons attacking me.

The lounge has windows looking twelve stories down to the streets and buildings of the campus. The sun is blisteringly bright, especially for someone working on little sleep. Despite the fatigue, the blue sky and high sun make me want only to run outside, to leave the hospital and forget the leukemia. The television is on to some late-morning talk show, bringing me back to a reality I'd prefer to visit only as a tourist. I tell myself I'm probably going to die, which is only made worse by the realization that my doctor doesn't know what is killing me.

It is about three weeks after my diagnosis and two and a half weeks after my splenectomy. I walk into my office across the street from the University of California, Davis, Medical Center. It is about 8 A.M., before most of the others have arrived. I'd returned from Rochester the night before. Only my friend Al, who'd picked me up at the airport, and Karin knew I was back.

Karin had come over to see me within minutes of my arrival home.

"Hi, hon," she said, carefully placing her arms around me. She just held me then and didn't speak. We both stood still in my small living room, our arms wrapped tightly about each other, as if we were afraid to release ourselves, as if being apart would throw us far away. We kissed, lips, necks, hands. I looked into her eyes, felt her shaking, whether in fear or happiness. I pulled her back to me, held her fast again.

"God, I missed you. I'm glad you're here. I'm glad to be back."

"Should I have come out there? I would have."

"I know."

"Does it hurt? Your scar?"

"Not too bad. Want to see it?" I gave a stifled evil laugh.

"Sure . . . maybe later . . . but first I just want to look at you, hold you, see that you're still alive. Are you going to be . . . ?"

"To be okay? Yeah, I'm going to be okay. More surgery in May, but everything looks good right now. Actually, I'm ready to get back to work."

"Work? Geoff, do you think you can maybe slow down a bit? Just a bit?" We sat down on the couch, turning to look at each other.

"How? Ruth has been covering, and she needs time in the lab. There's nobody else. It'll have to be me. But, seriously, if anything, I should be stronger now, I mean, my counts are better; my strength is fine. I think work is what I should do . . . but I'll tell you something."

"What's that?" She looked quizzically at me.

"I'll try to take it easy . . . but I'm not in control of all of that, you know. I mean, what am I supposed to tell the patients? 'Sorry, can't see you, I've got to rest. Get sick some other time'?"

"Well, no . . . but you know what I mean . . . try to take it sorta easy . . . for me, maybe . . ."

"Like I said, I'll try. But you know, I actually ran a bit." She gave me a look, but I continued. "Well, not a lot. The hundred miler is out, but I'm not going to stop my running, even if I can't run that much just yet. So I'll take it easy with both the work and running . . . but I won't give either of them up. I wrote to Norm Klein, the race director, and told him I'd work the race as a doc. He said he'd save me a place in the race next year, although that's a long way away."

I looked down at my hands, then up at the face before me. "Can you stay tonight? I'm not sure if I'm good for anything, but it would be wonderful if you could stay. I'd just like to hold you as I fall asleep, see you when I wake up . . ."

"I've got the kids, and I told Jenny I'd be back in a few minutes. They're waiting for me. I really have to get home. But I'll see you at work tomorrow, won't I?"

I was disappointed. As always, I tried to accentuate the positive. "Of course. And any other time you want."

She looked away for a moment, then turned back to me, a trace of tears starting in her eyes. "I'm glad you're back, Geoff."

Aside from the lingering pain of my abdominal incision, I feel fine as I walk into the office in the morning. One of the secretaries is on the phone as I go past her, and she looks up suddenly with a startled gasp

"Dr. K.! Welcome back." She turns quickly to the phone. "No, I'm not talking to you; it's someone who walked in and . . . I'll call you back." She replaces the phone on its cradle and looks up.

"Hi, Janis. Good to see you."

"Doctor K.! Is that really you?"

"Yes, it must be me . . . I keep touching myself to make sure it's still me."

"Well, it looks like the surgery didn't change your sense of humor, at least . . . thank God. How are you? How do you feel?"

"It beats the alternative."

"Huh?"

" 'Old age isn't so bad, when you consider the alternative.' Maurice Chevalier."

"Oh . . . Oh, I get it!"

"Great. Is Monica in? Or Ruth?" I was trying to find my nurse and my partner.

"Haven't seen either yet . . . soon, though, I bet."

"Suzanne ought to be here soon, I suppose," I say, referring to my secretary. "Well, tell whoever gets in first to page me."

"Will do, Dr. K."

I keep moving down the unadorned corridor. The building is a small place that probably was a realty office until the university rented it to house the department. It has veneer paneling and thin windows that give it an air of impermanence. The department has been promised better offices for years, but we all know that'll happen "when hell freezes over." Our medical poverty isn't limited to our office space. We see our clinic patients in renovated trailers rather than in a real building. It's easier to put up temporary buildings (in the form of trailers) than go through the red tape of budget justification, environmental impact studies, and job bidding required in the University of California system in order to have a real building.

I get to my little office, turn on my pager, and call the operator to tell her I'm back. She screams a welcome and alerts the other operators of the return of Dr. K. I hear hellos in the background. I cross the street to the medical center and walk down to the cafeteria, where I have that rarity of rarities for me, a real breakfast.

Ruth soon finds me via my pager, and I retrace my steps to the office to find out the goings-on with the patients. Monica, the nurse specialist, is with her as I wander into Ruth's tiny office.

"Hi, sports fans."

"Hey, am I glad to see you," says Ruth, giving me a hug. Monica, who's been the nurse specialist for years and is nearing retirement age, smiles and shakes her head in agreement.

"Is that because the service is so rough, or what?"

"Well, it's not too bad. Rachel is back in, so is Kimberley. I just sent Jeff and Timmy home." Two of our sickest CF patients are in, two are out. "The ICU is quiet, no consults there, thank God, and clinic hasn't been too terrible."

"Okay. I'm back. I'm ready to start back on, now."

"Are you sure you're up to this? I mean I don't want to volunteer for more call right now, but . . . are you sure?"

"Yeah . . . yeah, I'm sure . . . I'll be all right. Anyway, it'll be good for me to get back to work. I need to work, some. Some people will do anything to get a few days off . . . get leukemia, get their spleen out . . . I mean it's terrible." I laugh out loud with the two of them.

Ruth quickly gives me the story on our patients as I take notes. It turns out the service isn't too bad, if you think that having only about seven or eight patients, with two of them suffering from severe cystic fibrosis, is not too bad. I go back across the street to make rounds. It's now about nine in the morning, and I get a second cup of coffee on my way to the ward.

As I walk onto the ward, you would have thought a visiting dignitary had arrived. I find myself thronged by the interns, residents, nurses, and some of my fellow faculty. It turns out that one of the residents had given an informal talk on hairy cell leukemia once my diagnosis was made known, and he asks if I've seen the recent article in the *New England Journal*. We compare notes for a few minutes, and then I make my way to the chart rack, after accepting the well wishes of everyone, to start rounds.

The "service," as it is known, the collection of patients, is small, but at least two of my charges are especially sick. Cystic fibrosis is a chronic disease, characterized by abnormal secretions that clog the lungs and pancreas, leading to progressive respiratory disease and mal-nutrition in most of its victims. Even though we've gotten better at treating it, it's still ultimately fatal.

I see the asthmatic children who are getting better and save the sickest patient for the end of rounds. Rachel's only three years old, and her cystic fibrosis has put her back in the hospital for another course of antibiotics. It's her fourth or fifth hospitalization in less than a year.

I had diagnosed her with her illness after she came to the clinic at three months with pneumonia and weighing only a few ounces more than her birth weight. Her parents, Grace and Walter, were deeply reli-gious, quiet, and overwhelmed as I doled out the medical verdict. Grace's hair was braided and wrapped about her head; her clothes were spotless and prim. Walter sat beside her, his short-sleeved white shirt was tautly starched, and his close-cropped hair made him seem a barber rather than a butcher. I remember their look as I told them their daughter had cystic fibrosis. In their eyes, it was pure hubris of me to assume any overwhelming knowledge in such things. I was not to be trusted; in fact, I was to be avoided.

"How do you know she's got this . . . cystic fibrosis. Can you be sure? Really sure?" Walter asked, piercing me with his eyes. He was strong enough and big enough to kill me, although I was pretty sure he wouldn't because of his spiritual beliefs.

"Rachel has the classic symptoms of cystic fibrosis. You told me yourself of how she eats all the time but has diarrhea and doesn't gain weight. And the pneumonia . . . that all goes along with it. Finally, the test we did shows that she has too much salt in her sweat. That makes the diagnosis."

"Can't the test be wrong?" Meaning, couldn't I be wrong. The answer to the first was almost certainly no, while the answer to the second was less secure.

"No. It's not wrong. Believe me, I wish it were. And we've got to do something about it. We can treat it. But we can't do it without your help. This will take a lot of work, and we have to start by getting her well, and the best way to do that is in the hospital." I had looked earnestly back and forth at both of them as I said this. Grace's gaze had been averted the whole time. This was a matter for her husband to decide.

There had been more talk as the other patients waited in their clinic rooms. Finally, after twenty or thirty minutes, Walter reluctantly agreed to allow me to admit Rachel to the hospital. I pushed my way through clinic, seeing the remaining patients, and then, late in the afternoon, wandered up to the ward to see if Rachel was settled in her room, to speak again with the interns and residents about the plans for her care. I went up to the nursing station desk and asked which room she was in. One of the ward nurses gave me a forlorn look.

"She's not in a room yet."

I suddenly found myself seething. I was sure there was a screwup by some administrative type, something unsatisfactory with the family's insurance, something that prevented me (again) from doing my job. "So why," I tried to show an outward calm, "isn't she in her room?"

"Well, Dr. Kurland," the nurse began, "we're having some trouble convincing the parents that their daughter will be okay here. I've spoken with them, but they still seem unsure. I think you better talk to them."

I looked over my shoulder and for the first time saw the small group of people: the resident, the head nurse, Monica, my pulmonary nurse specialist, and one of the social workers. Now, I knew there was big trouble.

"Listen, Dr. K.," said the resident. "I'm not sure what their problem is. I think they're worried about the medical student."

"Medical student?"

"Yeah. The student is going to work her up with the intern. After all, she's a new patient. I thought it would be appropriate. Anyway, the parents said they don't want the medical student in there."

I looked back at the gathering by the nursing station. The student pointed out to me was tall, round, and bearded. I'd seen him on the wards before, and he'd seemed interested, outgoing, and quite nice.

It wasn't the first time a family had refused to have a medical student examine their child, but the refusers usually were parents of children who were in and out of the hospital, over and over fighting a chronic illness. I could understand why they might not feel up to telling the long, involved story again to a student physician, one just learning the art of medicine. After all, in addition to finding out the immediate reason for the hospitalization, he or she would ask all sorts of probing questions that seemed unrelated. Small details of the family history, history of travel, pets, allergies . . . in short, all the extraneous facts that, while at times important, tend to drop by the wayside in the middle of a fight with leukemia, cystic fibrosis, chronic hepatitis.

Alone, I went up to the parents. Grace held Rachel , now asleep in her mother's arms, breathing hard. Walter looked at me with clear eyes and set jaw. "Hi," I started. "I understand there's a problem."

Walter did the talking. "Yes, Dr. Kurland, there is. We don't want Rachel in that room." He glanced to his left.

"Is it the room? Or is it something else? If it's just the room, we can change the room. If it's something else, then tell me what it is, and I'll try to help."

"Well. It's not just the room. We don't want the student there."

"I can understand that you might feel uncomfortable with a student doctor, but you know we also will have the interns and residents and me taking care of Rachel. This is a teaching hospital. This is how we train physicians. This is how I was trained as a medical student and intern. That's how I learned how to take care of Rachel. That's how all physicians learned."

"It's not that, Dr. Kurland. We understand that students have to learn." He acknowledged his wife for the first time. Grace looked up at me with him. "It's just that . . . well . . . he seems kinda dirty to us."

"Dirty? What?" I was totally taken aback.

"Well, it's his beard. We're worried about his beard, about it maybe being dirty and causing more problems with Rachel or something. Besides, we feel that our wishes should be taken into account. You know Dr. Kurland, I'm just a butcher, but where I work, the customer always gets what he wants; the customer is always right."

Walter's clean-shaven face turned a slight shade of red. I closed my eyes, took a deep breath, and said nothing for a few seconds. I thought of all the depictions of Christ I'd ever seen, each showing him robed, sandaled, and bearded. I thought of how I'd looked as a medical student, with my long hair. I must have scared a lot of people but never to the point of their refusing to see me, even when I worked at the Veteran's Hospital.

I looked at my watch. It was near five o'clock in the afternoon and I still had all of my rounds to do now that clinic was done. Was it as Walter said: the customer is always right? Are parents of sick children mere customers for medical care, like someone going into Burger King or a grocery store? Well, I told myself, probably not. On the other hand, was this a battle that in the long run was worth fighting, or was it more important to get Rachel started on treatment, placate the parents enough to where they would accept me as the physician, and get on to other things? I realized the latter was the better approach. I had to make peace with the parents and on the ward, too. I opened my eyes and took another breath, then turned back to the parents standing before me.

"Look, Jim is a fine medical student, but I can understand your feelings. I'll speak with the staff and rearrange things. I think it's very important to get Rachel started on medications, and then we can all talk about cystic fibrosis and what it will mean for her and you tomorrow. Let's let her get settled in, get a good night's sleep, then deal with it. Is that okay with you?"

"That's okay with us," was the reply.

I talked to the staff and placated as best I could. I spoke with the medical student, asking if he'd mind not taking this case this time. I hated doing it because it was a great case to learn from. But to his credit, Jim understood and would continue to follow Rachel 's course, albeit from a discreet distance. In conference, the resident, intern, Jim, and I discussed Rachel and the plan for her care: intravenous antibiotics to fight her infection, chest physiotherapy to unclog her lungs, and nutritional support to give her the strength to fight back against cystic fibrosis.

Over the next several days, Rachel improved, and the parents accepted the diagnosis as best they could. They accepted their daughter's fate as if it was their only choice at a cafeteria for the starving: the child they had wished for came with an unforeseen disease, one that, as I explained to them, moves constantly to kill and never takes a vacation. Their work to care for their daughter was only just beginning and would go on until the disease took her life. I spoke with the parents as if my words were floating on bubbles that might suddenly burst, startling Walter and Grace out of agreement and understanding. Their eyes never softened; their voices sounded the deliberate strains of fervent believers who would, along with and despite all the medicine I could muster, pray for their daughter's deliverance from this evil into which I, representing that cruel world of medicine, had thrown them headlong and unwilling.

She got better, but that admission to the hospital was the first of many. Some six or eight months later, her parents delayed bringing Rachel back to the clinic for evaluation. When I finally saw her, she was in dire straits, unable to sit upright in Grace's lap, fighting for each breath, her limbs thin enough to encircle easily with my thumb and forefinger. But even then, the parents refused to allow her admission to the hospital, promising to bring her back the following day. I couldn't take the risk of them backing out on their promise; besides, Rachel was too sick to wait another day for treatment. For the first time in my medical career, I invoked a police hold, called hospital security, and admitted her to the intensive care unit, where she very nearly died over the next twenty-four hours. The hospital police officer had come into the clinic room where the parents sat and calmly told them that Rachel would have to stay. The parents listened as if being spoken to by an alien being, a power that they acknowledged only on the surface. Their faith, I was sure, was silently damning me, the physician, forever to hell for doing this to them, for taking away their ability to be parents. I could barely speak to them, even when they admitted how much better Rachel looked after a week of treatment in the hospital.

But something happened to the parents and to me. Somehow we began to put aside all of the deep divisions and differences to work together for Rachel, who served as an object for our uneasy truce. But despite the admissions to the hospital and no matter how hard her parents worked to stem the killing tide of her disease, making sure she took her medications, giving her the twice or thrice daily treatments that required pounding her chest to get her thickened secretions out of her lungs, despite all that, we all saw the progression of her cystic fibrosis. It was slowly choking off her life, stealing her nutrition, and sealing her fate. Through this we, Grace, Walter, and I, all now worked as a team, bound together by the common foe.

And now, Rachel is once again sick and in the hospital. I read the chart outside her door and hear her weak cough within. I scan the notes, read the orders that have been written. Taking a breath, I knock on the door and poke my head inside. The shades are partly drawn and the room dim.

"Dr. Kurland. You're back." Grace speaks it with a finality, yet she looks up and smiles gently at me. She is, as always, dressed in a simple, clean, starched dress. Her hair is pulled around her head. She sits close to her daughter, as if protecting her.

"Hello. How are you, Rachel?" Rachel glances at me and pulls away, asking to be held by her mother, who obliges, placing her upon her lap.

"Not so well," Grace answers for her. "She's better than she was when she came in. But she's not getting as well as fast. Is that bad? I mean, normally she'd be better by now, after a week and a half of antibiotics. But she's still coughing a lot and isn't eating too well. Is that bad, Dr. Kurland?"

"I don't like it," I say. "Let me take a listen." I take my stethoscope and listen to the small lungs. I can hear the mucus filling the airways, the lungs squeaking and crying to be rid of their burden. Rachel's small heart is pounding, working hard because of the infection. She is more pasty than pale. And she is beyond thin, with a wasting body, nearly every bone visible. Her blond hair is pulled back from her face in tiny braids, making her blue eyes bulge from her face as if they might shoot into the room. Her fingertips are thick and round with the deformity called "clubbing," a sign of chronic lung disease.

I slowly sit down on the bed, wincing a bit as my abdominal incision rubs against my shirt. Grace intently watches my face.

"Rachel," I say, talking to her mother through her, "I can still hear some of the sticky stuff in your lungs. We should keep going with the IV's and the chest treatments. Keep up your eating and taking your enzymes. You'll probably get better over the next few days." I outline the essentials of her care, the same type of care we've had for cystic fibrosis for many years.

"We heard you were ill, Dr. Kurland. We heard you had to have surgery."

"Yes. I've got an illness. It's a form of leukemia. I just had my spleen removed. I'll be all right, I think . . . I hope."

Grace's eyes bore deeply into me. She looks into my face again.

"I know you'll be all right. You've got to help care for Rachel. And we've been praying for you, Dr. Kurland."

I look down at Rachel, then back up at Grace. "I thank you for that. And you're right, I've got a lot of work to do here. I plan to do the best I can."

"We know that. Thank you, Dr. Kurland. And God bless you."

"Thank you, Grace. And you, too, Rachel." I get up slowly and walk out of the room, back to the nursing station where I write my notes and discuss plans with the resident on call for the ward. It is getting late in the day. I take the elevator down a few floors to the satellite pharmacy.

"Dr. K.!" Steve exclaims as he sees me standing at the Dutch door of the pharmacy. "We heard you were back!" I spy Karin inside, smiling. She knows I hadn't just come by to see Steve, who knows it also.

"Hi, Steve. How you been?"

"How've I been? Boring, compared with you, that's how. You look great." He looks at me intently, nods, smiles, and says again, "You really look great. I mean it."

"Thanks. It's good to be back. Good to be home." I look over his shoulder, and Steve half turns his tall, thin body around and sees Karin approaching the door.

"Karin. Somebody here to see you." He grins as Karin comes over to the door.

"Steve, I think I'm going to go on a little break, okay?"

"Well . . . all right, this time. But don't be too long. Although I have to admit you haven't taken too many breaks for the last couple of weeks, I suppose," Steve chuckles.

"Back soon," Karin says as she closes the lower half of the door and gently puts her hand on my arm. We walk down the corridor, and she slips closer to me, putting her arm next to me.

"Want to go anywhere in particular?" I ask.

"As long as it's with you, anywhere's fine with me. How is it, being back at work. Are you tired? How's your incision? Did you have lunch?"

"Wait a minute, wait a minute. I'm fine, I mean, I feel fine. And yes, I managed both a little breakfast and a little lunch. I'm not tired, at least not too tired."

Karin pulls us to a gentle stop. "Geoff, can you maybe take it easy?"

"I can't take it easy. I don't know how; at least I don't think I know how. Look at me." When she turns back to face me, the smile is gone.

I know what I want, at least from work: some time off. Some time to think about other things, like research. My research career is a sputtering rocket, exploding on the launch pad before any good work is accomplished. Perhaps, I tell myself, I should forget about research and just take care of sick children. Several of my friends have pointed out that I'm good at clinical medicine and perhaps should be satisfied with it. Why can't I tell my research gurus, consultants, and advisors to just take the whole idea of my doing research and shove it? Why am I working so hard for my patients only to feel so frustrated because I can't do my research?

The answer, I tell myself, is that research is one of the differences between being an academic physician and a private practitioner. I could work in private practice as a pediatrician or a pediatric pulmonologist and probably make twice or three times what I earn at the university. But if I go out into practice, I'm afraid that seeing the same type of problems over and over will turn my excitement with clinical medicine into a mind-numbing sameness eventually robbing me of any enthusiasm for my work. But there's something else hidden below that argument. Maybe my friends have been wrong all along; maybe I'm not all that good a doctor. Maybe I can't really take care of those kids in a private practice that well. Maybe my stint as an academic, seeing the esoteric, had blunted my understanding of the common problems I might face as a pediatrician in the "front lines."

At the university, I am assured of having patients who've been referred by their pediatrician after the usual treatments hadn't worked. Maybe I'm best when a lot of diagnoses have already been ruled out. I can then pursue the unlikely, the hidden, the unexplainable. But perhaps that is all I can do. Perhaps the normal child with the common illness would be totally missed by me. The "Ivory Tower Syndrome," referring to the better-than-the-rest-of-the-physicians mentality held by too many of us in academics, might serve to trick my mind into believing that only the rare illnesses are of importance. So, leaving the university carries two risks: I might either become too bored or discover that I'm not up to the job.

There is another reason I want to continue doing research here. Doing nothing but patient care, I'll be treated as a second-class citizen, not as "academic" as those scientists working with test tubes. In my naïveté, I thought that all members of a university medical faculty are of equal importance. Basic scientists push back the frontiers of our understanding of the way cells and molecules work. Clinicians take care of the patients, applying scientific advances to patient care. But the university always seems to favor science as practiced at the laboratory bench over that performed at the bedside.

Karin probably reads my mind. "Listen," she says, "you know you're a good doctor. Your patients like you. All the other physicians like and respect you."

"Some of them."

"Oh, come on! Some of them? How 'bout nearly all of them? The house staff, the med students, they all like you . . . they respect you. Now you've got to take care of yourself, Geoff. They need you, your patients, the house staff. I need you."

"Karin, I need you, too. I really do. I'm not sure what to do with myself. I'm . . ."

"What?" she asks. "You're what?"

"I'm . . . I don't know." I'm scared, that's what. But I don't know how to tell her or anyone.

The fact that I can't get into the lab and do research is a strong sign that I'm not fully in control of the work aspect of my life. I've never been able to say no to patients when they called or to say no when the call schedule for the ICU featured my name. Now, facing a second surgery, the possibility of chemotherapy, and perhaps the forfeit of my life to the unwanted hairy cells, it doesn't take a genius to figure out that I am even more outnumbered.

I must look at a loss for words. Karin knows when to push and when to relax. She squeezes my hand, pulls me close, and kisses me.

"I better get back. You'll call me tonight? After you run?" She smiles, knowing that I am going to run no matter what she or anyone says.

I finish the final chores of rounds, talk with the residents about Rachel, then trudge back to my office. It is nearly six in the evening, still an early night for me. I begin to attack the enormous pile of mail on my desk, the accumulation of weeks. I am sure that my name is on dozens of mailing lists, by virtue of my being a physician, a pediatrician, and a pediatric pulmonologist. One would think that my increased level of specialization might have reduced the number of drug companies, book publishers, and equipment vendors seeking me out, but, in fact, the opposite has occurred. Pediatric pulmonology is a small specialty, with less than four hundred of us in the United States, and the competition for our individual attention is intense. I've received brochures describing books I can't practice without, courses I must take to keep current, drugs to ensure my patients' (not to mention the drug company's) well-being, and equipment that was a dream of some bioengineer only a few years before but now is absolutely essential to my practice. Most of these are summarily trashed. I gather up the cards and letters from friends and colleagues telling me to get well (and get back to work) and carry them to the car.

The club where I work out is about a ten-minute drive from the hospital. Some people are able to exercise at home, but I'm not one of them. Ever since my childhood, when swimming meant first driving to the nearest pool, I've found it easier to go somewhere with the express purpose of exercising. It is not efficient, and maybe that is one of the things that I like about it. I park in the lot that the club shares with a bunch of other small businesses in its mini–shopping center. I self-consciously walk into the foyer of the place, with the little bar for health drinks next to the check-in desk. The person on duty recognizes me and waves me into the locker room.

The club has weight-lifting equipment, stationary bicycles, an aerobics room, a tiny swimming pool, and a miniscule indoor track with banked, tight turns. I never run indoors except as an absolute last resort. I use the training equipment as stationary pillars to stretch against and never do the aerobics classes. I am an anomaly at the club. Before I'd gotten sick, I would usually show up around six or seven o'clock, change into running gear, and do my stretching exercises on the floor amid the weight machines. I would then call the hospital operator, tell her how long I would be gone and, carrying my beeper along with the necessary dimes for the pay phones I might have to use, head out the door. When I was training for the fifty-mile run, I would be gone for an hour or ninety minutes, running in the dark on the streets, my reflector gear visible a block or two away. On those rare weekend days when Ruth was covering the service, I didn't have a beeper to worry about, so I would run the five blocks from the club to the American River and then along the bike path that stretches some twenty-five miles through the woods. Sometimes shirtless in the soft heat rising from the river, my stride would open up as I felt my head clear with each successive mile, feeling as though I were far from the city through which I ran.

I start to take my clothes off, getting to my undershorts and T-shirt, and abruptly stop. The scar behind the T-shirt wants to hide, but there are a lot of guys in the locker room, several of whom recognize me. One of them comes over. Tom is a few years older than me, tanned from long workouts in the sun, with a hard-muscled physique that screams of the great shape he's in.

"Hey, doc. Where you been? Working too much again?" He laughs. I suddenly don't feel like I have anything to hide.

"Nah," I say as I calmly take off my remaining clothes and step into my running shorts. The room is very quiet, Tom's eyes wide, his mouth partway open.

"Holy shit! What the hell happened to you?" The other men in the room turn away, but I can sense them listening intently for the answer.

"You think this looks bad, you ought to see the other guy," I say, smiling.

"Sure, yeah, sure. So what's the deal?"

"Well, I just got diagnosed with leukemia and had to have my spleen removed. Anyway, I just had it done about two-three weeks ago. That's why the scar is so . . . red. But I'm late, I gotta get out and do a little run."

"You're gonna run?"

"What do you think I come over here for, to watch you jerks work out? Yeah, I'm gonna run. Not much, but I'm gonna run."

"Well, more power to you. Go get 'em. You're tougher than most." He's smiling and shaking his head. "I'm glad you're back in one piece."

"I'm not in one piece. I'm missing a spleen." The room erupts in laughter.

After putting on my shoes, I wander out to the area where I can stretch before my run. On the way out the locker-room door, I walk past a mirror and stop cold to look at my reflection. It is the first full-length mirror I've seen since the operation.

"Jesus . . ." My breath falls out of me. I scan the mirror up and down, slowly, as if called upon to judge a photograph. The reflected image is both me and not me, a two-dimensional, hard-edged, sharply focused portrait of someone I thought I knew.

Yes, it's me, but I am paler than I should be, thinner than I've been in years. My face looks older with my eyes now sunken, my cheeks drawn. My running shirt is yellow nylon mesh. The scar is plainly peeking between the netting, a thin, red, faded lipstick line brushed as a diagonal kiss from a bizarre lover who'd not yet finished with me before I broke away. I feel more tired than I should, and I haven't even started my run.

Then I look at myself again.

My legs are still strong, though pale, my shoulders squared, though my arms are thin. I am still alive, and I am going to run. I am back from surgery, and, by God, I am going to run, and even if it is only to be a half a mile today, then a half a mile it will be.

I get ready for my run by stretching my overworked, knobbish, and aging muscles on the gym floor, then go out into the yellowed light of the April late afternoon and set out to do a slow half mile at the high school track. I walk the three blocks as briskly as I can in the dry spring warmth that portends the brutal heat of the Sacramento summer soon to come. The sun is beginning to arc into the horizon as I arrive at the deserted track. I tell myself to walk-jog two laps, a half mile today. I jog only about one half of one straightaway, about fifty-five yards, out of each quarter mile, but I do the entire half mile. I then quick-march back to the club. My workout has been inside out: the time I had spent stretching and warming up was substantially longer than the actual time spent on my run. But I did my half mile, and I'll slowly increase the distance until I'm actually running miles instead of jogging straightaways. And this is how it will have to be if I am to get stronger.

Home, after that slow jog, I call Karin.

"How was it?" she asks.

"How was what, the run?"

"Of course. How was it? Did it hurt, I mean, did your incision hurt?"

"Not too bad. I could feel it pulling a bit, but it was okay. But I'm still pretty slow and tired. But I'll do fine, I think, as long as I can build back slowly."

"Makes sense. Did you have dinner yet?"

"No. Want to join me?"

"Sure. I don't have the kids."

"Could you stay with me tonight?"

"I was hoping I could."

The next morning, I again decide to have a real breakfast instead of my usual, which had always been a quick cup of coffee and a dough-nut slurped together as I walked from the cafeteria to the elevator. Instead, I am actually sitting in the cafeteria, facing a tray with cereal, milk, and buttered toast along with my seemingly mandatory coffee and doughnut. One of my colleagues, a pediatric intensive care specialist, walks through the line with his own cup of coffee and does a double take as he sees me sitting down with what looks like food. He saunters over to my table and sits down across from me.

"Welcome home, man. Some people will do anything to get out of call. How ya'll been?" His Nacogdoches, Texas, accent is thick and delightfully out of place in California. "What the hell is this?" he asks, indicating the food on my tray.

"Hi, Charlie. This," I look down, then back up at him, "is what I believe most of the world refers to as 'breakfast.' It's a curious habit some people have. They sit down, don't work for a bit, and eat food in the morning. I heard that getting calories on a more regular basis might be good for me, so I thought I'd give this a try. We'll see how long I last."

"Last? You mean eating regularly? Or eating what you're eating now?" he says, glancing down at the stuff on my tray. "Or do you mean something more sinister?" he snickers.

"Could be any of them, I suppose." We both laugh, then I look around conspiratorially. "What's going on around here?" Charlie was always the one with the local gossip.

"Not much, actually. You know, same shit, different day. Seriously, though, what is this crappy leukemia of yours gonna do to you, with call and all. Can't you take some time off?"

"Uh . . . I was thinkin' maybe you'd take some extra call for me." I can't stay serious, and he sees through it, smiling back. He's the only real pediatric intensivist here, and because of that is on call more than any of the rest of us. Besides, he doesn't do a lot of the things I do: take care of kids with cystic fibrosis and asthma (unless they happen to be in his ICU) or do bronchoscopies. He knows there's no way I can ask him to take my call. For that matter, the faculty is stretched so thin that there's really no one else to cover for me. Except Ruth, and she is trying to get her work done in the lab. Charlie and I both know it. But it doesn't stop him from asking the obvious.

"How about Ruth. Can she do some extra call?"

I think about it for a moment. Just before she'd started work as my partner, she'd been awarded a large research grant that stipulated that

80 percent of her time was to be spent in the lab. Within seconds of finding it out (the news was announced at a faculty meeting by Spike Miller, the chairman), I asked for a third partner, as the grant paid for most of Ruth's salary. The university turned down the request within a few weeks, saying that I'd just have to manage most of the service time myself. I know that Ruth will have trouble covering for me.

"You know that she's in the lab. I don't think she could do the extra coverage. You heard I gotta go back for another round of surgery; she'll cover for me then, of course. But she's got to be productive in the lab, or else she won't continue to get funded, then . . . well, who knows what'll happen."

"Yeah, sure . . . but it's still ridiculous. I mean, you're just back from surgery; you've got a partner who's been successful at getting funding, so the hospital gets her as pretty much a free ride, but they won't give you another partner. It's worse than ridiculous; it's real bullshit. Those guys in the administration are idiots. Although I gotta admit, she's not the doctor you are."

"Thanks," I nod in agreement.

"Anyway, you should talk it over with Spike again. Even though he's leaving soon and the administration probably won't give him the fucking time of day, not to speak of another pulmonologist."

"Yeah. When's he planning on making the move?"

"Spike? Late June, I think. He starts in Pittsburgh July uno. How about you? Are you still looking around for something else . . . I mean will you still look when things settle down with you?"

"You mean, when I find out if I'm going to live for a while?" After a mock serious moment, I laugh. Charlie has a dumbfounded look, then joins me. "Well, I think I should still look around. I mean . . . well, you know I have looked around, and Spike himself told me I should. He told me that my days here are numbered. I mean I see a lot of patients; I take a lot of call. But when it comes to deciding whether I can move up the ladder, the university will ask where my research papers are first, second, and third before they get to the patient stuff. I'll be a lost cause.

"Like I said, Spike encouraged me to look at the job in Pittsburgh. I took that as a compliment, with him going there as the new chairman.

But I'd want to get the job on my own merits, not riding his coattails, that's for sure. But I'm not sure I want to leave. I mean, I kinda like this place . . . despite how they're screwing me. I kinda like this city. No, that's not right: I love this city. And then, there's Karin . . . there's Karin."

Charlie looks a little harder at me. I'm almost finished eating; his cup of coffee is down to the grounds.

"But are you happy with the job? Serious, now."

I lean back a bit. "Serious, now," I repeat. "I think I do a good job."

"Of course you do a good job," Charlie says, almost brusquely. "I didn't ask you that. I asked you if you are happy with the job."

"I work too much. I feel like I'm always on call. Probably because most of the time, I am on call. I'm tired of making rounds seven days a week. I'm tired of wearing the goddamn beeper twenty-four hours a day. I'm tired of always being 'It' in this game. No, I guess I'm not as happy as I want to be."

"Listen, Geoff. I know and you know and for that matter everybody here knows that you are a good doc. And we all know that you are overworked. Overworked and underpaid, that's us."

"No, not underpaid. I don't complain about my pay." Charlie's giving me the 'yeah, right' look. "I am stone cold serious about that. I've always felt that I've gotten enough pay for my work. Not that I was ever paid a lot of money, so maybe I'm used to the crummy salary I get, compared with some folks. But I know what most of the parents of my kids earn, and I feel happy enough with what I've got. At the same time, lots of people feel that doctors are totally overpaid, and I suppose some of them are, but I'm not one of them. You're not one of them either."

"Amen, brother."

My salary from the university is about seventy thousand dollars a year. A lot of money, I think. But my labor is pretty cheap. I once sat down and calculated what I got per hour, assuming I was being paid for carrying that beeper, for staying up all those nights, for being available to come into the hospital at any time. It came to less than twelve dollars an hour. For that twelve dollars an hour, the university (and my patients) got someone who'd gone to Amherst College, had studied hard enough to get into Stanford Medical School, had spent an extra couple of years there doing research before going on to do a year of internship, two years of residency, and then four more years of fellow-ship training during which my pay was only slightly more than I got during residency. It came to a total of twelve years of school and train-ing *after* college. I was cheap labor, indeed.

"All right, all right," Charlie says, "maybe not underpaid. But over-worked. And you're not happy with it. We all know it. Listen, I like you too much to lie to you. I'd like to tell you that you should forget about looking somewhere else for a job, that you should stay here. But that's crap. I mean we'd all miss you a lot and we'd be losing a great doc. You're crazy if you don't look for another job. This place is suck-ing your life out, and if you let it, you won't be any good for yourself, your patients, or, for that matter, Karin. As a matter of fact, the only way for you to stay alive with your work is to stay happy with it, and I don't see you doing it here. I, of course, am not the best example to follow for happiness on the job."

I nod again. Charlie's bitching and moaning about how much work he has and how little support from the hospital he receives are legend, even if all his complaining happens to be right on the mark. But he's certainly right about my own work and how it affects my life.

"Yeah, maybe," I say. "But Karin is important, real important to me. And maybe things will get better here."

"Hell, you think I don't know that Karin is important to you? But look at yourself. Look at what's happening? If I were you, I'd take this as a sign: you get leukemia, you get surgery, and you're right back on call. You think this place really gives a rat's ass about you? They just see the work getting done. You need to find a real job, one where you'll get some semblance of the respect you deserve. Karin could join you. You'd be happy or at least have a shot at being happy."

I just look at him, sitting back in his chair across the table from me. The cafeteria is nearly empty.

"Yeah. I suppose . . . I mean, you're right. But it's hard to decide. Karin can't leave Sacramento. Maybe I should talk with Spike. Maybe

I can get things straightened out or at least start to get them straightened out."

"Good idea. Listen, I got to get up to the unit. People are trying to die up there."

"So I've heard. Well, you just tell 'em to stop, okay?"

"Okay. See you around. Come on by the unit later on. Let me know what Spike says, if you see him today. Or come by the unit anyway. I want to hear about the surgery, all the gory details. I can't wait." The Texan laugh again.

"You're a sick man. But I'll see you later. Thanks, Charlie."

He waves as he takes off for the stairs. I place my tray on the conveyor belt and follow.

Before I start rounds, I call Spike's office and arrange to see him that afternoon. I make rounds over the next four hours or so, finding out what had been overlooked by the house staff the night before, seeing a sick patient in the walk-in clinic, working into and then beyond the lunch hour I'm supposed to take. I call Karin and convince her to take a quick coffee break with me.

"How's it going? You feeling okay?" she asks as we sit down.

"Not too bad. Not too . . ."

"What?" She asks to my silence. "What?"

"I talked with Charlie this morning. I'm meeting with Spike in a few minutes." I tell her of my earlier conversation as she silently hears me out, nodding. We both know that my future here holds next to nothing. Still, she nods with me, even as she finishes her coffee and looks down at her watch, her face hidden.

"I better get back to the pharmacy. I promised Steve I wouldn't be too long," she says as she stands up. I stand up also and walk with her to the door.

"Can I see you tonight, after I run?" I ask as we approach the elevator.

"You can see me tonight even if you don't run. But I know you will . . . run, that is. Call me." She gets in the elevator and is gone.

I walk out of the main hospital and head over toward the clinic building where Spike's office is. The sky is brilliant blue, the deep color of California spring, cloudless and clear as an unused swimming pool. The sun, high and bright, floods me with light as I walk across the parking lot, which already is starting to store the heat, as if saving it for the inferno of the summer to come. The grass in front of the clinic building seems to feel the oppression of the sun despite the daily efforts of the grounds crew to provide enough water. I enter in the side door and take the stairs to the third floor. The carpeted corridor leads down to Spike's office, along with those of a few other members of the department. Marjorie sits typing, short and round in her seat in Spike's anteroom, as I poke my head in. I stare, silently, until she feels my eyes and turns toward me. Her entire face widens in a grin.

"Dr. Kurland! Welcome back! How are you? You look great!"

"Good to see you, Marjorie. Is the boss in? I'm supposed to meet him, I think."

"Well, sure he's in. But he's on the phone. Wait a minute while I tell him you're here." She gets up and quietly enters the office. A minute later she beckons me inside.

I'd first seen Spike nearly ten years before, when he received a research award at a scientific meeting in Carmel, California. He'd given a talk describing his work, the almost serendipitous discovery of the cause of a rare disease. He had become, through hard work and genius, a world authority on the immune function in infants. His scientific papers and books had formed the foundation for our understanding of some of the reasons that babies are especially susceptible to infections.

Soon after I got to Sacramento, Spike had been recruited from a hospital in the Los Angeles area to become the new chairman of pediatrics. He singled me out as a faculty member who needed help, for at the time I was the only pulmonologist. He promised to help me recruit a partner but went even further, suggesting that we do research together. Even before he came to Sacramento, he flew me down to the L.A. airport, where we met in one of the snack bars so we could plan research projects to be done as soon as he arrived up north. My first presentation of a scientific paper detailing our initial project, ironically, was in Carmel, at the same meeting where I'd first heard him speak.

Spike had been one of the first people to call me after my surgery. A perpetually busy man, who seemed never to stop thinking or moving, he had taken the time to call my parents at home, while I still lay in the hospital, just to give them words of encouragement. It was typical of Spike: he always went the extra yard for people he cared about.

I walk into the office and see him in his customary shirtsleeves, tie askew, thick black hair curled close to his head, face expansive and open. He stands up, coming around from the desk, his hand extended to me, smiling broadly.

"Geoff! Great to see you! You look terrific, you really do. How do you feel?"

"Actually, pretty good. Pretty good. It's good to be back. Thanks for the calls. What's going on here?"

"Oh, the usual. I hope I didn't bother you or your folks with the calls. You're pretty special to us, you know."

"Well, thanks. My parents were happy you called; it really helped."

"Anyway, are you going to be all right? What's happening with you? You'd mentioned more surgery when I called. I don't know if you remember all of the conversation; you were still a little wiped out."

"Hell, I'm not sure I want to remember any of what went on. But I think I will for a long time." I tell him quickly about surgery past and future. I tell him about the possibilities of chemotherapy, including Pentostatin. Spike leans forward in his chair; even though this is serious business, his mouth is in a near grin, a sign of total attention as his eyes are fixed on me. He nods with the information.

"Spike, I wanted to touch base with you to get some advice."

"I figured as much," he answers. "It's time for you to decide what to do. I suppose the leukemia has to enter into your decision, and it should." Now it's my turn to nod in agreement.

"Yeah, it does. But I'm not sure what kind of future I have here. I know you told me I'm supposed to come up for tenure, and I don't have a lot of publications. Plenty of experience on the wards and in the ICU, however. But you and I both know how much that counts in this place."

"Let me tell you something," Spike says, sitting back in his chair. "Tenure in the medical school doesn't mean anything. You know I was in the California system down in L.A.; it's the same University of California system, the same university as here. I didn't have tenure. What's tenure, anyway? It means they will always have a position for you, right?" I nod. "Well, believe me, that doesn't mean much, because it can be a position with almost no pay. In other words, being tenured as a physician does not equal job security."

"So I shouldn't worry about getting tenure, right?"

"No, that's not right. Since you're in the tenure-track, it means you have to come up for tenure, like it or not. If you don't get tenure, then you either have to change your direction in the school, like transfer to the so-called clinical line, or, alternatively, you'd have to leave. The next chairman might help you move to the clinical line. It's not impossible, although there's a lot of bureaucratic stuff with it.

"But there are more important questions you have to ask yourself. Do you like your job? Is this the best place for you and your career? Will you be able to do the things you want to do here, or should you look somewhere else?"

"Those are the questions, I guess. You know I like Sacramento. I like the people I work with. I like working with you."

"But I'm leaving, even though I like Sacramento, too."

"Yeah, I know. I feel like I'm going nowhere, or at least I feel frustrated in trying to do things other than just patient care."

"Look, Geoff," Spike says, "you do a great job taking care of patients. And there's nothing wrong with that. But I think I know what you mean, about being frustrated. You haven't had enough time to do the research, to even really find out if research is what you can and should do. When we got Ruth here, I thought that would help, but her grant stipulates that she's in the lab most of the time."

"And she should be. The grant says it, and she does good work. I remember asking for another person when she got the grant."

"Sure, and the university said no. In a way, that was one of the things that wound up forcing me to look elsewhere. I took it as a message, not just to you, but to me . . . to all of us. I think you should take the message to heart. You'll never know what you can do until you try, and you can't try unless you're given the chance. I think you should continue to look at other positions. I know you already had your first visit to Pittsburgh just before you got sick. I spoke with David Orenstein after that visit. I know he and I would both like to have you there. One other thing is when should you look."

"When? Like now or in two or three years?"

"Well, that's the question. I know that David would like you out there now, or at least soon. So would I, for that matter. But things are a bit different for you now."

"That's an understatement," I agree.

"Listen," says Spike, "if you decide to stay and you wind up getting tenure, you'll be set if you want to stay here. If you don't get tenure and have to change the title of your position, then your CV would have to reflect that. At the very least, it might make it a bit more difficult to get another academic position. Unfortunately, that might include Pittsburgh. Of course, I'll be in a position to help you if you decide to move to Pittsburgh under those circumstances."

"In other words, being turned down for tenure would make it harder for me to get another job? Maybe even in Pittsburgh?"

"Well, to some extent, yes. For that reason," he begins.

"I shouldn't wait to be turned down. I should get out first," I finish.

He looks over at me. We both know that all my hours spent taking care of patients or teaching medical students won't mean much when it comes to the tenure committee considering my application.

"Yeah. My advice is prejudiced, you know. But I really think it'd probably be best for you to seriously think about making a move sooner rather than later. Especially with the amount you are overworked here."

I look out his window for a moment. "I'll be able to say, 'You can't fire me; I quit.' You're right," I say to the window and the world outside.

I look back at the walls of his office, which are relatively unadorned. Spike has never needed to be reminded of how good he is, and he's never had to try to impress anyone. On the wall, instead of diplomas, commendations, and awards, is only a single, large framed print, showing a drawing of John F. Kennedy in a small sailboat, as if he were sailing away from us. The quote, from Kennedy, is something like "Each man can make a difference, and every man should try." Spike is right: the only way to find out how much I can do is to get into a situation where I have the chance and the time to see what I am capable of.

"You're right," I say again. "I've looked at Pittsburgh. But I know that there are a lot of jobs out there for guys like me. Is Pittsburgh really still my best option? I'm wondering if I should see what the market might hold for me."

"We both know it's not the only place looking for a pulmonologist. I'm sure that you'll be recruited heavily for that job. I spoke to David Orenstein only a few days ago. He told me he'd called your folks and told them that he'd like you in Pittsburgh in any condition."

"I assume he meant 'live' condition."

"Yeah," Spike laughs back, "I'm sure that's what he meant." Spike looks back hard at me. "But at the same time, I really think you owe it to yourself to see other places. That way, you'll get an idea of just how valuable you are. I think you're going to be an asset anywhere. And I think that after you look around at a bunch of places, you'll realize the potential and challenge that Pittsburgh offers. I think David Orenstein is great, and so is his partner, Ed Pattishall. I think you and I could get a lot of research done together. But I'm serious when I say you should look at other places. You've got to convince yourself of what's best for you. For that matter, you should also consider staying here. If that's what you want, if that's what you think is best for you, then I'll help you all I can." He's silent, sitting there, his near grin gone, his face firm and set tight upon him. I, too, am quiet for the moment.

"Okay," I sigh, "I'll be thinking. And calling around. I hope I can talk things over with you some more when I get a better idea as to where I'll be looking."

"Great. Just call Marjorie, she'll set up a meeting whenever you want."

I walk out of the office, down the hall and the steps, and finally outside into the afternoon sunlight. It is spring in Sacramento, a season that would pass for a pleasant summer almost anywhere else, but I know that the blistering heat of the Sacramento summer comes early, sometimes as early as May. But by that time, I'll be getting my chest cracked at Mayo.

Over the next weeks, I get progressively stronger, working full-time, which means long hours at the hospital, making rounds, taking call, wearing and answering the beeper. Most of the people with whom I work are surprised that I continue my long hours, my patient care.

Some of my friends privately tell me that my illness is a sign, a message, from my life or from God, telling me to slow down. Karin continues to tell me to rest more or take better care of myself, but she knows as well as anyone how stubborn I can be. Each time we talk, I agree to take it easy or at least make some concessions to being sick, even though I feel fine.

The paradox is that I am probably healthier now than I was before my operation, and (aside from Karin) few of my friends told me to take it easy back then. After all, my blood counts now are better than they'd been before my surgery. But it is more than my blood counts that gets stronger. The very phrase *blood counts* sounds too fixed. My innermost feelings are part of my strength, a sort of self-portrait within me. I have been allowed a brief glimpse of the picture, parts of which I now can change. I have the renewal of life that only comes from feeling and to some extent knowing the cool shadow of death. As long as the leukemia cells busy themselves in my marrow and my blood, my choice is to fight to the end until they or I perish. I find myself determined to remain alive.

People talk about fighting cancer. Entire books have been written telling of how cancer can be cured based on the strength and attitude of the patient. I'm not talking about that. I do not feel that I can get rid of my leukemia just by visualizing the leukemia cells dying, by willing their demise, by merely having a positive attitude. I know, however, that it won't hurt me to keep my mind set on my future, to have goals, to work, to run. One part I don't like is that my future may have to be spent somewhere other than Sacramento.

Several months ago, right after Spike's startling announcement of his planned departure to Pittsburgh, I'd called around the country, seeing what jobs were available. Pittsburgh was certainly not the only place in the market for a pediatric pulmonologist. I'd also talked with Dennis Nielsen in Salt Lake City, and we'd agreed that I should go out and visit there. Now, I call him again and tell him of my changed fortune, my diagnosis, and my recent and future surgery. Despite that, Dennis still wants me to come out, and we agree that I'll visit in the summer, after I've recovered from my chest surgery.

How many places do I have to visit? I liked Pittsburgh, and with

Spike going there, it's the main place I'm interested in. I decide I should plan my visit to Salt Lake City, but Pittsburgh's still the main place for me to look. I call David Orenstein once more.

"Hey," his chipper voice says as he realizes it's me. "How are you? Did your folks tell you I'd called?"

"Yeah, they did. Thanks. Did you really mean that stuff you told them?"

"Stuff? I don't think I'd call it stuff. But if you mean the part about wanting you out here in any condition . . ."

"Alive," I add.

"Well, okay, if we're gonna put constraints on it, alive. Yeah, I do mean that. I think you'd be great out here. And I think we have the kind of place you'd be able to work in, fit in, you know."

"I spoke with Spike a few days ago."

"I know. He called me that afternoon." Spike is nothing if not thorough.

"I figured he would've gotten in touch with you. Did he also tell you he suggested that I look at a bunch of places?"

"Actually, no, he didn't. But I'd tell you to do the same. After all, we want you to come here because this is the best place, not the only place."

"Okay. But I'll be honest; I don't want to take a lot of time looking at places I'm not truly interested in. I promised Dennis Nielsen that I'm going to visit Salt Lake in the summer. Other than that, I'm not planning on other places."

"Sounds reasonable to me."

"Okay, well here's the deal." And I tell him of the next surgery, the need for recovery, and the probability of my visit in the summer.

"Geoff, we should keep in touch . . . before your next surgery as well as after."

"Agreed. I'll let you know how it goes. You know how to reach me . . . and my parents."

There are some aspects of life now unavoidably surrendered to the care and feeding of my leukemia. My blood counts have to be monitored every couple of weeks, and I must play the role of patient. Fred Meyers in hematology-oncology had accepted the task of looking after

me in Sacramento. He'd received the letter from Tom outlining my
history, the details of my operation, and the plan of treatment, or, more
accurately, the plan to watch and wait. In a way, Fred is a second opinion at my own institution, although I hope he will go along with Tom's
plan. I don't want to find myself in the middle of a disagreement
between two physicians.

On the appointed day, I walk over to the clinic building in the middle of the warming afternoon. Being a member of the medical staff has
its privileges: I'd had my counts done by the lab earlier in the day.
Rounds for me are not done, so I'm hoping this first meeting won't
take too long. After removing my white coat, I sit on the exam table.
The clinic room is equipped with the usual accoutrements: glass con-
tainers with tongue blades and Q-tips; cabinets containing syringes,
needles, and anesthetics; the opthalmoscope-otoscope to examine eyes
and ears; the blood pressure cuff. There is an outlet for oxygen and an
intake to a vacuum line. The fluorescent lights leave little room for
shadow.

Outside in the corridor is the crash cart, carrying the equipment to
intubate the fallen and resuscitate the near dead. I had stared at it as I
entered the room. The nurse had asked if something were wrong. After
all, I am a physician, so surely I shouldn't find a crash cart unusual. It's
not unusual; it's just too close to me, to the door of the room I'm in.
I've worked for so long in similar surroundings, with the same equipment, blind to it all for so long. Now I am just another patient in a
clinic. Having all the equipment around means it is there to be used.
Will they ever have to open the crash cart to pull me back to the
world, or will I fade into the nothingness that is beyond it all? Will it
hurt? Will I want them to try to save me? I've never thought much
about it before. I've never had to.

There is a sudden knock on the door and a simultaneous opening of
it as Fred strides in. He seems even younger than Tom Habermann, if
that's possible, and is brimming with energy. I stand up, and he grabs
my hand.

"I've read the letter from Tom Habermann. Wow, some story . . ."

"Yeah. Some story. I'm feeling too much like a story these days, not
so much like a person."

Fred smiles at me for a brief moment and then is serious.

"Well, I think Habermann's right about just observing for now. Your counts certainly improved after the splenectomy. How's work? I know of you, but I've never met you . . . this is a pretty big place here."

"True. I've been here a bit longer than you. I don't know what you've heard about me."

"Oh, good things, trust me."

"Is that like 'Trust me, I'm a doctor'?"

"Gee, maybe. I know you're busy, so let's take a look at you." I take off my shirt.

Fred listens to my chest and heart, looks in my throat, feels for lymph nodes, and then starts to gently prod my belly.

"Let me know if you find a spleen in there," I say.

"No problem. Do I get a prize if there is a spleen in there?"

I sit up and put on my shirt. "Hmm. Maybe I get the prize. I'll have to think about that."

Fred sits down at a small desk in the room. "Your counts really do look great. Like I said, I agree with Habermann. Let's find out what the chest mass is and go from there. No chemotherapy right now."

"Is this Pentostatin really as good as the article in the NEJM suggests?"

"Well, so far it looks pretty good. It'll take some time to be sure. That's another reason to wait before we treat you. You're heading back to Mayo in early May, right?"

"Yeah. I'm due to see Habermann on Friday, May eighth, and have the mass removed the next Monday. I'm not exactly looking forward to it."

"I don't blame you. But I agree it's gotta come out."

"Oh, I know that. It's just that now I'm just starting to get my strength back, my running's getting better . . . and I'll have to start all over again."

"But . . . well . . . yeah, it's got to come out. I'll need your counts every week or so until you head back to Mayo. I'll drop a note to Haberman and Pluth."

"Thanks." I put my white coat back on. We are suddenly equals in the room. "I'll get my counts done next week then, if that's okay with you."

"Fine with me." We arrange my blood work around my schedule, and I walk back across the parking lot toward the hospital, to the pediatric ward, to work.

Again it is evening and I run, now with more strength, more distance. I call Karin and have dinner with her. Her kids are with their father, so it is just the two of us, sitting in one of the booths at my favorite natural food restaurant in Sacramento. We gropingly talk around the knowns and unknowns in my future; for me, it is easier talking about the kids, about anything but our future together when my own future is itself so uncertain.

I really don't want to talk about all of this stuff: my illness, my looking for another job, the chance that I might have to leave Sacramento and Karin. Like my father, I find it easier to approach feelings through metaphor. Avoidance is easier than engagement. I've thought of myself as a fortress that has to withstand the onslaught of anything life will throw at me, including my newly diagnosed leukemia. I am, however, a hollow fortress at best and probably not a fortress at all, for in so many ways, I am literally and figuratively running away from any help I am offered. My life is mirrored in my running: I do them both alone, even when surrounded by others.

Having grown up swimming, it's amazing to me that running would have ever assumed importance in my life. We all move down our own paths, with choices of side treks, junctions, and possible turns to take. Most of our decisions are not irrevocable: we can almost always turn back or take another course. But in another way, all of those twists and turns we take define our own peculiar journey of life, and the choices are not only irrevocable, they are irreplaceable, inevitable, and uniquely and necessarily ours. Entering the tenth grade, I was a year ahead in school and therefore a year younger than my classmates. I was a year smaller and a year further from any hint of pubertal growth. I saw myself as a short, scrawny, intelligent but not too canny kid a long way from any semblance of manhood. I had prepared myself merely to get through that first year of high school without making too many waves, without achieving ignobility in the classroom, in short, to survive. It was a big school, and I was but a little fish.

That first day, all of the tenth-grade boys were herded into the gym for lectures by the various team coaches, who were there to encourage any of us who'd somehow missed the opportunity to go out for a team to do so now. One of the last to speak was Mr. Davis, the cross-country coach. I'd never heard of cross-country until that moment. For that matter, I don't remember ever having seen anyone run competitively before in my life. Mr. Davis was somewhat short and a bit stocky with a chiseled face and a black crew cut. As he stood before us and told us that cross-country was a sport where people ran two miles along golf courses, I thought he, or anyone who would do such a thing, was crazy. But then he said that it was a sport where each individual was alone in proving himself. And finally, he spoke to me, the scrawny kid, telling me that in cross-country, unlike football, size didn't matter; it was talent combined with hard work that counted. All five feet three inches and ninety-five pounds of me was grabbed by the thought that this small body could actually compete in a high school sport. I decided to try out for the team.

I was a terrible runner. But I was lucky, making the team only because the total number trying out was less than the capacity of a school bus, which, full or nearly empty, would take the team to any meets. Much later, I learned that Mr. Davis felt sorry for me, always at the back of the pack of runners, sweating, cramping, and trying so hard. Clandestinely, he called my parents one evening and told them that I'd never be a runner, but he didn't have the heart to cut me from the team. He hoped that perhaps my parents could convince me to give it up. His tactic failed, as it was a lucky rebellion against the advice of my parents that steeled my resolve not to quit. I told my parents that the only way I'd be off the team was if I were cut or if I flunked my courses. I look back on that decision as one of the best ones I ever made in my life. Running was to become one of the definers of my self, a veritable limner of my soul. Early on I learned the power of persistence, for when I was out running in a race alongside the fairways of the golf course that served as our home course, no one could help me but myself. Success or failure came down to me alone.

My life now is being run out in the same way: I avoid any help, even from Karin, when it is offered. I think of my refusal as a sign of my self-reliance, just as running is a way to prove myself. In reality, I know, it signifies my inner fears, fear of intimacy, fear of failure, fear of showing myself as a human being with real feelings, hurts, hopes, dreams, and needs.

Karin sees through all of it and somehow knows how to give me the help and support I need while allowing me to have my "space," as they say here in California. She knows of the blows my body and ego have suffered over the years: the loss of the woman I'd lived with to my former partner; my being worked to a frazzle; the leukemia and surgery. She knows that I will need help, just as she recognizes how hard it will be for me to accept it.

I feel better knowing she'll be there for me after I'm out of the hospital. I am starting the delicate process of learning to walk all over again, to step outside the fortress that I pictured myself to be, to embrace those whom I've kept outside the walls for all these years, to allow myself to be taken care of.

The surgery I face in the next few weeks is, as chest surgery goes, straightforward, with a relatively low risk. But low risk doesn't mean no risk. And the area of the operation, my chest, has some important organs and blood vessels that could conceivably get injured during the surgical procedure. Although I have all the confidence in the world in the Mayo Clinic and in Jim Pluth, I am a realist. I know the dangers of surgery and the risk to my life from the illness I am facing. So I do something pragmatic: I arrange with a lawyer to draw up my will.

8

Returning for my second surgery, I face another run across the Minneapolis terminal to make the Rochester connection. My training must be paying off as I make the plane easily. The sky is clear, and I feel the warm midspring sun as my mother and I walk to the car in the Rochester parking lot.

"Dad'll be home after work. Unless you'd like to meet him for a swim before dinner," my mother says as we leave the lot.

"No. Maybe I'll run a bit. I'm back up to about four miles a day."

"Four miles already? I wish I could walk a half a mile!"

"You can, Mom, if you want. You know what they say, the hardest step is the first one out the door."

"Are you sure that's the hardest?"

She looks over at me, but I look out at the Minnesota farmland. Dust rises where tractors are plowing the soil that only a few weeks before was solid beneath the snow and now seems almost eager to accept the gash of the plow. I feel my breastbone, beneath which lies the mass soon to be removed by Jim Pluth.

After my run and over dinner, my father probes the specifics of my health. My counts have been fine. My running strength is returning.

"I'm not so sure that's such a good idea," my father says. "Your running so much, I mean."

"Dad, I've been running for so long, I just can't quit now."

"I know, but don't you think you could cut back? After all, you have lots of stresses. I'm just saying that your running might affect your immunity or your ability to fight this . . . this thing."

"There are scientific studies proving that running affects immunity any way you want. I mean there are papers saying that running improves immune function, worsens it, does nothing to it, protects from cancer, I mean, you name it, it's out there. Don't worry, I'm not planning on another fifty-mile run, at least not right now."

"Okay," he sighs, "Now I've already set you up with your lab work tomorrow. Seven-thirty in the morning and nothing to eat before. Then a chest X ray, then you see Habermann and then Pluth after that. Don't stay up too late." He looks at his watch. "I think I'll get some sleep. See you in the morning."

Not heeding my father, I stay up and talk with my mother, the night owl. "Your father's really worried about the running," she says over a cup of tea. I only nod, looking into her rheumy eyes. "He says that because it's something he can see. It's not just the running. He really is worried about you, you know. We're both worried. You too, I suppose."

She supposes right. I look at her graying red hair, the hands, now puffy and blotched, that held me as a child. Her voice is scything into my heart, and I wonder how much longer I will hear it. I cannot talk or listen much right now, but I must be here with her. She is worried. My dying, I realize, may prove itself more her concern than my own.

We sit, she speaks, and I listen. She tells me some of the history of our family, as if my role as bearer of the secrets will insure my survival. Gradually, her voice goes soft, and we look at each other, knowing that I have no choice but to follow my fate.

The next morning, my blood work and chest X ray are done, and I sit again on the brown leather couch waiting for Habermann. He's his usual enthusiastic self as he pours into the room.

"You look great!" he exclaims as he sits down at the desk and opens the lab sheet. He looks back and forth from it to me, smiling all the while. "Your counts are fine. How are you feeling?" He keeps talking as he does a quick but thorough exam, feeling my belly, my armpits, listening to my chest, my heart. His enthusiasm is contagious, and I am pulled along, feeling myself better by the moment.

"I feel okay. I'm running about three to four miles already. Not too fast, but . . . I guess I'm still recovering."

Habermann laughs, "I wish I were able to recover like that. Four miles at a time?" I nod. "That's impressive, that's impressive. Listen, you look good; your counts are good. I think our timing's right to get that mass out of your chest. You okay with that?"

"Sure. I guess so. I'm not going to be the doctor, but it sounds good to me. Part of me wants to know what that thing is. And part of me doesn't. I suppose you understand." I'm putting my shirt back on, standing there in the room trying not to look scared.

"Well, I'm not sure I really can understand, so I won't tell you I do."

I silently breathe "thank you." It is too easy for a doctor to look back at the frightened patient and roll out some platitude, like "I know just how you feel." How many times have I been tempted to say something like that?

When I was an intern, I tried to comfort one of my patients, a thirteen-year-old girl with cancer. She was being prepared for another in a series of surgeries in what turned out to be a vain attempt to halt the tumor already pushing her bladder out of its way as it homed in on her abdominal aorta and intestines. It didn't even allow her to pee without a catheter. The chemotherapy had thinned her skin and hair, making her brown eyes with long lashes that much larger. She clutched a small doll as the nurses readied her for the surgeons. She pulled her legs up, rolling into a small ball, all fifty pounds of wasting flesh.

"Sarah, you're going to be all right," I said, looking at her belly instead of her face. It is harder to lie when you look someone in the eye. She knew better and was silent. My gaze slowly moved up until her stare went into me. I took a step back, put my head down, then brought it back up to face her again.

"Sarah . . ."

"I don't want to go. I'm . . ."

"Don't be afraid, you'll be all right. I know how you feel."

Her eyes filled with tears, her body shook with fear and anger, fear of pain and death, anger at dying before she had a boyfriend, before she finished school, before she could drive a car, go to college. Her tears fell onto a cheek white from chemotherapy and cancer.

"You know how I feel? You know how I feel?" I stood there dumbfounded with the obvious truth that she was telling, my mouth open, my skin flushed, my breath short. I looked into her eyes, deep brown and swimming, reddened, flashing with spite. Her hands gripped her belly and again her doll. "God, I hope you never have to know how I feel!" She half yelled, half choked at me as she pulled the blanket up over her head, hiding herself, now shaking and crying, from my view. I reached my hand out, gently touching the blanket outline of her thin shoulder.

The nurse had watched silently. She now went to Sarah's head.

"We're going now, Sarah," she said and gave me the look that said that they were both going, getting away from this callous, self-important, nonunderstanding fool of an intern.

"Pluth's going to see you next," Tom says. I look at him with a mild start. "I think the surgery should be pretty straightforward, but Pluth'll know better about that than me."

"Yeah," I say, reaching out my hand. Tom shakes it as I tell him, "See you in a bit."

"Right. Keep the faith."

I step into the corridor, wander to the elevator, and within minutes, I'm ushered into another exam room with yet another brown couch, this time in cardiovascular surgery. My wait is short.

Jim Pluth swings into the room and sticks out his large hand, which engulfs my own.

"I've seen your X ray. There's no change in the mass since March. It's right beneath your sternum. Median sternotomy. Shouldn't be too big of a deal."

A median sternotomy means a splitting (that's the *otomy* part) of the sternum, which is medicalese for breastbone, down the middle from top to bottom. This allows the chest to be entered easily by pulling apart the rib cage. I'd heard from colleagues, especially my friends in surgery, that a median sternotomy is not as painful as other chest surgery that involves cutting the muscles of the chest wall. I have a feeling that what Pluth means by it not being too big a deal is different than what I would think is not too big a deal. But, after all, he gets to have the fun of doing the surgery. I will have the other, less enviable, part of the job.

"I understand you've been feeling pretty well since your splenectomy," he says, sizing me up again.

"Yeah, I've been doing better since the splenectomy. Back running a bit. I know I've got a ways to go, though."

"A bit, huh? More than I can do. Habermann called me after you left." He chuckles a little, appreciating the understatement of it all. "Well, I think you'll do fine with this." He talks as he gives a quick listen to my chest, placing a hand and a knowing eye upon my sternum. "Now," he says as I replace my shirt, "you have to go register. You'll be the first case on Monday morning. I want you in St. Marys on Sunday afternoon because there's a lot of stuff we have to do the night before. It'll be a lot easier if you're in then rather than having you come early Monday morning."

I go off and register, my mother now with me, her knitting needles clicking the seconds and minutes in the lobby as we wait. Again, the efficiency of the Clinic is proven, and I am home, running, and then having a light dinner just as my father gets home.

"So, what's on tap tomorrow?" he asks after I fill him in on my planned entry into St. Marys two evenings hence. "There's a pediatric neurology conference on Saturday morning; want to go?"

"Why not? I'll learn something, and it'll take my mind off other things."

"Sure," my mother offers sarcastically.

The next morning, I am sitting in the back of the conference room, unable to concentrate, wondering if I'll ever be able to learn anything in medicine while I've still got leukemia. My father, sensing my detachment, drops me at home afterward, saying he has some things to do at the office. I turn down the offer of a swim. I'm going for what may be my last run in a long time.

It is less than forty hours until my surgery. Rather than the short distance I all but crawled only six weeks ago, I set out to run several miles, around the municipal golf course and up a long hill home. I am far away from any thoughts of surgery, of leukemia, here in the sun of spring. I want instead to grasp the day, to hold it tightly in my mind, to save the sounds I hear, the sights I see, the feel of the pavement beneath my feet. In what seems like a few minutes, I find myself running past the golfers still stiff from the oppressive winter. I turn toward the hilly street that will take me up to the house, now only a mile and a half away. A light wind is in my face, and I feel strong, fast, and indestructible as I tear up the sidewalk. I know what running gives me: the illusion of escape, invincibility, and control of my life, my mind, my future. Children laugh as they play on a lawn. One of them looks up and smiles at me. A few houses ahead, a score of sparrows sit pecking for food on the lawn. Suddenly, the birds fly off in unison, heading for me. One of the birds chases another, both just inches off the ground as my right foot descends. I am running perfectly, my strength concentrated in my legs, my breath feeling young and unlabored, the leukemia magically gone. The first bird flies directly under my left foot, the second arrives as my heel strikes the pavement.

It is over in an instant. The cracking of the body rises through my shoe and up into me, as I vainly try to take back the step. I look for an instant over my shoulder; the limp wings, twisted legs, and shattered body on the pavement return my glance. I am suddenly tired, empty, old, and afraid, my strength gone. My stride is shorter, quirky, and ungainly as my breath catches in my throat, nausea rising. I feel the mass rearing within my breast, as if to rid itself of me. The sun is suddenly much too hot, but I still have over a mile to go, uphill. I make it home drenched in sweat.

I walk quietly into the kitchen where my mother makes dinner, a sort of Last Supper, on my last evening before entering St. Marys. I reel, overtaken by the sad smells of my mother's kitchen. I wonder, how much more time will I be allowed to share with my family, with Karin? Am I to die alone in the midst of those who love me?

And I later sleep in uneasy, alternating waves, with troughs of deep, silent slumber, peaks of twitching alertness as I peer at an unmoving ceiling, and torment in between. In the darkness, like a hail of unforgiving arrows, the world rushes forward to meet me.

The next morning, I sleep late, unable to awaken, my fear burdening my body. I finally pull myself out of the bed and upstairs to coffee, toast, and a quiet morning with my parents. My brother, his wife, and my nephews and niece come by, and I vainly try to play the riotous uncle with them. By the afternoon, I find myself ready to go to St. Marys, to face the surgery, to get it over with.

The admission formalities take only a few minutes, and I am soon escorted to my room. It is a copy of my postsplenectomy room: plain beige walls, a single casement window, and the chair on which my mother will, I am sure, await my awakenings with her knitting in her lap.

I am sitting on my bed when a thin, clean-shaven young man with short, blond hair, wearing a scrub suit and white coat, walks in. He's holding a medical chart.

"Dr. Kurland?"

"That's me. And you're . . ."

"I'm Tom," he said, reaching his hand out to me. "The physician assistant. I'm working with Dr. Pluth. I'm here to examine you for your surgery tomorrow."

"A PA?" I ask, giving his title the accepted shorthand. "Will there be a resident, also?" I figure the PA is just the first of many to see me tonight.

"No, sir. Just me. I see you're having a sternotomy and mediastinal mass resection tomorrow," he says, speaking "doctor" to me. He sees my reluctance. "I've been the PA for Dr. Pluth for about eight years now."

"Eight years is a long time," I say. "You don't look old enough to have been doing it that long." This PA, although not a physician, has more experience than most residents in cardiothoracic surgery.

"And you don't look old enough to be here, either," he says. "Your chart says you're forty-one. Is that correct, sir?"

"Yes, and you don't have to call me sir, sir." We both laugh.

"I would've thought you were ten years younger or so."

"Well, I try to stay in shape."

"Yeah, I read your chart. Anyway, let me take a look at you, and I'll tell you what'll happen tonight and tomorrow morning."

Tom goes a bit more into my history. I'm probably a lot different from most of the patients he'll see tonight. I'm one of the few he'll see who isn't overweight, doesn't smoke or drink excessively, doesn't have high blood pressure, and actually exercises. He finishes the history and physical exam, then sits back down.

"Well, Dr. Kurland, I think things should go fine tomorrow. You're the first case of the day. Someone will come here later in the evening to prep you; you'll have to get shaved from the neck to your waist. But before that you may want to go to the conference room down the hall. We have a short video describing some of the postoperative care. A lot of it doesn't pertain to you, stuff about the ICU, ventilators, suctioning, and all that. I think the plan is to have you extubated after surgery and not send you to the ICU. Anyway, you may want to take a look at the video; it's up to you."

"Thanks, Tom. I think I will. I can always learn something. Thanks for your time."

"My pleasure. Good luck tomorrow, sir. I mean . . ."

"I know. Thanks." I watch as he walks out.

A few hours later, I walk into the conference room and join some ten or so others. Some are obviously spouses or children accompanying those destined to go "under the knife" tomorrow. I am by far the youngest of the patients; I look like the healthiest. Some sideward glances shoot toward me as if to ask, "And what the hell are you doing here, kid?" I try to ignore them as the video starts.

The video tells how we'll all be taken to the operating room, a trip I'd made before. It then shows us the immediate postoperative course of a typical patient, in this case a white male about sixty-five or so. The video shows him still intubated, breathing through a tube in his mouth. A ventilator sighs rhythmically next to him as it forces air into his lungs. Other thin, plastic tubes enter the chest through the skin. These had been placed in the pleural space, the tiny area between the lungs and the inside of the chest wall. The tubes drain fluid and apply suction to keep the lungs expanded. Nurses give medication for pain, help the patient communicate his needs, help him relax. The video reassures us that we will all receive the best of care, as we each individually recover from the planned intrathoracic intrusion tomorrow. I sit, watching, looking around at the other rapt faces, each of us saying a silent prayer that things will, indeed, all go well. Occasional wet coughs sound in the room, the effect of years of smoking. I tell myself I'm not like these other people. The video isn't directed at me. I'm not supposed to be here, I say under my breath.

I'm not planning on waking up with a tube down my throat, with a machine breathing for me, with the nurses speaking kindly to me as they push other tubes into the tube in my throat, forcing me to cough as they suction the secretions building up in my lungs. I'm not planning on waking up in the Intensive Care Unit. I've worked enough in one, taking care of children clinging to life, making the decisions, watching the deaths, and dealing with grieving and unbelieving families.

The video over, I return to my room for the pre op shave, for hair can harbor bacteria that can infect surgical wounds. Shaving off the body hair in the area to be operated on is part of the routine of surgery. The orderly who shaves me from neck to groin does it quickly and expertly, using a disposable plastic razor and ordinary soap and water. He's probably shaved hundreds of others before me. I feel a peculiar nakedness, as if the hairs on my chest previously hid me from the ravages of the outside world. Even wearing my hospital gown in bed with the covers up to my chin, the wind insinuates itself down my neck onto my truly naked body.

My sleep again is an uneasy torment. In my dream, the bird flies free before me, then in the same instant is shattered beneath my feet, which become painful chimeras, sprouting feathers from the bones. The bird looks back up to mock me, its feathers dropping off, its eye an empty hole. Like me only two months ago, it had lived without thinking of death, but now accepts it as a part of life itself. For death is nothing if not that sharp edge against which each of our lives is measured and then cut. I am startled awake, the black room greeting me as another hollow eye. The corridor outside the room is silent save for the echoing footsteps of someone, a patient, a nurse. Sleep returns, but not as the rescuer I seek.

Early in the morning, as it was only six weeks before, an orderly with a gurney awakens me. A feeling of déjà vu overtakes me as I climb aboard, and, watching the ceiling pass rapidly overhead, I am delivered to the preoperative area. Again, I am greeted by a friendly, if unknown, anesthesiologist; and I am wheeled into the operating room, where I crawl off the gurney to lie upon the narrow, cold table.

The bright lights shine into my eyes, and the masked anesthesiologist leans down toward me.

"Dr. Kurland, I'm going to start some lines. An arterial line and a central venous line."

A *line* is medicalese for a catheter, a thin, plastic tube placed into a blood vessel. An arterial line usually is in the artery in the wrist, and it allows the anesthesiologist to sample arterial blood to measure oxygen and carbon dioxide. The arterial blood oxygen and carbon dioxide tell the true tale of how the lungs are doing and how well the anesthesiologist is breathing for the patient. A central venous line goes into a major vein, usually in the neck, and is pushed in far enough so that it is in or near the heart. It can be used to administer drugs and to measure the pressure in the veins before they enter the heart, which, in turn, gives an indirect view of how well the heart is pumping.

Both the arterial and central venous lines are standard for heart operations, but I hadn't thought about them before the anesthesiologist told me he was going to put them in. I am suddenly afraid, not wanting to experience them mucking about my wrist and my neck. The lights seem to double in intensity, and the room suddenly reeks of the alcohol from every doctor's office I'd been in as a child. I feel a panic sinking into me. There is a blood pressure cuff inflated around my arm. Someone is putting an IV into the back of my hand. I just want to go to sleep, to miss any chance at pain. Or, if I have to be awake, I don't want to remember any of it afterward. But I don't want to appear too afraid, for I still have to show myself that I can take it, whatever "it" is. I turn my face back to the anesthesiologist.

"Um . . . I was just wondering . . . Is there any chance you could put the lines in after I'm asleep? If you can't, well, that's okay. I just was wondering if . . ."

He looks back at me, calmly. He's been through this drill before, I'll bet. "Sure, we can. No problem. We'll make sure you're comfortable. Now, you're going to start feeling sleepy, Dr. Kurland. Don't worry about a thing."

I will myself to sleep, but my will has nothing to do with it. The IV is in, and I feel the effect of the first drugs. I look up again at the voice speaking to me. The expressionless masks conceal the unfamiliar faces. The light above is now blinding as the voices around me become more quiet, more reassuring. I feel the bed and then the room move gently, and the world, the operating room, my leukemia are all in perfect harmony, and everything, I am sure, is going to be great. My eyes feel sleep rushing toward me as the lights above me double in intensity, only to suddenly dim. A voice above my head is saying something, but I don't hear him as the walls move away into a dark distance and disappear altogether.

I awake to a deep burning within my chest. It is as if I can feel, even see, the two cut edges of my sternum scraping against one another with each breath. The rest of me is cold and stiff, disjointed, as if brought back into a reality out of phase with the one I'd left seemingly only moments before. The light in the room is a pale yellow leaving no shadows. I hear no clicking of knitting needles and am aware of my feeble attempts at breathing. There is a muffled bubbling on the floor beside the bed. A nurse comes in and notices that I have rejoined the conscious world.

"Hello, Dr. Kurland," her voice smiles. I can't quite focus on her face. She is at my side. I can only grunt in return.

"I hate to tell you this," she says, "but we've got to do some chest physiotherapy to keep your lungs expanded."

Chest physiotherapy is one of the main treatments I prescribe for my patients with lung disease, particularly those with cystic fibrosis. Chest physiotherapy is nothing more than putting the patient into different positions and pounding the chest with hands or a mechanical percussion device. Its goal is to help move secretions from the small airways to the bigger airways, where they can then be coughed out. For patients with cystic fibrosis, their thick secretions are hard to cough out easily, and chest physiotherapy helps. During my training in pediatric pulmonology, I'd had chest physiotherapy, just to see what it felt like. Back then it wasn't too bad, but back then my chest hadn't just been cut into, opened up, and wired back together, either.

"You can have some morphine if you want, before we do your chest PT," she says, using the common medical shorthand. "Since you just woke up, perhaps we should try it first before we get the morphine." Again, I ask myself, why is it that nurses so often say we, when it's the patient who will get the treatment?

I try to talk. After a moment of breath-catching sternal burn, I manage to say "okay." Then I add, "You're the boss. Although as far as I'm concerned, Bruce Springsteen is still The Boss." The nurse chuckles, but just for a moment.

Because I am lying on my back, she has to turn me to one side. An aide, summoned for the task, joins her as the two of them set out to turn me like a sack of potatoes, head, shoulders, chest, hips, legs, all at the same time. My chest screams out again as those cut sternal edges scrape, pulling on the wires holding them together. Just as I'd been afraid that my belly would open up after my splenectomy, now I have the dread feeling that my chest wound is going to give a loud Pop! and open, exposing my heart as it beats a last drumbeat knell. I try to repress images from the film *Alien* that suddenly flood my mind. Several minutes later, I'm turned to my right side, by which time I can only gasp, my eyes shut tight, my hands clenched into fists, my entire body exhausted. I take tiny breaths, the only ones that are in any way tolerable.

"Dr. Kurland, are you all right? Comfortable?" The nurse asks, then corrects herself in a voice that tells me she somehow understands something of the pain I'm experiencing. "I mean, comfortable as possible?"

I again grunt and breathlessly murmur something she takes for "Yes."

"I'll try to be gentle, but you know, we don't want you to have any atelectasis."

Atelectasis is a collapse, or loss of air, in areas of the lung. Normally, most of the lung is filled with air. If thick secretions totally fill an airway and the patient can't cough them out, the air in the lung beyond the blockage is absorbed and the lung collapses, becoming dense (white) on an X ray and unable to exchange oxygen and carbon dioxide. Atelectasis can lead to yet another problem: pneumonia. Atelectasis can occur if something outside the lung, like a tumor, presses on it and prevents adequate expansion. More commonly, however, it's mucous secretions, particularly in someone who's just had chest surgery, blocking the airway that leads to atelectasis. Chest physiotherapy will help keep my mucus moving.

I lie there on my right side, knowing that the chest physiotherapy I will receive is really, like the old adage says, "for my own good."

Even though she said she'd be gentle, it seems to me that the nurse begins with a vengeance. The gentle tapping on my side is transformed by the cut edges of my sternum into a pile-driving weight percussing into my body, which reels from the blows. I try to hold my breath, then, when that fails to ease the pain, I try to time my breaths with the rhythmic pounding. The nurse talks to me even as she beats upon me.

"I know it hurts, Dr. Kurland. But we'll be through soon. I promise. Do you think you can do a bit more?"

I grimace, wince, and say I can do a bit more. I'm not going to be a wimp, I tell myself. I'm not going to get pneumonia. I'm going to make it out of here. I grit my teeth, shut my eyes, and wait for the percussion to cease. After a few minutes, it's over. Or so I think.

"Okay, Dr. Kurland. Now we'll do the other side; then I'll leave you alone for a bit."

The aide returns, and the two of them again roll me like a sack of potatoes. Again, I think my chest is going to split open. I receive another five minutes or so of the pounding; then with my teeth gritted, I am rolled upon my back.

"Now you try and get some sleep. But I've got bad news for you."

"Huh?" is all I can say.

"We've got to do this every four hours, Dr. Kurland. Now try and rest."

I look forward to another treatment in four hours about as much as I'd like to have surgery again. I groan and watch myself breathing carefully, trying to calm my chest as I teeter on the brink of sleep.

"Honey, are you okay? You really got the treatment, didn't you?" It is my mother's voice. She's been here the whole time, and I haven't known it.

"I'll make it," I offer. "Do me a favor. Remind me to take morphine or something before the next treatment." Yet almost as I say it, I feel myself falling back to sleep and that, despite the pain, my chest is intact, and I am not about to fall apart. I hear a distant voice saying something about reminding me, she promises, but by then, the voice is too far away to be heard clearly.

Some time later, which I suppose in my twilight state is about four hours later, the nurse comes in and offers morphine (in the muscle of my hip) before she beats me again. I accept, and in the fog of the morphine that follows the burning in my hip, I feel the rhythmic pounding once again on my chest. I again hear a distant bubbling at my bedside and realize for the first time that I have two large, clear, plastic tubes entering my body just below my rib cage, one on each side of my abdomen. Each is nearly as wide as one of my fingers, as if I am being explored or sexually violated by machinery directed by some extraterrestrial being.

As a pulmonary physician, I've seen many chest tubes in many patients. Chest tubes are placed into the pleural space, itself a "potential space" because most of the time there just isn't any space there. Air or fluid in the pleural space keeps the lung from expanding adequately, and chest tubes connected to suction serve as conduits to drain the hindering fluid or air. After chest surgery, if the pleural space has been entered, the surgeon places a chest tube to make sure the lung stays expanded. Suction is maintained using a special device with a water compartment that air bubbles through. This bubbling is the susurrus I hear next to my bed.

I'd put a lot of chest tubes into patients, usually premature infants who'd needed them because of a leak in the lung that caused it to collapse. In those babies, many weighing less than two or three pounds, the tubes were put in fairly high on one side of the chest. I look down at my own chest and see that my own tubes enter a lot lower and closer to the front of my body.

I also see the incision, one day to be a scar, on my denuded, pale, and totally defenseless chest. The incision itself is not quite midline as it tracks over my breast. It is angling more to a sort of magnetic north rather than to the true north pole of my head, but it is magnetic north as drawn by someone whose measurements are subject to frequent minor changes. The edges of the incision are red, fresh, and puckered to grow into one another, a lengthy kiss of skin edges. My mother must have seen me looking.

"How is it?"

"I thought of having it moved and done up in a different color, perhaps mauve, or perhaps magenta." I hear a stifled laugh, but it is not close by.

"At least they didn't remove your sense of humor."

"I think that's the next operation." Another chuckle, a little further away.

And I find myself again in a twilight between the burning in my chest and narcotic-induced dreams that aren't enough fun to be dreams but aren't scary enough to qualify as nightmares. Every once in a while, I am more awake than asleep, and I realize that, unlike the bird of only a few days before, I have not been crushed by a trick of fate. For now at least, my flight and fight continue.

9

Healing from major surgery is both rapid and slow. Some things happen overnight. The edges of my skin incision knit as if guided by
unseen fingers (my mother's?) into a thin, red scar that can withstand
the normal push and pull of my breathing as well as the jar of a sudden
cough or a laugh. On the other hand, it will probably take months
before this same thin, vertical line on my chest fades from bright red to
pink and weeks before the clear-cut forest of my chest hair returns.

Bone takes longer. There are wires lacing my sternum like a shoe,
holding its edges close enough to allow them to merge. But still the
rough-cut margins rub and scrape with nearly every breath and every
turn of my body. I also have unannounced reaffirmations of the wires
themselves. They insinuate themselves into or next to a nerve, sending
a knife into my chest, causing me suddenly to stop my voice, hold my
breath, and wait the moments until the screeching disturbance passes,
like a train.

There are more than five clips of silver, each tightly strangling a
small artery that formerly nourished the mass, now removed. They will

be a signature of white flecks upon my chest X-ray, remaining for the rest of my life.

After a week in the hospital, my chest still tender, my scar still red, my leukemia still worming inside my marrow, I go home to my parents' house, to my mother's cooking. Turning from side to side in bed, coughing, or nearly any other vigorous activity still produce a sternal rhumba, a fire within my chest telling me to stop. But I am still strong enough to walk, and I know that walking foretells running, itself one of the keys to my future. Even with the price paid for every bit of extra exertion, even with the weakness of my legs, the pain in my chest, I am resolved now to get on with this life. I begin again the daily ritual of taking out my running stuff, stretching my legs in my mother's kitchen, and going outside into the heat for my workout. I start back as I'd done less than two months before: the first few days managing a slow walk-jog for an eighth of a mile, then a quarter mile the next days, then finally a third, then a half. Each day I reenter the kitchen to my mother's cooking and hear the same question.

"How was it?"

And each day my answer is nearly the same.

"Not bad. I'll go farther tomorrow."

"I know you will," she answers and then asks if I'll have some soup after my shower.

My mother and, despite his often expressed misgivings, my father, now approve of my attempts at walk-jogging. They see me as I finish: only slightly sweaty, for I am in good enough shape that the quarter or half mile I "jog" isn't far enough to tire me. Like me, they know the purpose of my daily routine. The slow steps of each workout trace the path leading me back to the possession of my own life.

There is more to help me cope, to help me heal. Karin, as she had promised, is visiting her parents. She is driving over to see me, now only a week after my discharge. I've been sitting with my mother, trying to seem interested in our conversation.

"Relax, will you? You'd think the president was coming to visit you."

"The president's not as important. But, seriously, you've never met her."

"Don't worry, it'll be fine. Listen, she's not due here for half an hour. She only left Austin forty-five minutes ago, right? Tell me again what Habermann told you yesterday in clinic." She's trying anything to get my mind back home.

"What Habermann told me? Oh, about the path on the mass?" I offer, speaking medicalese to her again.

"Yeah. What'd he tell you?"

"The mass was a thymic cyst. It's not malignant. It's not a thymoma, which is what he thought it would be."

"So what does that have to do with leukemia."

"Nothing. It's not related at all."

"You mean you had two things going on, the leukemia and this cyst thing?"

"Well, you can look at it that way. But I look at it that I was lucky."

"Lucky? Two things going on, one of them leukemia, and you're talking 'lucky'?"

"Yeah. It's all a serendipitous convergence."

"A what? What did you call it?"

"Mom, what I mean is that I was lucky I had something on my chest X ray to get me to a doctor. Think of it this way: if my chest X ray hadn't shown anything, including a rib fracture that I thought I had, I could've just gone about my business, my running, all that, until the leukemia made me really sick. I mean I was walking around with a very low white blood cell count. It could've gotten lower, and I could've developed a really bad infection that might have killed me. But I had this cyst in my chest and that led to getting the CT scan, which showed the big spleen and . . . well, you know all the rest. So I figure I'm pretty lucky."

Her eyes are fixed on me. I look away, then back at her.

"And now, I really am lucky. I mean, here I am, spleen out, mass out, chest healing, with my parents, waiting for a beautiful woman to visit. What could be better?"

"How about all of the above plus 'no leukemia'?"

"Well, okay. But I'll take what I've got now and deal with the leukemia down the road. My counts are good. Habermann told me before this surgery that he doesn't think I need any chemo right now. He wants to watch and wait."

"You still okay with that, too?"

"Absolutely. The longer I can put it off, the better I'll like it. Of course, Habermann could change his mind. I've got to see him before I head back to Sacramento."

"Well, I hope he doesn't change his mind. At least I think that's what I hope. At any rate, I know he'll do what's right."

A white car glides to a stop in front of the house. My mother looks at me, smiles, and says, "You should go outside and bring her in."

I walk out the door and up to the window on the passenger side. Karin looks across at me even as she opens her door, watching me then walk around to her side. She steps from the car, stands before me in the street. I hold her as firmly as I can. She can feel the care with which I pull her to me. She takes a step back, looking me up and down.

"Well, you look pretty good for what you've gone through." Her blue eyes flash at me as she turns her smile into a grin.

"I've got a shirt on, dear. I look lots different with it off."

"I hope I get to find out."

"So do I. But first, come inside and meet my mom. My dad's still at work."

We walk arm in arm slowly to the house.

"Does it hurt a lot now?"

"A bit, but I'll be okay. I have to be careful."

"Hmmm, I wonder what that means," she smiles. We are at the front door.

A lot of the next half hour or so my mother talks with her, much as she would a prospective daughter-in-law, which is what she is, after all. They talk about Rochester, Karin's family and her children, about whom my mother had heard a lot, and, of course, my health. After a while, I feel like the third wheel and decide to make myself scarce so they can get to know one another. But I can only last about ten or fifteen minutes before I wander back up to the kitchen. The two of them are sitting over glasses of iced tea, speaking in quiet tones. My mother looks up.

"Oh, and speaking of the devil . . ."

"Right, here I am," I finish for her.

My mother turns back to Karin. "Well, I'm sure you two would like a little time together. I know you have to get home in a while. Sure you can't stay for dinner?"

Karin smiles, shaking her head. "I wish I could, but I promised my folks I'd get their car back this evening. My brother is coming over."

"Well, you're always welcome, you know that. Now I've got a few things to do around the house. Like I said, you probably both would like some time together."

We both say, almost together, "Thanks, Mom."

We go downstairs and into my room. Finally, we have time alone. With all the desperation and desire to see her, I am at a loss as to what to say, how to say it. We sit on the bed, side by side. The bedspread, the walls, the curtains are white, the room seemingly filled with light. She turns to face me, looking me in the eye, as if that will strengthen her in the face of my illness and what it might mean to my health, to our relationship, to my work. She has always been more pragmatic than I, better able to push aside emotion and replace it with reality. Yet she, like me, seems now to want reality, itself a palpable presence in the room, to disappear.

"So tell me, really, how is your chest? How do you feel?" she asks.

"Like I said, it hurts. But believe me, it's a lot better." I tell her a little about the day or two just after the surgery, of the chest pounding, of the bones scraping against one another, of the morphine.

"Well, I guess you appreciate what some of your patients go through, now."

"Yeah, though this isn't the best way to have to learn the lesson. I do have a bit better understanding of all that. But . . . I don't want to talk about that any more."

"Oh, so what do you want to talk about?"

"Well, nothing . . . everything." I grip her hand, then put my arm around her slowly, feeling my chest creak within, feeling my heart about to explode. I hold her to me, kiss her. "I really needed to see you. I'm glad you're here; God, I'm glad you're here."

She stops me. "I love you. Let me help you heal. Let me start your healing now." She is soft and kind as we lie back on the bed holding each other closer and closer. I am ashamed of my scarred chest and keep my shirt on. I can hardly move, but we both want and need each other. I feel my strength returning as I hear her breathing, her body now surrounding me as we hold each other, making love slowly on the narrow bed in the white light of the room. It is as if her presence itself is enough to fight back my disease, to clarify my being into a fullness and new strength. Afterward, we are lying together on the bed, and she looks at me, smiling.

"Are you going to take your shirt off now?" she asks.

"You sure you want to see?"

"I'm pretty tough, you know."

"I know." And she is right, for she is one of the toughest and truest of all. True to herself, her children, her family, and me. I pull up my shirt slowly. Her eyes scrutinize my violated chest. She gazes with the eyes of a mother, offering unspoken support and quietly unpronounced love.

"Well, doesn't look too bad to me," she laughs. "What's the big deal?"

"Uh . . . I don't know," I offer and chuckle back at her. I pull her again to me, kissing her once more. Then I look away.

"Geoff. Are you okay? Are you . . ."

"Yeah," I interrupt. "At least I think so. I'm just not sure how to go about this."

"This what?"

"This 'us.' I'm still not sure what we can do. I don't know what to say right now. I mean, you know how lousy I am with my feelings and all."

"Like most men, I'd say. Listen, neither of us can expect too much right now. You're still a ways from getting back to normal." I start to grin at her, and she sees it. "Not that 'normal' is a word that fits for you. And I have the kids and they have a dad and . . ."

"I know all that. I just wish there were a way I could make it easy. But I don't know how to do it."

"I'm not sure I can expect you to know how to do it. I don't know, either. No matter what happens, I still feel the same way. No matter what happens." Now it's her turn to look away, but not before she peers into my face, kisses me, and holds me to her gently, mindful of my wound. I turn around on the bed, putting my feet on the floor.

"We'd better get upstairs. What time do you have to be home?"

"Pretty soon, but let's not hurry too much." She pulls me around, and my feet leave the floor again.

A few minutes later, we wander again into the kitchen. Karin talks a bit more with my mother, then I reluctantly lead her to the door. We walk slowly again out to the car, my caution returning in the short distance across the grass. I am silent until we reach the car door.

"Listen, I'm going back to Sacramento in a week or so. Do you think you can get back over here before I leave?"

"Well, I'm not sure. I'll call. I have to go back soon, too. The kids want to do some stuff with my folks, and I should be there with them for that, so it may be tough to get back to Rochester. I'll call, or you call. Maybe you could come over to Austin."

"It depends on how I'm feeling. I'm not sure I'll be up to driving for a few days, at least. But we'll see. Thanks for coming over. I really needed to see you. Say hi to the kids for me." She is in the car. I carefully lean down to kiss her before she leaves.

I walk into the house, alone again, even though my mother is here somewhere. The sense of aloneness in the face of my illness, despite the support of my parents and Karin, is palpable and overpowering. I walk as if drugged down the stairs and into the bathroom. I peer at myself in the mirror and see my reflected face, pale now after the days in the hospital, my blue eyes settling back into their own uncomfortable distance. How long will it be until someone really shares the mirror with me? Will I ever be able to give up enough of myself to let it happen? Again, I pull my shirt up, inspecting my reddened scar. The line upon my skin is a mocking vertical smile, garish and tight, its silent, derisive teeth hidden along with the wires clamping my sternal edges together. I can't look myself in the eye, at least not right now. I can't stand the lonely person I have become, suffocating myself with an unwillingness to freely breathe the love that is mine to have and to give. The thought of intimacy, of sharing my life, my thoughts, my dreams with someone else, terrifies me, and I am learning the price of giving in to that terror, allowing it to dictate my being.

It is several days later when I pay my last visit to Habermann before my return to Sacramento. I wait again on a brown couch in a room high in the Mayo Building. A hand outside the door flips through my chart; then he bustles in.

"Your counts are terrific," he smiles. "I don't think you should start any therapy yet."

"No therapy? When . . . how will I know? I mean, will I need chemotherapy . . . I mean, ever?"

" 'Ever' is a long time. I can't see the future, you know. But remember, this is a chronic, slow leukemia. Since your counts are good, we're not pushed into anything right now. I want Fred Meyers to continue to follow you, get your counts, and keep in touch with me. I really think you'll do fine for at least several months. It could be longer before your counts drop. Then, if we need to start treatment we'll be able to do that. I'm close to getting this interferon-Pentostatin protocol approved. If it turns out you need to be treated, then I'd like to get you in on that combination."

I feel simultaneously relieved and unsettled. He sees it all over my face.

"Look," he says, now leaning forward again in his chair. "I can't tell you if you'll ever need chemotherapy. The longer you can go without it, believe me, the better it is. You probably know that, too. And I'll tell you again, as soon as you need it, we'll be able to start you."

"Okay. When I found myself with this diagnosis, I told myself that I would be the patient and not try to be *the* doctor, or even *a* doctor. I trust you. I've come this far, and I'll go the distance."

"Sounds like a runner talking."

"It is. A long-distance runner. When I was first diagnosed, it all felt like it happened so fast. I mean I had my spleen out only a couple of days after I'd been told I had leukemia. It has seemed like a sprint up until now. But now, it's looking more like a marathon."

"Well . . . I can't help . . ."

"No, don't get me wrong. I prefer the marathon, or even longer. I hate sprints. With the long run, I feel like I can somehow keep up better. But I have to be honest with you. Even now, knowing that I'm not sick enough to get chemotherapy, knowing that I have to wait and see, all that still bothers me some. But what really bothers me is that every day I live now is a day spent with leukemia in me. And I want to get rid of it, finally, once and for all."

"And I believe you have a good chance to do just that. But not right now."

"But at least you can see my point of view?"

"Sure. And you can see mine?"

"Absolutely."

Plans are made for my follow-up, and the visit is finished. My counts will be done at least once a month when I see Meyers. I now prepare to return to Sacramento, to work, to my search for another job, and to Karin, who is already back there with her children. I jog in the afternoons, circling the block a bit faster and trying to go a bit farther each day. Each night, I lie down on my bed with the utmost care, still fearing the splitting of my skin, the exposing of my bones. I stay awake reading into the night and sleep with care, as any turning awakens me to the strain and pull of wires holding my sternum together. I awake in the late mornings, climbing the stairs to find my mother sitting at the kitchen table, waiting for me.

Now back in Sacramento, I move a bit slower, but soon the demands of the job speak louder than the internal cries of sternal wires and bony edges. Clinic, call, procedures, medical decisions, all come back to me, and no matter how I tell myself to take it easy, I work progressively harder each day. Part of my hard work is explained by the fact that there is so much to do. But part of it is my need to perform at a certain level and to deny to myself and to the world around me that I am at all sick. And part of it is my reassertion of power and control that had been wrested from me by my leukemia and its treatment, pulled out with my bone marrow biopsy, splenectomy, and the removal of the mass in my chest. The spleen and mass are gone forever; my bone marrow will eventually have to be purged of the leukemic cells invading it. My life is held hostage by a foe I don't fully understand but who seems to understand me all too well.

10

The hour-long drive from Sacramento to Foresthill takes us from the city into the western slope of the Sierras. Leaving the massive hot valley named for the Sacramento River, Karin and I climb first to Auburn and then into the pine forests of the foothills cut by the American River and its tributaries. These rivers and streams are cold snowmelt, and there is a place called Rucky Chucky where the icy waters of the American must be crossed on foot by tired runners who've already endured the first eighty miles of the Western States Endurance Run. The little town of Foresthill, its houses interspersed among surrounding trees at three thousand feet up in the hills, would usually be a sleepy place of less than four thousand souls resting in the modest heat of an early summer day. But today, as every last Saturday in June for more than ten years, it is the location of the sixty-two-mile mark in the race. It is eighteen miles from the river crossing and thirty-eight miles from the finish in Auburn. In the parking lot in front of its small schoolhouse is one of the major aid stations, where tired runners meet their crews and get some nourishment. As part of the station here, the runners also have a mandatory medical check, and since I can't run the race, I've volunteered to be a doc.

It is noon when we arrive, and the station is just being assembled. The first runners won't be here for another one or two hours, even though the race is already seven hours old. We walk up to a man carrying boxes of equipment. He's large, sweating with the work, but brings himself to a laugh as I introduce Karin and myself.

"Howdy!" he yells. "I'm Bill. I'm running the medical station. Norm told me you'd be coming up. Said you'd qualified but gotten sick or something." Norm is Norm Klein, the race director, whom I've never met. Bill is a physician assistant who works in nearby Georgetown, one of the many small towns in the foothills.

"Yeah," I offer. "You might say that. A combination of leukemia and surgery, otherwise, I'd be running."

"So Norm said. Well, we'll need all the docs and help we can get. It looks like it'll be a hot one. Sacramento's heading over ninety, so it'll be at least a hundred in the canyons. We'll have our share of dehydrated runners here. I understand you've never worked an aid station in the race before."

"Right. So tell us what to do."

"Help me set up, and you'll both pick it up as you go."

Over the next hour, as more volunteers arrive, we set up an open nylon-mesh pavilion as well as a table and chairs and three weighing scales in front of the school. We commandeer one of the schoolrooms for our treatment center, stocking it with needles, syringes, plastic bags of intravenous solution and tubing, army surplus cots, blankets, clipboards, blood pressure cuffs, stethoscopes, and other first aid material. The rest of the school parking lot is incorporated into the areas that together will be the Foresthill checkpoint. There are separate tents for runners to be checked in and out of the station. There is a set of long tables with the ultrarunner's version of race food: potato chips, candy, small sandwiches, oranges, bananas, grapes, cokes, electrolyte replacement drinks, coffee, and hot soup. The runners will arrive hot and tired, having run the sixty-two miles from Squaw Valley to Foresthill over mountain trails with more than twelve thousand feet of uphill

and nearly as much down. They will have endured temperatures rang-
ing from 36 degrees at the start to as much as 105 in canyon depths.
They will have carried all their fluids and food in their hands or in
fanny packs. Despite their best attempts at drinking as they run, many
will come to us depleted of salt and sugar, hot and dehydrated.

By now it is 1:30; there are perhaps eight of us at the medical tent.
Bill gathers us together to go over our jobs.

"Listen up," he says. "Our main job is to make sure the runners are
okay to go on from here. Every one of them comes to us first, and we
get their weight. Runners will have a wristband, which'll have their
heart rate, blood pressure, and weight they had at the check-in yesterday, the day before the race started. We compare the weight we get
with the prerace weight. As long as they're close and the runner looks
okay, we send 'em on. If they're down 5 percent, they have to stick
around and tank up, then get rechecked before they can leave. Any-
body down 7 percent is out of the race."

"Do we take them out of the race ourselves?" someone asks.

"We can. Actually, I'm supposed to be the one to do it," says Bill. "I
cut off their wristband and give it to the guys at check-in over there."
He points to another pavilion twenty feet away. "Most of the time, the
runners know that they're going to drop out and they don't give much
fuss. Every once in a while, you have to talk some sense into them,
'cause some of them just look terrible, even if they're not down 7 percent. The runners who're really in trouble get taken into the schoolroom for IV hydration. They're automatically out if they get that done.
The first runners will be here in an hour or less. Things'll be slow at
first, but from around 7:00 to 9:30 tonight, this place'll be hopping.
We've got some sandwiches and cokes, so you should get some food
into yourselves now. Remember, the absolute cutoff here is midnight.
No runner leaves for Auburn after that. If it's 11:50 and someone is
okay to go and has the guts to do it, we should let them. But try to
make sure they have a chance to make it to Auburn in one piece.
They'll have a better shot if they have a pacer, and if they don't have
one arranged, the other race officials will try to help get 'em one."

A pacer is another runner who volunteers to accompany the official
runner for the last thirty-eight miles of the race. Most of the runners

have arranged for a pacer to join them at Foresthill. Four years ago, I'd volunteered to pace for a friend of mine, but he dropped out before making it to Foresthill. The year before that I was part of his crew and had my first taste of Western States. I haven't been able to let it alone since.

Thirty-eight miles is a long way to run, and the pacer is there more for the runner's safety and company rather than for speed. After running the sixty-two miles to Foresthill on trails that include most of the major climbs in the race, the runners will not be setting any land speed records. And that final thirty-eight miles includes downhills and steep climbs as well as the river crossing. For the majority of the runners, it'll be mostly run in the dark while the runner and pacer carry flashlights. Speed under these conditions is out of the question.

We get ready by the scales and wait nervously. We have clipboards with forms to enter runners' numbers and weights. We have pre-printed tables attached to the scales that give starting weights and weights corresponding to drops of 3, 5, and 7 percent. It is now over 80 degrees, and there is a cloudless sky above. I can only imagine how it feels in the heat of the canyons.

A car pulls into the lot, and a short man with a healthy tan comes over to us.

"Hey, Norm," shouts Bill at the race director.

"Hey. You guys all set?"

"Ready as usual."

I walk over to Norm and hold out my hand. "Hi, I'm Geoff Kurland."

He looks me full in the eye, then up and down, smiling all the way. "Hey, great to meet you. I really appreciate your help. And if you want to run next year . . . if you're okay . . . then you've got a place guaranteed."

"Thanks," I say, "but I'll only take it if I qualify for the race." I know that a fifty-mile run in less than nine and a half hours is the qualifying time for someone of my age.

"That's fine with me. Keep me informed. And good luck here today. Stick with Bill. He's done this a few times, you know."

"I'll do my best. And thanks for letting me volunteer." Norm goes to chat with others at the various stations in the checkpoint, then leaves to make sure the other, more distant ones are set up and ready to go.

A few minutes later, a loudspeaker at the check-in pavilion announces that the first runner has reached Bath Road, a mile away. Some ten minutes later, the lead runner comes into Foresthill to a cheer from the gathered crews of the many runners behind him. He passes off his bottles to be refilled with fluids, races up to the scales, and steps up to be weighed. He looks like he's just been out for a short, hot run; his shirt and hat are sweat soaked, his shoes dusty, his legs covered in dirt, but he's grinning and joking with his crew. His weight is identical to his prerace weight.

"How do you feel?" I ask.

"Great!" is the answer. He turns and runs off with his crew and pacer before I can tell him he can go. Perhaps some day, I hope, I'll be the one standing on the scales. Perhaps next year, I tell myself. My sternal wires are silent in agreement.

Through the afternoon, the heat builds, and the trickle of runners becomes a steady stream around 6 P.M., just as Bill predicted. Karin and I are almost too busy to speak with one another. She is at the scales, weighing runners in; I am often in the schoolroom caring for dehydrated runners who have been carried in for intravenous fluids. Most of them submit willingly to the needle stick; others want to try to drink enough to give them the strength to continue on to Auburn. Most of them can't keep any fluids down, vomiting almost as soon as they try. Only a few succeed and get back on the trail. The day becomes night, then midnight as the last of the runners come in to the checkpoint only to have their race end in Foresthill.

Few, if any, of the runners we pull out of the race seem overly saddened by what might on the surface appear to be failure; instead, most of them are happy to have been able to participate, to run this far. I have little idea of why they have the look in their eyes that speaks of contentment and satisfaction along with the frustration and pain they most obviously feel. There must be something out there, on the trail, in those mountains, that does that to them.

At a little after 12:30 in the morning, Karin and I volunteer to take a couple of stranded runners to the finish, where their crews can find them and where they can get some rest. We've closed up the makeshift shop; the pavilions are down, tables and chairs folded, cots put into boxes. Foresthill will return to its quiet ways for another year.

The four of us get into Karin's little Honda. The two runners in the back have hobbled slowly out of the school, carefully folded themselves into the back seat, and stare into the night as we head down the road.

"Are you okay back there?" Karin asks. "Do you need anything?"

"Fresh legs," a voice answers. Then he says again, "Fresh legs."

"First time?" the second voice asks.

"Second. Maybe the third time'll be a charm, and I'll finish. Two years ago, I dropped at Michigan Bluff," he says, referring to the tiny town at the fifty-six-mile point in the race, just over Volcano Canyon from Foresthill. "How 'bout you?"

"First try. Maybe I'll give it another go. I don't know. I thought I'd trained enough . . . the heat wasn't all that bad for me, but there aren't any hills like these where I'm from in Florida."

I turn around a bit. "What's it like?"

"What's what like?" a voice from one of them echoes.

"The course, the race . . . I mean, I qualified but got sick so I couldn't run. I'm thinkin' maybe next year . . . so what's it like?"

"It's hard to say, 'cause there's so much of it. Hills, rocks, heat, trees . . ."

"That's not what I mean. I'm not sure what I mean . . . except . . . are you glad you did it? Was it . . . I don't know if this is the right word . . . fun?"

Silence for a moment. Then one of the voices softly says, "Fun isn't the right word. Magnificent is more like it. Just to think that you're out there, alone, in a place so beautiful is something that's hard to describe."

"Alone? But there were about 350 in the race."

"Yeah. But you're a runner, aren't you? You know what I mean when I say alone. And most of the time I was runnin', there was nobody near me. And even if there was, I was doin' the work myself."

"I think I understand. But I suppose the only way to really know is to do it."

"You got that right."

The rest of the thirty-minute trip to Auburn is quiet, and Karin and I hear soft snoring from the back when we get to the high school. Even though it is after 1 A.M., the football field with its track is lit as for a night game. There are tents and cots set up on the infield and an electric timing clock over by the stands where the finish line is. There is a handful of people in the stands, crews waiting for their runner to appear at the far gate and make the slow run around the track to the finish. We help our runners as they walk stiffly to the medical tent at the finish.

"Should we go home now?" Karin asks.

"Let's watch one or two people finish, then go." We walk around the track, holding hands, waiting.

A voice on another loudspeaker from the press box at the top of the stands announces a runner entering the field. A whooping cheer goes up from some people in the stands. Karin and I watch the runner and his pacer labor for the last three hundred yards to the finish. He crosses the line, gets hugs from his crew and his pacer, gets his weight checked, and is helped to the medical tent.

"Do you wish that were you?" Karin's voice pulls my gaze back to her. "It looks to me like you do."

"You're right. I wish it were. I wish for a lot of things, don't I?"

"It's okay to wish for those things. I hope you always get what you want."

"God . . . I feel like I have a lot of what I want." I look her in the eyes as she smiles back. "I'm not sure I deserve it or if I can ask for more."

"I won't be the judge of that."

"I wouldn't really ask you to be the judge. But what do you think? Think I'm crazy for wanting to do this?"

"Honestly?" We start walking around the track again.

"Sure, honestly."

"Well, it's not something that I'd want to do. At least not right now or maybe ever. A lot of those runners we saw in Foresthill were pretty wiped out. I'd worry about you if you were to run it, especially . . .

especially after all you've been through." She was looking at me as she started but now looks away. "I worry about you enough without a hundred miler. And the way you work . . . anyway . . . So, yeah, I'd be a little scared for you. But I know you, too. And I would never stand in your way if it was something you wanted that much. I've told you before I'll always be here for you. That goes even for crazy stuff." She turns back to me, and I enfold her carefully in my arms.

"I promise, if I do this, it'll only be because I'm convinced I can. I'm not stupid enough to risk myself on running this without being ready. I only hope I can get well, over this leukemia, and then be able to run it. And I hope you can be with me when I do."

"I'll second all of that. Now, maybe we should get home."

We drive back on Interstate 80, which is all but deserted at 3 A.M. I look out the window as Karin turns the radio on, but I don't hear any of the music. All I can think about is the look in the eyes of the runners, the strange mix of pain and exhilaration as they lifted themselves carefully onto the scales, working to balance themselves, to stop moving. I see the faces of the runners who dropped out and came into the schoolroom for fluids, vomiting, exhausted, covered in the runner's mixture of sweat and dust that caked over their limbs and their clothes. I see the crews, the wives, husbands, friends who have stayed up since the early morning to get the brief glimpses of their runner at the checkpoints along the way. I'd heard that the main job of the crew, aside from giving the runner the fresh shoes and socks, the refills of water bottles, and encouragement is to lie as convincingly as possible. Over and over, I heard it at the aid station as crews told runners "You're lookin' great! Fantastic!" even as they stumbled and hobbled up to us, their expressions telling me how they were probably really feeling. And the runners, true to form, usually answered, "I feel terrific!" and they'd turn to their pacer and yell, "Let's go to Auburn!"

We are home, and as I fall asleep, I hear a voice, my voice asking, "Do I really think I can ever do this?" I remember how I felt after doing my first fifty-mile run. It was the American River 50, from Sacramento in the valley up to Auburn in the foothills. In April, it is usually hot, and this was no exception. I ran out of all energy at thirty-two miles and was on the ground at the aid station, almost unable to move, for forty-five minutes. It was only through the cajoling of John, who paced me the last eighteen miles, that I got up and started down the trail in more of a slow jog than a run. Amazingly, I soon started to feel better and was able to run, somehow eating and drinking enough to replenish myself so that I could finish. But my finishing time was a slow ten and a half hours. I'd have to cut an hour off that time just to qualify for Western States. How would I feel after fifty miles into States, with another fifty to go? As I drift into the blackness, I tell myself that there is only one way to find that out.

The marble lobby of the California Pacific Medical Center is cool and bright in the afternoon. Even in July, San Francisco has a bit of hidden winter. I search for the information booth and learn that the coronary care unit is several floors above. The elevator ride is swift, and I feel lost when the metal doors slide apart, facing a clean, white wall in a corridor without obvious signs. I wander around briefly until a man pushing a floor cleaner points me in the right direction.

I go up to the desk at the nurses' station. A clerk is checking some reports, filing them into charts as she spots me and calls out.

"Excuse me, sir. Are you here to see someone?"

"Yes . . . I am . . . I'm looking for Dr. Miller."

"Bed seven, around the corner. Let me check with his nurse to make sure he can take visitors now." She puts the phone to her ear, speaks with a voice on the other end, and turns to me. "You may go back and see him now."

I slowly walk into the unit, past beds with sallow patients breathing with the help of murmuring ventilators, their intravenous solutions running and their monitors softly beeping. None of them looks like the exhausted and beaten runners I took care of only a few weeks ago. None of these patients is going anywhere soon.

It was only a couple of days after Western States that one of my colleagues told me the bad news. Spike, no longer the chairman of pediatrics, was taking his first vacation with his family in about five years. He was getting some much-deserved time to relax before starting his new job as chief of pediatrics in Pittsburgh. The night before his family's flight to Hawaii, while they were all in the hotel at the San Francisco airport, he was striken with chest pain and collapsed. Rushed to the nearest hospital, he was found to have sustained a massive myocardial infarction, killing much of his heart muscle. With difficulty, he was transferred here where the cardiac unit could perhaps stabilize him. The other reason they told me he's here is that they do heart transplants, which may now be his only hope for survival.

I inch around the corner and see a glass-enclosed bed space. A pasty-faced, dark-haired, unshaven man is lying with his head propped on two pillows. A monitor screen above him whispers his blood pressure, pulse, and hemoglobin saturation that tells if his blood is oxygenated. Several IV lines run from plastic bags down to enter his hands and his neck. There is catheter tubing with urine draining into a bag on the right side of the bed. On the left side is a white box plugged into an electric outlet. A large, white tube snakes from the box and under the covers toward the man's groin. The box issues a soft whoosh that seems timed with the man's heartbeat. He's watching TV on the wall near the foot of the bed. I approach slowly.

"Spike . . . ," I nearly whisper.

He turns his head slowly, then brightens and smiles, simultaneously talking as he fumbles briefly for the TV control to turn the thing off. "Geoff! Great to see you. Thanks for coming." His voice is much stronger than I anticipate.

"How . . . how are you feeling? . . . I mean . . ."

"Pretty good, considering. Scared, but waiting."

"Waiting?"

"For a heart. I'm waiting for a transplant. My heart took too big a hit. That's why I've got the assist device in." He nods toward the box on his left side.

The box is connected to a long balloon that has been threaded into an artery in Spike's groin and from there back up into his aorta, the main artery leading from the heart. With every attempt of the heart to pump, the balloon suddenly is inflated, propelling blood forward to supply his body. It makes up a portion of what his heart no longer can do.

"Is it helping?" I ask.

"Well, I'm still alive."

This is the man who has served as my mentor and leader for five years. His life is now held in balance by a tiny balloon with a wall less than a millimeter thick. I can only stare for a moment as the frailty I see before me is made manifest. He cannot move from the bed without help; in fact, he cannot do much more than talk and think, allowing the machine to help pump his blood.

"Spike, I . . . I don't know what to say. I'm so . . . sorry about this . . . is there anything I can do? Hell, I know there's nothing I can do."

"Actually, I've been waiting for you to visit. I need your advice and expertise."

"My what?"

"I need your advice. Listen. I'm listed for a heart transplant. My surgeon tells me they've never waited more than a week or so before getting a heart, so I'm allowing myself to be optimistic." This, I confirm, is a man who definitely sees the glass as half full. "So I know you've had a sternotomy, which is what I'll have when I get my heart. Any suggestions on recovery? I mean, you're the expert here."

"Suggestions?"

"Yeah, warnings, ideas for helping me to get through it, you know, stuff like that. I'd really appreciate any help here."

"Well," I start, asking myself how much I should tell him and then realizing that he wants the truth so I blurt it all out, "it hurts . . . but unlike me, you'll probably be on a ventilator for the first day or so, so they'll keep you pretty snowed with meds to ease the pain. Make sure you can get your pain meds IV or, if possible, with an epidural block. Take meds before they turn you for your chest physiotherapy. And get up as soon as you can take the pain . . . it'll lower the risk of pneumonia." I stop and realize I am shaking with fear. Spike looks to me to be the picture of calm.

"Thanks. I'll try to remember that."

"Spike . . . tell me . . . is a transplant what you want?"

"No. No, of course not. But I have only two choices. Get a heart transplant or stay on the balloon pump until I get some other problem like an infection, renal failure, or something else bad, and then die. For me there really isn't much choice. All I can do is go forward. I'm not ready to die."

"I'm not ready for you to die. Lots of us aren't ready for you to die."

"Thanks again. Now, enough about me." Enough about him? What else is there? "What are you up to? I know this isn't a great time for you, but how are you?"

"I'm fine . . . fine."

"You don't need chemotherapy right now?"

"No . . . not now . . . Spike, we don't have to talk about me. My problems are nothing compared with . . ."

"Wait a minute," he interrupts. "I just want to know if you're still considering the job in Pittsburgh. I worry about your future, you know." He's waiting for a heart transplant and is worried about *my* future?

"I've got a visit planned to Salt Lake City, and then I'll decide if I'll visit Pittsburgh again. I'm not sure what to do."

"Listen to me. Your future in Sacramento isn't necessarily secure. You and I talked about that a couple of months ago. You've got to keep your options open. I think you're doing the right thing to look in Utah . . . and then maybe Pittsburgh. I'm trying to recruit you there myself, you know."

"You've got some surgery in front of you first, I think."

"Yeah, that's right, but I'm keeping a positive attitude about all this. Things happen for a reason, they say." What reason could there be for this? I ask myself. The balloon pump murmurs away on the other side of the bed, and the monitor shows an EKG tracing with small blips representing the weak electrical signal of a dying heart, yet the pale face before me carries a faint smile amid the heavy cheeks and lids that have all but lost the energy to rise on their own.

"I hope you're right. About all of it. About recruiting me to Pittsburgh. About you being there. God, I just hope you're right."

"So do I."

I leave soon afterward, as his exhaustion shows and he drifts to sleep. I wander back to my car and drive the hour and a half to Sacramento. All the way I hear his voice, telling me to keep my options open. How will that include Karin? I know she can't move; the kids have their father in Sacramento, and she's told me that for the foreseeable future she must stay there. I tell myself that things will somehow work out and try to agree with Spike that everything happens for a reason. It's late when I get home. Keeping my options open, I decide, may not be as easy as it looks.

11

The air is crisp in Toronto as I step out of the taxi. It seems years since I've found myself in an autumn where blue skies overhang trees whose leaves are red or gold. A park surrounds the hotel, and a large sign welcomes the participants in the North American Cystic Fibrosis Conference. Although I'm here for the meetings, I have much more important business. After unpacking my bags in my room and going for my afternoon run on the nearby trails, I search out David Orenstein.

"Hey, Geoff," he says soon after we meet, "can you join us for dinner tonight? I'd like you to meet some of the folks from Pittsburgh."

"Yeah. I'd like that, I think."

"So would we."

We set the time and place. I go off to think, alone. The last four months have been tough. My visit to Salt Lake City was good, but it didn't leave me ready to move there. Spike waited longer than a month for a heart, and by the time it arrived, he'd had at least one stroke and developed renal failure. It will be difficult for him to make it to Pittsburgh, or anywhere, assuming he makes it out of the hospital, where he's been since his heart attack in June. But Spike's always been tough, and he might just be able to pull it off.

The situation with Karin, however, has been nearly impossible for me. So many times we tried to talk about my future, so many times it came out much the same way, as it had just a week or so before my trip to Toronto.

I had spent the weekend day with her and the kids, taking them ice skating, itself a surreal experience in the eighty-degree heat that constitutes fall in Sacramento. Not having skated since childhood, I looped slowly around the uneven ice of the only indoor rink in this part of California. Karin and the kids, all closer to winter sports thanks to the Minnesota grandparents, flashed by as I wobbled along. After dinner, the kids were in bed, Karin and I sitting on her couch in the soft light of a single lamp. I stared out the window, again uncertain of what to say.

"Well, you're pretty quiet. You want to talk about anything?" She looked up at me.

"You know I'm going out to Toronto to the CF meeting, and then I'm going down to Pittsburgh." She was silent and knowing. "I'm . . . I'm thinking that I may take the job. I'm worried that . . . I'm worried that you and I . . ."

"What are you worried about? Are you afraid that I'll forget about you? Or you me?"

"No. I just worry about being apart."

"Listen, Geoff. You and I know that your job here is killing you. And that the kids and I have to stay here, at least that's what the court and their father say. You've got to be in a place where you're happy to work."

"I know. And if I could stay here . . ."

"God, you know I'd love that. You know that, don't you? But you told me yourself that you probably can't. I remember talking with you after all those discussions you had with Spike. Your days at the med center are probably numbered, he'd said. And anyway, if you stayed, what would they do to you? Abuse you more, if that were possible? Make you even less satisfied with the amount of work you're doing?"

"Yeah, I know. It's easy to rationalize it all. But life isn't always about rationalizations. I only wish that you and the kids could come with me." She was about to speak, but I kept on going. "I know you can't. I know Roger's still here. I know about the court order about how far from Sacramento they can live. It doesn't change how I feel."

"I would hope it wouldn't change how you feel. About me . . . about us . . ." She shifted on the couch and sat up, her eyes boring into me. "Listen, I would rather have you somewhere where you're happy working than staying here to be with me, winding up miserable, and hating not just your job but me, too. I don't think I could take that. We can somehow work this out. I don't know how or when right now, but we can . . . we will. I'm patient. Once we know where you'll be, we can work on it then. But for now, you've got to make those decisions about your work based on where you'll be happy. Then we'll see."

I leaned back into the couch, knowing that I would have to decide my future for myself and hope that it would ultimately include Karin.

Now, back in Toronto, I wait for David and some of the others. I get to the restaurant a bit late and spot the group over at a corner table. David's hand is in the air, waving.

"Hey, nice of you to join us. I kinda hope it might be permanent. Let me introduce you to everyone." And with that, I meet some of the trainees, nurses, social workers, and nutritionists who make up the CF team in Pittsburgh. The conversation is polite, restrained at first, but my sense of humor meshes too well with David's for that to last too long. The next several raucous hours are spent trading stories of our time at Amherst, of how we discovered we'd both wound up in the same specialty, of how we'd each tried to recruit the other over the last couple of years.

Three days later, I ride to Pittsburgh with the whole group stuffed into a van borrowed from the university. Every seat is filled, bags are under our feet and filling every available spot left inside the van, and, if that weren't enough, Tassos, the Greek first-year fellow, is at the wheel, asking directions, changing lanes without always looking, taking suggestions for where to stop for dinner outside of Buffalo (fast food wins in a minilandslide). We pull into Pittsburgh late in the evening, and David takes me to his house, which he and his wife, Susan, share with two very large, outspoken, and overly friendly German shepherds. I find myself welcomed almost too vigorously.

Over the next several days, I do the usual round of interviews and dinners, but the best part of the visit is my run through the park with David and Susan. The trails are covered with leaves, the trees obscuring the roads that are close enough to hear. It is hard to believe that I'm in the middle of a city, expecting to see deer run out in front of us at any moment. As it is, the woods are filled with birds and squirrels; the dogs strain against their leashes for a chance to chase. I could live in a city that has this, I tell myself.

My visit ended, David drives me to the airport. Between us on the seat we share french fries from the Original restaurant, a Pittsburgh landmark whose neon sign boasts that they sell thirty thousand pounds of the fries each week.

"Well, I hope you enjoyed the visit. I don't have to tell you that everyone who met you was impressed. I hope you can accept the offer." During this, the second trip of mine, an actual appointment with salary was floated to me.

"And my leukemia? Aren't you worried about it?"

"I don't think I'm the one who's supposed to be worried about it. You say you've been doing well and your counts are okay. That's good enough for me. Anyway, I . . . I mean we, want you under any circumstances."

I look out the window for a minute or two. The sky is gray with clouds, and the air is chilled with autumn. "I promise you'll have your answer in less than a week."

"Okay . . . okay . . . I hear you," I tell her. "It doesn't change anything, my moving, yet we both know that it'll change things." The kids are with their father. Karin and I are at a late dinner after my long day at the hospital, followed by a dark run through the rainy streets. Although it's 9:30 at night, the sun's been down for four hours. Even in sunny California, it gets dark early in January.

"Sure, I know it'll change things. But it won't change how I feel.

And you know you can come out here. At least, I hope you'll be able to come out here!"

"I will," I promise.

We've been readying ourselves for this for the last months or even more, for we both knew inside that I'd be moving. The stress of it is weighing down on us both, as I've arranged to sell my house, pack my stuff, and move to Pittsburgh by mid-February. Every spare moment seems a bit more precious to me. I look across the table at her.

"We can do this. Somehow, we can do this."

She nods slightly even as her eyes turn red.

Within a month, I am in Pittsburgh, though the first weekend I return to Sacramento to run a fifty miler that will qualify me again for Western States. Now the sound of Karin's voice coursing over the phone line is one of the few things that keep me going. It is a long way back to Sacramento, but there's a lot of work to do here. I have to make myself known to the patients, nurses, respiratory therapists, as well as the complement of medical students, residents, and attending physicians. I throw myself into the hospital, making rounds, taking call, doing bronchoscopies, teaching. I plan to get some research going in the laboratory of one of the adult pulmonologists at the University Hospital. Within a few weeks of my arrival, I feel inundated, entwined.

But I need my own physician to look after me; I have to find a replacement for Fred Meyers. I ask Cindy, one of the pulmonology nurses, whom she'd recommend. She tells me to talk to Larry Ellis. His office is only a couple of blocks away. I set up an appointment and arrange to have my records from Mayo and Sacramento sent to him.

Late in March, I'm sitting in a small examining room in Ellis's office suite. Unlike rooms at the Mayo Clinic, this room is too small for a couch. There is only a single chair and an examining table. A small metal table holds an opthalmoscope-otoscope, as well as a glass jar containing the mandatory tongue depressors and Q-tips. I hear the papers shuffle outside the door.

"Well, nice to meet you. I've got your records here," he looks down at the papers in his hand. "Interesting story" is all he can add. He looks like he should be a character actor, in his late fifties, tall, thin, with silver gray hair, piercing blue eyes, and a complexion that suggests he gets a little too much sun, although for a moment I wonder if it's from a little too much alcohol or a little too much of both together. His thick baritone speaks of experience and confidence, a hematologist who's seen it all. He wears a white coat, and his stethoscope dangles haphazardly from the pocket on the side. He smiles rather than grins and shakes my hand with a strong grip.

"So, from what I can see, you've done pretty well since your splenectomy and sternotomy. When was your last blood work? Oh, here it is, a couple of months ago. You got here when?"

"Mid-February."

"From Sacramento? Wow, I bet that was some change!"

"Yeah. My mother helped me drive out to Minnesota, then I took it in from there. When I left Sacramento, it was rainy and in the fifties. When I got here, it was something like fifteen, and it had just snowed about six inches or so. I thought I had enough warm clothes, but I had to borrow some to run in."

"Oh, yeah, I remember reading in your record something about you running a lot. Actually, it sounded like it was more than a lot."

"Well, it is what I do, when I'm not being a doc."

"You are a pediatric pulmonologist, right? Like Children's so far?"

"Yes and yes."

"And have you bought a house yet?"

"Well, actually, I found one soon after I got here, and I'll close on the place in April and move into it in late June. They got me an apartment to live in for now, but it's actually more like a shoe box masquerading as an apartment. As they say, it's so small I have to go outside to change my mind."

Ellis laughs with me and then does a quick exam. "Okay, listen, I want your blood work now. My nurse can draw it right here. I'll want to see you in about a month, but for now, I don't think we have to do anything, assuming your counts are still okay."

"It's a deal," I say, and I walk down the corridor to the lab.

A few days later, Ellis's nurse calls me.

"He wants me back next week?" I ask.

"Yes, Dr. Kurland. Dr. Ellis said your white count and platelet count were a bit lower than your last set, and he wanted to check them sooner rather than later."

I am stunned but have to shake it off, for I'm in the middle of rounds and still have several patients to see.

On the appointed day, I'm in Ellis's office. My blood drawn, I'm led into an exam room. Only a few minutes later, Ellis strides in.

"Thanks for coming in today. I just wanted to make sure your counts aren't as low as they were last week."

"How low?"

"Low enough to have me bring you back." He looks at me, his eyes shine behind his glasses. "I'm presuming nothing other than it has to be repeated." Enigmatic enough. He examines me and pronounces all to be well. "I'll have these results by tomorrow morning. I'll call you one way or the other."

It is morning, and I slowly walk the two blocks along Fifth Avenue back to Children's. The street is wet from last night's sleet and drizzle as winter tries to stick around. The temperature is in limbo, just as I am, neither cold nor warm. I go through the day, see patients, work out at the gym I joined, sleep fitfully, and wait.

True to his word, Ellis pages me in the morning as I am back on rounds.

"Geoff, your counts are still too low. I think I'd better see you later today so we can decide the next step. Can you come by, say around four this afternoon?"

Next step, I think. I can only think of one next step. "I can finish rounds and have someone cover for me. I'll be there."

We sit in his office now rather than an exam room. There are photos on the bookshelves, but I don't look at them. I am falling back into the chair, listening as he is talking.

". . . too low. I already called Habermann, and he thinks you can be on the protocol for interferon and Pentostatin. But before you can start, we have to have another marrow."

"Another one?"

"Sorry, but that's the protocol. Can we do it tomorrow?"

"Well, we have a few bronchoscopies set up in the afternoon."

"How about eleven in the morning?"

"Won't I be woozy from the premedication?"

"Premedication? I don't use any. Trust me, I've done so many of these, I guarantee you won't need any premedication."

I have no choice. "Where do you do it? I mean, do you do the marrow here in the office?"

"No. They give me a room at the hospital." He gives me the directions. I try to get up from the chair but find myself sitting down again, disbelieving. "Geoff." I look up. "I can't take away the shock, but I think we're catching this early, and I think the best thing is for us to deal with it now."

"Oh, I agree. I know. But it's just that I was feeling . . . feeling so good. I just did a long race only a month ago or so. This is just like it was when I was first diagnosed a year ago."

"Except for one thing," Ellis says.

"What's that?"

"We know what we're dealing with."

Ellis is right; we do know what this is. And now I've just had my second bone marrow done, this time without premedication. Ellis was right about not needing any. He gave me enough local anesthetic to have delivered a baby through my bone. I lay down on the bed in the otherwise abandoned room on the ward. Ellis told me to relax for about half an hour, putting my resting weight on the site in my iliac crest, down in my lower back, through which he bored the needle to sample my leukemic marrow. I am asleep when a nurse comes in to remind me that I can leave. I walk slowly back to Children's and help oversee the fellow as we do three bronchoscopies.

My phone call that night is a late one, after rounds, after I walk back to my apartment and get in my evening run. Fortunately, Sacramento is three hours earlier, so I don't awaken Karin. I tell her the news of the last several days.

"Why didn't you tell me earlier?" she asks.

"I didn't want you to get upset for no reason. I feel fine. It was only my blood counts that alerted Ellis. Otherwise, I'd never know."

"Are you taking good care of yourself? You're not working too hard already, are you?"

"No," I lie. "I'll be fine. When can you come out?"

"When do you want me out there?"

"Yesterday. But I think we should wait until I know more of what's going on, if I even need any medications, and get a time when you can come out for more than just a quick weekend while the kids are with their dad. By the way, how are they? The kids, I mean, not their dad."

"We're all fine. But don't change the subject like you always do. You take care of yourself. I mean it."

"I'll call you when I know more about what is going on. I promise."

The next week, marrow results back, I visit Ellis's office again. I'm on the exam table; he's in a plain metal and plastic chair, like something from a high school cafeteria. He's writing in my chart, then looks up at me.

"Okay. Here's what I've found out. Your marrow, no surprise, still shows hairy cell leukemia. I checked again with Habermann, and we've got you on the protocol. It calls for interferon-alpha for twelve weeks, a couple of weeks off for some other testing, then Pentostatin every two weeks."

"It's not just Pentostatin?"

"Nope. Pentostatin may be good, but we know that interferon leads to a clinical response in a high percentage of patients. Maybe you won't even need Pentostatin."

"Do I need more lab tests? When can I start?"

"You're set. You can start today or tomorrow. We'll help you get the interferon, and you can give yourself the first injection, unless you want my nurse to give you the first one. In any event, you'll be giving your own injections."

"My own?" I've administered only a handful of injections, although I started lots of IV's as an intern and resident. I have heard about injection woes from patients with diabetes.

"Don't worry. You give this sub-q." It's under the skin, not into the muscle. I breathe a sigh of relief. "It'll be only half a milliliter per dose, three days per week. We'll check your counts every two weeks at first, then every month. The only thing you need to know is that interferon makes you feel like you have the flu. I suggest you take some Tylenol when you get the injection and about four hours later. That should prevent too many symptoms. My nurse can go over the details with you. You can get syringes and needles at Children's, right?"

"Right." We shake hands, and I go out to the nurse with the prescription. I will start my own treatment tomorrow afternoon so that if I get a fever, it'll be in the evening. After my instructions, I head back to home, for it's now nearly 5:30 in the evening. I decide to skip my run, get dinner, and wait until Karin is home for the call. I sit on the couch in my little apartment, peering out the window at the gathering darkness. I have been waiting for this for about a year. Tomorrow, I will have my first chance to fight back at the leukemia with more than just my will.

12

The road curves before me as I wind the car down from Pittsburgh's north hills toward the airport. Karin looks over at me, then away out the window. Neither of us has looked forward to this drive since she arrived three days ago.

I had picked her up at the airport Friday afternoon and, after our hungry embraces, drove her into the city, hearing her gasp as we came out from the Fort Pitt tunnel and were presented with the city spread before us. We went to my tiny apartment and tried to make up for the months apart as soon as we were alone, holding each other close, making love in the afternoon.

She went with me to the hospital and met the staff, visited the house I'd bought but not moved into and met my soon-to-be neighbors. We slept together in the same bed for the first time in too long, awakening to each other. And now, after joining me at the Pulmonology Division's spring party, she has to return.

"Did you have a good time?" I ask.

"What do you think? Of course. I just hope I can come out again."

"When?"

"It'll depend on my vacation schedule, the kids, Roger, you know, the usual stuff."

"I know. We'll work it out. I can help with the money."

"I know, but I don't want you to have to do that too much. And besides, you've got a lot of stuff to do here, on call every third weekend."

"True, but that beats being on call nearly every day in Sacramento. We'll figure out when you can come back. Maybe next time you could bring the kids, stay a bit longer. It'll be lots easier when I'm in the house."

"I'll say. That place is huge. I know the kids'll love it when they see it. They've always had to share a bedroom, but your house . . . I mean five bedrooms is pretty big."

"I bought it with us in mind."

"I know, but you have to do things with just you in mind right now. We can't predict what'll happen. We don't know. . . ." her voice trails off and there is silence.

"Anyway, I'd like to bring them out, although I'm not sure how they will like the city. You know, they're pretty used to Sacramento." We laugh as the airport comes into view. The good-byes are difficult, but we both know that she'll be back.

Now, with Karin gone only a week, I have another weekend alone. It feels warm for a Saturday night, and I awaken suddenly in the early morning hours of Sunday and kick the covers off the bed. A few minutes later, I feel just as suddenly cold, and I wrap myself up in the blankets that were on the floor. My arms and legs are shaking; my teeth chatter; my head aches. In some ways, it feels like an exaggerated aftermath of each interferon injection without the intervening protection of Tylenol. Ellis warned me of this, but my last injection was Friday and was without any of these symptoms. I probably have a little cold, I tell myself as I fall back to sleep.

Sunday is a blur of fatigue as I spend most of it in bed, but without the chills of the morning. I even go out and ride my bike a bit, only to return to the apartment more exhausted. I drop into bed early and fall asleep almost instantly. I walk the half mile to the hospital in the morning and get to clinic. My schedule is full, yet the patients don't present too many problems to me today. My bladder, however, suddenly has developed a mind of its own, and I seem to run to the toilet five or six times during the morning. Dragging by the end of clinic, I wander into the office a little after one in the afternoon.

"Hey, Diane," I call. The administrative assistant looks up. "I'm not feeling too well. I think I'll go home early."

She looks over at me across the office, then walks to me as if to get a closer look. "Are you okay? You don't look that great. Do you want to call Dr. Ellis?" She, like the rest of the office, knows my diagnosis and my physician.

"No . . . no . . . I'll . . . I think I just got a cold or flu or something. I'll go home and take a nap. It'll probably be much better by the morning."

"Well, okay, but let one of us know if you start feeling worse."

"Deal," I say and walk out. But before I've gone ten feet, my bladder tells me to detour for the men's room again. I walk in and suddenly I am in one of the two stalls, on the floor. The green paint of the walls is peeling, the tiled floor is ice, and my breath fails as my teeth chatter. I cannot gather the strength to rise for several minutes. The room is silent except for the staccato in my head. I grab hold of the railing in the stall, pulling myself upward, unsteadily erect, now cruising along the wall, holding on step by step until I am out of the room and lurch across the corridor and back into the office. I sit down and am silent.

First Diane and then Cindy see me. I am not sure how I look until I see their faces.

"Get a wheelchair," Cindy says. "I'll call Dr. Ellis's office." They each move to a phone. "Geoff, do you want to lie down?"

"On the floor?" I inanely ask, as if it would be considered in poor taste. "No. I'll sit. I don't think I'm going to go home yet." Cindy looks at me even as she says something into the phone, then nods agreement with the person on the other end. She makes another quick call, then comes to my side, looking down at me.

"Geoff, we're going to the Presby ER," she says, referring to the University-Presbyterian Hospital, which is attached to Children's. I offer no resistance to the idea, which now sounds like a pretty good one. A wheelchair appears. I am delivered in a few minutes through the connecting corridors.

The gurney on which I lie is in a corner of one of the many rooms, a thin curtain visually insulating me from my several neighbors. The nurse has visited and told me that my temperature, taken with a new infrared thermometer placed in my ear, is nearly 104. Several syringes full of my blood have been taken, and I have produced a requested urine sample as carefully as my shaking limbs would allow. An X-ray machine has come and gone. A cheerful dark-haired woman in a white coat is at my side; she's the medical resident, and she's talking to me, seemingly silhouetted by the fluorescent light that floods the room. The only other sounds I hear are soft moans, snores, and occasional startled cries mixed with the rattling and whirring of equipment and the frequent ringing of telephones. Everything is happening very slowly, I think, but I'm not really sure.

". . . urosepsis, so we'll start some IV antibiotics. Dr. Ellis knows you'll be coming in." A few moments pass. She says other things, but I'm not concentrating enough to hear them. "Is that okay? Dr. Kurland, is that okay? Should we notify anyone?"

"What? Oh, it's okay." Whatever it is. "I'll tell people in my office." I've only understood that a bacterial urinary tract infection is busily disseminating through my body. I've already received my first dose of antibiotics. They're admitting me to Ward 123, called Twelve 3, as it's on the twelfth floor of the hospital.

Several hours later, after several other house staff have had their go at me, questioning and examining, I finally am able to make some calls. Karin wants to come out. I tell her it's not a good idea. My parents are due to leave for a European trip in two days. I tell them to have a good time, because I'll only be hospitalized for one or two weeks and I'll be fine. Am I sure? my mother wants to know. Yes, I am sure. The antibiotics should kill the bacteria, and I'll be back to work soon.

It is evening, and in addition to my antibiotics, I've gotten some fluids. I feel as great as one can feel on the uneasy edge of an infection. But fatigue overtakes me and I fall asleep.

And in the middle of the night, it begins. I am suddenly awake and my body shakes with fever and chills as my temperature reaches for the heights: 40.3 degrees Celsius or 104.5 degrees Fahrenheit. Either way, it is a mean way to awaken. My bed is soaked, the nurse worried, the blood tech busy taking more blood to send to the lab to grow the bacteria that must be responsible for this.

The days go by, turning into weeks, and despite the antibiotics, the fevers, chills, and sweats persist. I have more tests: a CT scan of my head, followed by a spinal tap, ultrasound examinations of my kidneys, repeat chest X rays; all are negative. A nuclear scan designed to light up areas of infection shows a faint glow around my windpipe, possibly because of my previous surgery. Ellis is reassuring but clearly puzzled. He's stopped my interferon, telling me that whatever I have, it isn't the leukemia doing this to me. It must, he thinks, be some side effect of the drug or a strange infection allowed by my immune suppression.

The nurses look at me with eyes betraying a compassion for the dying. And, as if to accommodate them, I start draining away physically and emotionally. My physicians don't know what I have, so they can't treat it. The two-week course of my antibiotics has been completed; my condition is unchanged. People from the office come to visit and find me hollow, fatigued, and weak. I see my fear reflected in their eyes. I can't tell them to leave, but I don't want them to see me like this. Karin's voice is far away, and it is more difficult to be cheery, even with her.

I am pretty sure I will die, for the nightly fevers, a hollow appetite, and apathy have conspired together, leaving me silently anguished and empty. I tell myself that this is what it is to die slowly. I am not afraid of dying as much as I thought I'd be. Instead, I feel a sadness that the cause—the infection, the tumor, or whatever it is—eludes my physicians. Perhaps this is what those who died of consumption in the last century felt, dying of what we now know is a treatable infection. And like the consumptives, I've been wasting away. I've lost ten pounds from a frame that doesn't have too much to lose. The days fall into nights that in turn fall into one another. No day is different, yet each is painfully long, boring, hopeless, and discouraging. My nightly sweats break apart my sleep just as they drain my strength. But I somehow force myself out of bed for a walk around the ward at least once a day. I wander slowly to the windowed reading room overlooking the campus. It seemed a beautiful view the first few times I went there. Now the sun is too bright, and the heat of late June insinuates itself through the glass into me, giving me a daytime reminder of my night-time terror. Whatever is doing this, be it infection or hidden tumor or something else, it is relentless and overwhelmingly effective.

After nearly three weeks, I get a call.

"Geoff . . . are you there?" It is my mother. "I've talked to Dr. Ellis. I'm coming out there. Dr. Ellis has agreed to let you go with me to Rochester. I also spoke with Dr. Habermann."

"I'm not sure that's necessary," I say without conviction.

"Listen, I don't care what you think. I've talked with Dr. Ellis and Dr. Habermann. They've talked with each other and it's okay. I'll be there in two days. Be ready to go."

I wonder what I could possibly do to be ready to go; I can't go home. In fact, I have to vacate my apartment and move into my new house in two or three days. But I can't think much about that now. I can only try to hold on for another few days. I somehow arrange to have the movers, hired before my hospitalization, await my mother. I'll let her figure out where all my worldly goods should be placed in the house in which I may never actually live.

I am sleeping in the afternoon and hear a soft voice call my name. I look up at my mother's face, worried but relieved. After all, I am able to return her gaze, speak to her, and actually sit up. I gather my clothes and, on a brief pass from the hospital, show her the house, my apart-ment, and the storage place where I've left most of my belongings. She and my real estate agent do the move in the morning. The following day, we leave; I carry my latest X rays and a discharge summary ticking off the myriad tests that have been run to search for my fever's source. The flights take us from Pittsburgh to St. Louis and then on to Rochester. En route I sleep fitfully, walk from a gate of arrival to the gate of my connecting flight with the blank stare and measured gait of what must be a zombie. Others in the airport avert their gaze, for I can only imagine how hollow I appear, as one who has faced down a high fever. At home, I can barely sit and speak with my father, tending to want to sleep instead. I spend only a few hours at home before check-ing into the Methodist Hospital, the second of the large facilities used by the Clinic. I am given the going-over again, this time by the house staff and attending physicians of the Clinic. The past few weeks have blurred into a lethargical nothingness, and I can do little more than recite my case and let them look at my multipage discharge summary and my sheaf of X rays.

Habermann isn't the attending physician on my case, although I think he's calling a lot of the shots from the Clinic. But in any event, the Clinic physicians don't seem to have that much luck in pinpoint-ing the cause of my fever, either. But they manage to come up with some additional tests to run. My arm is pricked with needles to see if I have tuberculosis. On each of several mornings, I am awakened well before breakfast and taken to a room where an experienced nurse feeds an intimidating plastic tube through my mouth and into my stomach in order to see if I have any acid-fast organisms.

Although most of us equate tuberculosis with lung disease, looking at stomach contents after a night's sleep is another way of diagnosing it. As we sleep, we swallow small amounts of mucus that has been delivered up our tracheas. Patients suffering from tuberculosis of the lung may have the bacteria in their swallowed mucus. Sampling the stomach in the morning is another way of finding tuberculosis because the bacteria can be seen with a special stain named for those who dis-covered it: Ziehl and Neelsen. The tuberculosis bacteria retain the stain even when washed afterward with an acidic solution, hence the title: acid-fast. Even though I've ordered the test on some of my patients, I now have a much better appreciation for it. Having a tube pushed down your unwilling gullet first thing in the morning can only diminish further a diminished appetite for breakfast.

Finally, after three or four days, with my nightly fevers continuing, my physician comes in to have another talk with me. He doesn't look happy.

"Dr. Kurland, so far we still aren't sure of what is causing your fevers and chills." I nod but say nothing. "Even though your chest X ray is negative and you have no pulmonary symptoms, we think a bronchoscopy might be useful."

"A bronch?" I say, using the shorthand term. "Great!" I look up to see a startled gaze. "I mean, I do them all the time on kids. I've never had one! Sure, when do we do it?" Then I realize that "we" won't be doing it.

"Tomorrow morning. We'll arrange it all now, if that's okay."

"Absolutely . . . I mean, sure. I think my calendar's open for tomorrow." A wry smile from the other side of the bed. "Sorry. I couldn't help it. I guess I'm a bit frustrated with all this." I hold out my hand. I am smiling for the first time in a long while. He shakes it and smiles back.

In preparation for my bronch, I'm not allowed to eat or drink anything after my meager breakfast. An hour before it is scheduled, a nurse comes in with a large syringe.

"Dr. Kurland, I have to give you an injection of Demerol and Glycopyrrolate."

"Now? Where?"

"Yes, now. In your gluteal region," she says, referring to my buttocks. "I'm sorry, but this is the protocol we use for the procedure."

I say nothing but roll on my side. I hold my breath, and the injection takes me back to the morphine: a deep burn that goes through me and seemingly into my entire leg. I roll onto my back to wait for the drug to work, but after an hour I don't feel too different. A gurney arrives, and I journey again to the operating room, where an anesthesiologist spends twenty minutes numbing my mouth with a combination of foul-tasting medications, warning me to spit them out rather than ingest them. I couldn't agree more.

I am wheeled into the operating room and meet, for the first time I realize, the team who will actually do my bronchoscopy. So far, it is quite different from what happens when I am doing the bronchoscopy, for I always see the patient long before the procedure. There are no injections or mouth gargles for children. Instead, they receive medications intravenously and are made, as I like to say, "comfortable."

I feel anything but comfortable as I am asked to lie down on my back. A red-lighted probe from a device known as a pulse oximeter is put around my finger to measure my blood's oxygen level. It sounds how high the level is with a musical pitch that rhythmically pulses with my own heartbeat. It is playing a clear, high, and reassuring note.

My eyes are covered with a cloth, and a voice asks me to stick out my tongue, which is gently, but firmly, grasped by a pair of fingers (whose?) and pulled forward. The bronchoscope, which is itself passed through a soft rubber tube, is put into my mouth and then into my windpipe. The soft rubber tube is also inserted, keeping my airway open for easy access, should it prove necessary to remove and then replace the bronchoscope.

I first feel the bronchoscope in my trachea, and then a wash of fluid, the lidocaine, to numb my airway. I desperately want the local anesthetic to work, but I continue to feel my breathing and know the bronchoscope is there. The pitch of the pulse oximeter is lower, the rate faster, as my oxygen level drops and my heart rate speeds.

Voices talk to me, directing rather than reassuring. "Dr. Kurland, keep your hand down, please. Only a little bit more, then we'll be done. Dr. Kurland, just a few moments more." The eternity slips by as they finish.

My eyes uncovered, I look toward my physicians, but they are busy with the samples they've taken. One turns to me. "Everything looks okay, Dr. Kurland. We got a good sample." Hopefully, I tell myself, they won't need another. The anesthesiologist wheels me out to the recovery room, and I'm eventually whisked back to my bed, where I collapse, as the Demerol, better late than never, takes hold and puts me under.

My fevers continue, my bronchoscopic results are negative, and my physicians and I remain frustrated. After another few days, I am discharged, with no diagnosis, no specific treatment, and only a little hope. My only instructions are to record the times, duration, and height of my fever. Within the week, I am in Habermann's office for my follow-up appointment. He finds me huddled, nearly asleep, under a thin blanket on the couch in his office. The look on his face betrays my own sad strait. The exam is perfunctory, and he sits heavily down, close to the couch on which I lie shaking with a combination of fear and weakness.

"Geoff, I'm still not sure what's causing the fevers. I'm sure it isn't the leukemia. All your studies have turned up nothing, or at least nearly nothing." I look up. "I reread the discharge summary from Pittsburgh. I had your scan sent over to our people to read. There is a small chance that the areas lighting up in your chest are not simply the result of your surgery."

I pull myself up to a sitting position. "What are you saying?"

"It's possible that the areas are actually infected lymph nodes, which might be able to give us the answer to explain the fevers. Getting at them will be difficult, but I've checked with one of our surgeons, and he thinks mediastinoscopy is possible. I'd thought it was out of the question, given your past surgery. But he said it could be done. However, you have to know that if he can't get anything with a mediastinoscope, he'll have to be prepared to do a thoracotomy."

Of the two, the mediastinoscopy sounds best, for it will result in only a tiny scar at the base of my neck, through which the thin mediastinoscope is inserted under my sternum. A thoracotomy is the medical term for opening the chest with an incision between two ribs, which would result in another chest tube and a longer recovery time. But I won't have much choice, for my vote won't count, and besides, I'll be under anesthesia for the mediastinoscopy. In less than an hour, I've met my surgeon and agreed to be readmitted the following day for surgery.

I am wheeled into an operating room for the fourth time in less than sixteen months, and I do not know if I will wake up with one small bandage over my neck or with a second larger dressing on my right chest. I am too tired to fight; most of my fight has been sucked out of me. I move from the gurney onto the surgical platform as if onto a gallows, looking around the sterile room as if it were the countryside of a desolate frontier, with no friends and no hope.

When I awake, my hand goes to my neck and feels a small dressing perhaps two inches square. I listen and hear no bubbling of a chest tube and realize that my breathing is fine; my chest has no incision. The surgical fellow comes by a few hours later and reports that a few lymph nodes were biopsied successfully. The night falls, and my fever returns but seems a bit less hectic than my usual shaking chill. Perhaps, I tell myself, it is because I received an anesthetic that dulled my ability to generate a fever. The following day, I am discharged once more to my parents.

I am back in Habermann's exam room four days after my medi-astinoscopy, but today I am sitting on the couch rather than lying in a pile upon it.

"Well, you look a bit better," he says, after sitting down.

"I am." He looks intently at me as if to see whether I'm telling the truth. "No fever last night. I slept fine. First time in more than a month." I hand him a paper on which I've recorded my nightly tem-perature for the past several weeks. He studies it for a few minutes, noting that even though last night was the first without any fever, the nightly peaks have been diminishing over the week, even before my last surgery. He motions me to the exam table, listens to my chest, feels my neck and groin for lymph nodes, presses on my belly. I return to the couch.

"The lymph node biopsies they got are so far negative. Nothing's growing. The stains are negative . . . nothing. And now it seems your fever's going too." He sits, pensive in the chair, looks up, then out the window, then back at me. "I think you are close to going back home. The question is . . . or the questions are . . . do we have you finish the twelve weeks of interferon for the protocol . . . and should you go on after that to start Pentostatin?" He is thinking, silent.

"If it'll help, I'm probably going to have to pass through Rochester later in the summer."

"Yeah, it might help. When?"

"Late August. I am going to Oregon to meet some friends at a Shakespeare festival, and then I'm planning to drive a car I left in Sacramento back to Pittsburgh. I was hoping to visit my folks here on the way."

"A Shakespeare festival?"

"Yeah, it's a big deal in southern Oregon, and I've been going for over ten years. My friends and I meet, and we get culture for a week. And I can use it . . . culture I mean."

"I guess you can," he says laughing. "Okay, when are the dates? I can send information to Dr. Ellis; I'm sure he'll be agreeable."

We make the arrangements there and then. I will start up my inter-feron in two weeks, finishing my full twelve weeks just as I leave for Oregon. By the time I get to Rochester, a full two weeks would have passed, allowing me to get my first dose of Pentostatin at the Clinic. The main requirement will be another bone marrow to be done by Ellis just before my trip west. And I must remain fever free.

I tell my parents of the plan, including my return to Rochester in late August. Only my promised return extracts the parental okay.

13

I have been driving all night, and the windows of the red 1963 Porsche are down in the heat of the morning outside of Salt Lake City. My mind is numb from concentrating on the road, sad since leaving Sacramento, having watched as Karin waved good-bye in my rearview mirror. She was sitting on the curb around the corner from her house, alone as I drove past on my way out to the interstate.

I bought the restored car two months after my second surgery, now more than a year ago. I would show them who was going to live. "It's an investment," I told the folks at work. They all looked at me as if I'd purchased a hundred acres of land in the mountains of Nepal: beautiful country but would I ever get a chance to see it?

I'd come back out to take Karin to the Shakespeare festival in Oregon before bringing the car, stored this last year in Sacramento, back to Pittsburgh. Now I'm going home via Rochester: it's time for me to start Pentostatin. The week in Oregon already seems too far in the past.

Because I don't want anyone messing with the car and because it isn't air conditioned, I've decided to drive at night and sleep during the day. Dog-tired, I find a small motel where I can flop for six or eight hours before getting back on the road to push through the Great Plains into Iowa and finally Minnesota.

My parents are waiting as I pull in, hugs all around, and my mother steps back.

"You look a lot better than the last time I saw you."

"And feel a lot better, too." I tell them of Karin and the long drive. My father fills me in on my appointment time with Habermann. I get some much-needed sleep.

I decide not to sit on the brown couch in Habermann's exam room, and I'm at the window when he enters. He looks both happy and serious as he motions me to sit.

"You look good. Your counts are good." He'd already gotten my labs, drawn earlier today. "But we have some decisions to make."

"Like when I start Pentostatin?" I ask expectantly.

"I've got to decide if you should start it."

I sit down on the couch, slowly. "What do you mean 'if'? I'm not in remission, am I?" My hope rises.

"No. There's something else." He pauses, sitting at his desk. "Geoff, we found out recently what was causing your fevers earlier in the summer." Another short pause, but he has my attention. "Mycobacterium avium-intracellulare. I just got the report of the culture of the lymph node they got at your mediastinoscopy. I've made some calls around the country and to the infectious disease experts here. I'm waiting to hear from one or two other people, and then I'll decide which way we're going with this."

Mycobacterium avium-intracellulare, known as MAI for short, is one of the so-called atypical mycobacteria, harder to grow and far less common than its cousin Mycobacterium tuberculosis, which causes TB. As a medical student, I'd heard of atypical TB as an aside in the lectures focusing on one of the main scourges of man, TB. Atypical TB was always included in the differential diagnosis, or list of possible causes, of fever, though near the bottom of the list. But things have changed now with AIDS, and the medical literature is full of talk of MAI, because it is a common, usually fatal, infection in that population. It seems that even though MAI might be a prodigal member of the TB family, when it comes home, it is with a vengeance, for it is resistant to most anti-TB drugs.

I sit still. I search Tom's face for clues of anything. How can this be happening? I kept my end of the bargain: no fever since I left Rochester in July, my bone marrow done just a few weeks ago confirming that I still have hairy cell leukemia. Do I have AIDS, too? Is this brief break from fever just a tease before the infection takes over, moving in for the kill? Tom reads part of my mind.

"I've reviewed your records; both HIV tests, here and Pittsburgh, were negative. I think you got MAI because the interferon did its job too well, knocked out too much of your immune surveillance." He uses the term that signifies the silent housekeeping service of cells and antibodies that are on continuous alert, sweeping up any and all intruders, to the point where potentially threatening infections never even get a small toehold in our bodies. "It could be that the MAI is gone now or is and will remain quiescent. On the other hand, Pentostatin might allow it to return, and we don't have as much experience with Pentostatin. There is some risk involved."

"I'm willing to take that risk."

"Maybe so, but I have to be willing, too. Listen, as I said, I've got some calls out to some others in the field. I should have an answer by tomorrow. Can I call you at home?" We agree to wait a day.

I try to ignore the burden of waiting during the day as I play with my nieces and nephews, visit with my brother and sister, and try to relax even though I churn with uncertainty. All I can do, I tell myself, is wait for Habermann's call. It comes, as promised, the following day.

"Okay, Geoff, I've called around the country and we're all in agreement. You start Pentostatin tomorrow. You'll get the first injection at the infusion center at the Clinic. I've spoken with Ellis, and he knows to keep close tabs on you." I tell myself that I'm sure he will after my feverish performance of the summer. Habermann gives me the particulars of when I'm to show up for my first shot of Pentostatin.

The infusion center of the Clinic is geared to give lots of intravenous drugs to lots of patients. Soon after I arrive in the morning, I'm ushered into a small cubicle with a comfortable reclining chair with large arms. An efficient nurse prods my arm, finds a vein, and places my intravenous line. She hangs up a plastic container of fluid; I look up expectantly.

"When do I get my Pentostatin?" I ask as the fluid drips into my vein.

"First, we have to give you five hundred cc's of D5," she says as she indicates the half liter of 5 percent dextrose, or sugar water, hanging above my chair. "Then you get the Pentostatin, and then you'll be done." She opens the valve on the IV line, and I can feel the slight tingling coolness of the liquid mixing with my blood. I lean back in the chair and am soon asleep.

I am awakened by the nurse pulling gently on the IV site. I instinctively pull my arm away. "Dr. Kurland," she apologizes, "I'm just here to give you your Pentostatin." She's holding a small syringe filled with clear fluid, and I offer her my arm. Using an alcohol swab, she cleans off a port on the tubing, then inserts the syringe and slowly pushes the Pentostatin into my vein, following the medication with a saltwater chaser to clear all the tubing of medication. She removes the IV and hands me a bandage.

"You want to do the honors?"

"Sure, thanks."

"First time?"

"First time what?"

"First time for Pentostatin?"

"Yeah."

"Well, you're done. I hope it works."

"You and me." I get up and walk out to the waiting room, retrieve my mother, and head home with her.

It is in me. I feel no different, yet my step is lighter. I smile broadly out the window of the car while my mother drives. I tell myself I can feel the hairy cells dying by the thousands or millions. "Die, you bastards, "I hear myself whisper.

Six hours later, I'm the one who's sick, in the bathroom, vomiting. But in the morning, I am once again fine. "I'm still here, and you're the ones who're going to die, not me," I say to my unwanted cellular cargo. "This is me talking. The long-distance runner. I'm here to stay." The hairy cells choose not to answer, at least not now.

• • •

I am standing by a bed in the Pediatric Intensive Care Unit at Children's Hospital. It is late morning, Friday, the day after my third Pentostatin injection. My fellow and I have been called to the unit to see a very sick young boy with pneumonia, hoping that we can bronchoscope him to find out what is making him sick. We've agreed that a bronchoscopy is needed, the parents have been told, and we've gotten consent from them. The child is already on a ventilator, so the procedure should be fairly straightforward. In any event, I'm going to make sure my patient doesn't feel the bronchoscope in his airway. I've spoken with the ICU staff; they will give the boy medications to sedate him and keep him comfortable. I told the parents as we obtained consent that I myself had had a bronchoscopy, I know how it feels, and we will not even start until their little boy is ready.

Our technician has brought the cart with the bronchoscope and the equipment to videotape what we find during the procedure. In all, the cart with its equipment is worth the price of a very good new car.

Tassos, the Greek fellow working with me, is directing the ICU staff and nurses in readying the patient. He looks over at me when we're nearly ready to start.

"Okay, Dr. K. We're set." Then he looks at me again. "Are you okay?"

"I'll be back in a minute, then we can start. Can you hold on for a bit?" I ask the ICU team. One of them nods. I walk into the bathroom located only a few feet away and close the door. I am on my knees, hands on the cold floor, then vomiting violently into the toilet. After a minute or two, I am emptied, worn, yet feeling much better. I get up, wash my face and hands, and walk calmly out to the patient's bed. Looking first at Tassos, then the ICU nurse, I say "Let's go." We do the procedure; there are no complications.

Afterward, Tassos pulls me aside. "Dr. K., are you really all right? Before the bronch," he uses the medical jargon, "you didn't look too hot. Did you . . . ?"

"Vomit? Yes. I'll be okay. I just have this problem the day after I get my medication. I mean, it's only every two weeks and lasts a day or so. But I have to admit my nausea the day after is getting worse rather than better. I've talked to my doc, and we're trying some different meds, but so far nothing's worked that well."

"Well, at least is the medicine for your leukemia doing anything?"

"Oh, God yes! I just found out that my blood is clear, no more hairy cells that they can find. Ellis wants me in for another marrow next week."

"You're in remission?"

"He doesn't think so. The protocol I'm on says that he has to do a marrow once my blood is clear. Who knows, maybe I am, but I'm not getting my hopes up. I'll find out next week."

"Well, good luck. But seriously, do you really think you should be putting yourself through all this work on the day after your infusion? I mean, couldn't you just take the Friday off after your infusion? Or maybe they could give it to you on Friday, although I suppose that would really make your weekend a joy," he says sarcastically, laughing a little as he says it.

"I asked about that. His office is closed, although he's around on Fridays. It makes more sense to get the drug on Thursday, then if I have a problem the next day, at least I can find him fairly easily. But I've thought about talking with David about taking Fridays off after my Pentostatin. After today, I will probably have to start doing that. I feel as though I'm in a daze some of the time, and that's not good for the patients or for me. Actually, I feel like I can't keep up with all the things I've got going. I mean, my research isn't doing too much, because I seem to be either on service, post-Pentostatin, or just too busy with . . . I don't know what. My lab tech keeps trying to show me data, but I am having trouble getting over to see her."

Tassos looks at me and says, "I don't see how you can get anything done at all. And I sure think that you should take off the day after your Pentostatin, especially with the effect it has on you." I nod back, knowing that he's right. That afternoon I speak with David, telling him of my need to stay home on the day after my chemotherapy. He agrees that I should do it.

• • •

Late on a Thursday afternoon nearly four weeks later, I'm sitting on the exam table in one of Ellis's back rooms. Between myself, Ellis, and Susan, his nurse, we've figured out a combination of medications to combat my nausea, and they are at the ready at home. Susan walks in and greets me with the IV tubing, needle, and bag of dextrose in water.

"The usual spot, Dr. Kurland?" She asks.

"Yeah," I say, rolling up my left sleeve. She places the tourniquet as I squeeze my hand repetitively into a fist. The veins on my lower arm beckon to her. She cleans me off with alcohol and holds the plastic needle and catheter she'll insert. I turn my head away, for I never like to watch. "Give me fair warning," I half whisper, now pressing the fingernail of my right middle finger hard into the pad of my right thumb. It's a habit I learned to give my mind something to focus on other than the IV start.

"One, two, three," she counts as she slides the needle under my skin, entering the vein. I feel the tourniquet fall free and look to watch her tape the short catheter as securely as she can to my hairy arm. "That wasn't so bad, was it?"

"For me or for you?" I ask. She rolls her eyes. "Okay. Let me hang this D5. I'll be back in about twenty or thirty minutes. You want to lie down?" She pronounces the last word "dahn" courtesy of her Pittsburgh accent.

"I probably will. I've been working a bit."

"You guys busy over there?"

"Yeah, it's been getting worse with the winter coming in. Everybody has a cold. We've had a lot of our CF patients in with infections." She nods, then leaves me alone in the brightly lit room.

I edge down the exam table and look out the window at the darkening gray sky of Pittsburgh. Snow will be upon us within a month, but it looks as though it could arrive any moment. Eleven floors below, a few leaves whip down the street, driven by the wind and the passing buses on Fifth Avenue. Like me when I walked here from the hospital, the people on the sidewalk are dressed for the worst, either a cold and windy rain or an attack of sleet, their coats buttoned up, their hats pulled down, their scarves tucked in.

I reach into my coat pocket and pull out a box of Christmas cards and try to write but cannot. Somehow, I'm just not in the Christmas spirit as the sugar water flows into my left arm. I lie back on the table and turn my face to the wall. I wonder what Karin might be doing. It has been more than a week since I've heard from her. The distance is weighing on us both, and time is becoming more our enemy than our friend. What, I wonder, will happen to me, to her, to us? I see no clear answer, much as I search, but as I try to ponder, my eyes become heavy, and in a moment I am asleep, floating, but for the first time in a while free from leukemia.

I dream of being in a lake whose cold water is weighing down my arms and legs, and I am trying to swim to shore. I look about and see someone motioning to me, calling my name. It may be Karin, but I can't be sure. I redouble my efforts, and suddenly I am on the sand, exhausted, yet fully dressed. I hear my name again, and now it is coming from the opposite side of the lake. I turn back into the water, but I am immediately pulled beneath and cannot rise. My lungs are bursting as I fight to regain the surface, but something or someone holds me below, grasping my arm, pulling me deeper. I will die here, never reaching the voice calling for me. I awaken in a panic as the nurse is pulling on my arm with one hand, her other holding the syringe.

"I'm sorry, Dr. Kurland, I didn't mean to frighten you. But it's time."

I sit slowly, breathing hard, but gaining control. I hold out my IV to her, take the medication, and then help remove the IV and its tubing. Thanking her, I put on my coat and scarf, hold my hat, and give my good-byes as I walk out, confirming that I'll be back in two weeks. Nervous smiles from the staff follow me into the waiting room and out the door.

Now the true race is on, and I walk as quickly as possible to my parked car across the street in the garage owned by Children's Hospital. I drive home, cursing the red lights and slow drivers. The twenty minutes seem like an hour. I walk into my dark house, clamber the steps to the second floor, prepare for bed, and take the combination of medications that have been so laboriously arrived at by trial and error.

The capsule of Benadryl and the tablet of Ativan will do the job, keeping my vomiting to a minimum and putting me to sleep. I drop my clothes at the foot of the bed, pick up my phone, and hit the memory number for home.

"Hi, Mom," I say as she answers.

"Geoff, I was waiting for your call. You're home? Did you get the Pentostatin?"

"Yeah, I'm home. I just got here from Ellis's office. I took my other medications, so you won't hear from me until Saturday, and you shouldn't call. I just wanted you to know that I'm okay."

"All right. Promise to call when you're up to it."

"I will. Good night." I place the phone on its cradle, hoping that the medications will take effect before the Pentostatin makes me nauseous. The nausea has been arriving earlier and earlier following each injection. I'm not sure if it has something to do with the Pentostatin or whether I have a conditioned response, like Pavlov's dog; only instead of salivating, I vomit almost on command. I fall asleep.

Some eight or ten hours later, I awaken in the dark, find my way into the bathroom, and take more Benadryl and Ativan. I don't know if I've vomited because one of the other effects of Ativan is to help erase my memory. But I have dreams, which may or may not be real, of crawling on my hands and knees into the bathroom.

My next reasonable facsimile of consciousness is Saturday morning, when I awaken, groggy, thirsty, and bedraggled, my mouth feeling as though an army has marched through it after maneuvers in a swamp. My blanket is strangely tidy and unruffled, as if I had lain there for some thirty-six hours with almost no movement at all, as if I were near death for the entire time. I peer into the mirror and see a ghost staring back at me, mocking me with his smile. He may know whether the Pentostatin is working and, if it is how many more lost Thursday nights and Fridays I will have before I am done with this part of my life. But the ghost chooses to remain silent.

14

All of us in the Pulmonology Division are meeting on a Tuesday morning. Suggestions are being offered to improve the "patient flow" in the clinic. Someone suggests that we could have patients move to different rooms to see different members of the staff. Someone else says that the patients should stay in their rooms and the staff should do the moving. I tell the group that the problem isn't with who moves where, it's that some of us just like to talk too long.

"They're not here for social reasons; they're here because their kids are sick. Most of them want to get an answer to the problem and move on," I say. Some in the room, including the social worker, look a bit disapprovingly at me, as if I'm treading on their territory, deciding what the parents of our patients are really here for. One of the nurses starts to rebut me when my pager goes off. I look at the number and find it is one I've never seen before. The phone is over on a window ledge in the corner of the room.

"Kurland," I say in my soft, page-answering voice.

"Geoff, this is Bill Donaldson." Why, I ask myself, would the medical director want to talk to me? "Are you busy? Do you have a moment? I've got bad news."

"Bad news? What?"

"Geoff, I just spoke with Paula." He always refers to Spike Miller's wife in familiar terms. "Geoff, Spike had what sounds like a sudden pulmonary embolus at home. He's dead." The words crash into me through the phone. I groan and sit on the floor. I feel the eyes of the room turn to me.

"He's what? When?"

"This morning, early, just as he got up. Paula asked me to tell you." I am silent, eyes wide, staring, sitting on the floor. "The funeral will be in Davis tomorrow." Davis is the small university town some twenty miles from Sacramento.

"I'll be there," I say, not thinking. "I don't know how, but I'll be there. Thanks for telling me, Bill." I slowly hang up the phone and turn back to the group in the room. My eyes are wet; I'm sure I look as bad as I feel.

David is the first to speak. "What was that?" is all he can ask. I tell them, hear their gasps, tell them that I will go to Sacramento for the funeral and then return. David can only nod. In a daze, I walk out of the room and to my office, where I quickly book the flight to Sacramento for the afternoon.

By the time I arrive, it is late evening. I lower myself into Karin's car, waiting by the curb. "Thanks for meeting me," I offer. She takes a brief look at me and without saying a word leans over, embracing me over the gearshift for a long moment while the motor runs. I am silent at first on the drive to her house, asking only for any details of the funeral service in the morning.

"I'll take you there. I think it's best if you go in alone, if that's okay. I mean, you knew him much better than I did. I mean . . ."

"It's okay. I understand . . . and I appreciate the offer. This is too unreal. I spoke to him on the phone maybe three weeks ago. He sounded fine; we talked about some research project he wanted to do when he got out here . . . I mean there . . ." I look over at her. I want her to just stop the car, tell me that she'll be with me tomorrow, and that I don't have to go back home alone. But I remain silent while she concentrates on the freeway, and, as we pull closer to Sacramento, I turn away to survey the darkness that marks the river.

In the morning, the sun is blinding as we drive toward Davis and the funeral service. We had barely spoken last night, but I remember that when we lay down on the bed, Karin had said we had to talk sometime. I had mouthed my agreement just before falling into a deep sleep. I awoke suddenly, unsure of where I was until I turned my head and saw her sleeping. I pulled myself close to her, listening to her breathe, just watching for a few minutes in the gray light of predawn before falling back into sleep. When I awoke, it was to the smell of coffee and toast.

Davis comes into view, and we find the Jewish temple with cars filling the parking spaces on the streets around it. I see former colleagues walking somberly into the building. Karin looks over as she stops the car.

"Are you sure you can get a ride back?"

"Of course. I'll call you when I'm at your house." I reach into my pocket for her extra key. I lean over and kiss her, then turn and force myself out of the car and into the service, listening as she drives off.

In the temple, a few eyes turn to me, then others, as greetings are mouthed to me by my friends, now former colleagues. I arrive as one of the several eulogies is being given. The closed casket is standing alone amid a few flowers. The service ends, and I get a ride with Charlie as we follow the cortege to the nearby cemetery.

"You made it back. How are you doin' with all this? How's Pittsburgh?"

"Pittsburgh's fine but busy. I've had a tough year, but I'm better. The chemo I'm on is working, they tell me. I feel okay. But this," I gesture to the cars behind which we travel, "this really sucks. I was telling Karin that I spoke with Spike only a couple or three weeks ago, and he sounded great. I can't believe it."

"None of us can. How's Karin . . . I mean how are you and Karin. I see her every once in a while, but she doesn't look as happy as she was when you were here."

"She's doin' fine, or at least that's what she says. But I'm not sure. She told me we had to talk but didn't say what it was about. It's been tough, with me out there, her here. Hopefully, we'll have a little time to ourselves before I fly back tomorrow morning."

"You only answered part of my question. How're the two of you doin'?"

I pause to think. "I'm not sure, Charlie. I find myself so busy out there. Distance and time don't do wonders for a relationship, I guess. Like I said, it's been tough."

"No way she can go out there with you?"

"She's got to stay here, because the kids' dad is here. Part of the divorce decree says that for now she has to stay within seventy-five miles of Sacramento. Last I checked, Pittsburgh's a bit further away. I don't know . . . what to do about it all sometimes."

"I'm sure you could come back here," he offers.

"I'm not sure about that at all. I probably wouldn't be able to come back at the same academic level, and I'm sure some would resent my leaving and then returning essentially promoted without having gone through the usual take-no-prisoners bullshit. Besides, I've seen how a real children's hospital is supposed to work, and I'm not sure I'd want to come back here. I've gotten a bit spoiled and seen and done stuff I probably wouldn't get to do here. I've thought of it, but no, I don't think I could do it."

"Well, everybody has his price, right?" he says with a grin.

"Sure, Charlie. Everybody has his price." We arrive at the cemetery, park the car, and join the small crowd at the graveside. The prayers are short, for most of what had to be said was already said at the temple. It is over in a few minutes.

After a brief appearance at Spike's home to offer what condolence I can to Paula, I get a ride to Sacramento with Charlie. We talk more about his personal trials and tribulations at the hospital as we drive, but all I can think about is our earlier conversation and the conversation Karin wants to have.

The room is dark as I hear her voice next to me on the bed. "Geoff, you know I have to stay in Sacramento, and I know that you wouldn't be happy working here." I start to say something, but stop myself. "You know how I feel about you . . . about us . . . but we have to be realistic."

"Reality? This is a weird time to think of reality."

"I know. But I also know that it's not fair to either of us to have to wait and wait and wait to see what'll happen. You have to move on with your life, with or without me."

"I don't want to move on without you. Maybe . . . maybe we could get the right lawyer and fight the court's decision about you staying here."

"Roger would fight it all the way. You know how much that would cost? And I have to think of the kids. They'd probably suffer the most because of it. No, I don't think that's reasonable."

"Or realistic," I finish the sentence. "I'm just not moving on with my life. I can't think about that now. I still want it to be with you. I'll try to come out here more; you come back and visit me more. Somehow we can make this work."

"Geoff. I still love you. Sure, we can try. But we . . . you mostly . . . can't just sit around waiting for something to happen, for the kids to grow up so I can move. We'll both be a lot older then. I mean, Joseph's only four years old. I can't let you do that. I've already got the kids, but you . . . you're still alone. There's someone out there in Pittsburgh. . . ."

"No, there isn't."

"How do you know?"

"I don't. I don't know if I want to know."

"To be honest, I don't want to know either. But I know that what I've said is right." I hear her voice cracking as I turn and hold her in the darkness. My shoulder is wet with her tears as we fall asleep in each other's arms.

My runs, still mandated at no more than four miles, are easier and faster. The snow has been gone since late March, and the sun and spring have reappeared. Where my skin is exposed, there appear itchy welts, a complication of Pentostatin. I find myself rubbing my pruritic shoulder blades against walls. I stand in the shadow of telephone poles while waiting for streetlights. But I still run in shorts and a singlet, for that's the way I've always run when it's warm. My only capitulation to the Pentostatin is sunscreen, which doesn't work that well, anyway. The Pentostatin, however, is still working, although my vomiting comes sooner and sooner after each dose. A bone marrow biopsy in early May was read by the Pittsburgh physicians as completely clean, meaning I was in remission. It was sent off to Mayo. I'm in Ellis's office, hoping to find that the Mayo verdict is the same. Again the small exam room; again the papers shuffle outside the door. Ellis comes in and shakes my hand.

"Geoff, I just spoke with Habermann. He and several others at Mayo have looked at the marrow. They restained it and found a few hairy cells lurking around."

"I'm not in remission?"

"Not yet." He sees my face fall. "But Habermann is pretty confident that one or two more treatments should do it, and he's asked for another marrow after two more treatments. Actually, you had one of those two treatments two weeks ago, meaning you need today's treatment and then another biopsy. Even if you are in remission on that biopsy, the protocol says you still will have two more doses of Pentostatin. I'm sorry we have to continue, but we're really close, and I think we'll get there. We're just not there yet."

I look down, at first feeling sorry for myself. But I realize that a few years ago, I wouldn't be in this position because Pentostatin wasn't available at all. My chances of remission back then would've been closer to 30 or 40 percent instead of the over 90 percent chance I have now. I know I can do a few more rounds of Pentostatin.

"Fine. I mean, that's fine with me. I'll do whatever I need to do." I pull out my pocket calendar/schedule book I keep. "So if I have my dose today and one in two weeks," I hold the calendar open for him, "I could get my marrow done sometime around the thirteenth or fourteenth of June, and then get another Pentostatin dose on the fifteenth, right?"

He nods. "Why is that important?"

"I'll be going out to California to be a physician at that one-hundred-mile race the following weekend, and I don't want the Pentostatin to get in the way of the trip. I may be out there by the time

Habermann has a chance to check the marrow himself. I assume that he will be getting some of it, too, right?"

"Right. That sounds like a reasonable plan to me. Should we get going on today's dose?"

"Absolutely." I move into the injection room at the end of the corridor as he calls for the nurse to start my IV. After the Pentostatin's in, I race home again, do my emesis-avoidance drug-taking ritual, and sleep until Saturday.

Sacramento is hot in late June, and in Karin's rented house, the central air conditioning is off. It is Friday morning, and Western States starts tomorrow; I'm expected at Foresthill again at about 12:30 in the afternoon. Meanwhile, I am alone, Karin having gone to work already, her children with their father for the weekend. I sit on the floor in the small alcove off the kitchen, cradling the phone in my lap. The sun pours through the window, sheeting me in light. I dial Habermann's number at Mayo and get his secretary. I tell her who I am.

"Oh, yes, Dr. Kurland, I'll page Dr. Habermann for you. He told me you might call today." There is no indication as to whether that's because he has good or bad news for me. I sit in the light, waiting for a minute or two.

"This is Dr. Habermann."

"Hello. This is Geoff Kurland," is all I can muster. I am nearly holding my breath.

"Oh, Geoff. I'm glad you called." He's glad? "We restained your marrow and looked at it yesterday afternoon. You're in remission, my friend."

I let myself take a breath. My voice cracking, I ask, "Are you sure?" then regret my impertinence and quickly try to correct with "I mean, it's clean?"

Tom chuckles a bit. "Yes, we're sure. We saw enough to be sure. Congratulations. How do you feel? I guess that's a pretty stupid question."

"I can't tell you, except overwhelmed is close. God, this is great. Now what do I do?"

"Well," Tom becomes more serious, "you still have to have two more rounds of Pentostatin after this marrow to keep with the protocol. We all felt that the extra treatments would ice things if a few bad cells were around that we might've missed."

"Yeah, Ellis told me. We've already done one treatment since the marrow. So I have only one to go?"

"That math makes sense to me. Listen, I'll be in touch with Ellis and fill him in on the plan. Meanwhile, you have fun. Where are you now?" I tell him, and he answers, "You're not thinking of doing that race, are you?"

"Not this year . . . I was thinking maybe next year."

"Sounds like a bit of a challenge, but I have a feeling you might be up to it. You've got my okay to increase your distance. I've got to get going. Meanwhile, keep the faith."

"Thanks. I will. Thanks . . . for everything."

"No problem. I'm glad for you." He hangs up, and I'm alone again. I quickly make a series of calls. The first is to Karin, telling her the good news, then my mother, who agrees to pass it on to the rest of the family. Then I make reservations for a nice place to take Karin for a celebratory dinner.

I look outside again at a sky so perfectly blue and cloudless that it must be the harbinger of my future. The day is hot and bright, and I am going for a nice long run.

Karin and I arrive in Foresthill by 12:30, as the aid station is being put together. We both help set up the tents, chairs, and cots for the injured and dehydrated runners sure to appear over the next eleven hours. Last night we'd celebrated over dinner, choosing to talk of good things rather than the weight of distance upon our relationship. We both agreed that I would try to qualify for the race for next year. Our waiter, a friend, had run the race before and advised me against trying to do it.

"You risk injuring yourself by ramping up too quickly," he said, after I'd told him that I'd just gone into remission.

"Sure, that's right, but I don't know how long I'll stay in remission. This might be my only chance to give it a try."

He looked at me with a glint in his eye and a half smile. "Well," he said as he refilled my glass of ice water, "train on all the hills you can in as much heat as you can take. And stay in remission."

We could hardly wait to finish dinner and get home to be alone to really celebrate. We then slept a quiet night and awoke, ready to help with this year's race.

We have the station set up, Bill passes out the assignments to each of us, and we wait. We hear that the first runner is less than an hour away when Norm Klein, the race director, arrives to make sure all is ready. I wave, then walk up to him.

"Hey, Norm!" I yell as I approach.

"Geoff! Good to see you. We missed you last year, and I'm glad you made it today. We're really goin' to need you. How are you?"

"That's what I wanted to tell you. I just found out that I'm in remission."

"Wonderful!" he says as he shakes my hand, then gives me a hug. "You've got a slot in next year's race if you want it."

"Thanks, but the only way I'll do it is if I qualify. But if I do, then I'll take you up on the offer."

"The offer's good. You just keep in touch. I hope next year isn't as tough as this one's turning out to be." He looks up at the sky as I agree.

This year's race indeed looks like it'll be a tough one, as there are few clouds and little breeze as the dry, hot air rises from the valley up into the hills, turning the canyons into veritable saunas for the runners. Within five hours, we already have four people requiring IV fluids and another five or six trying to hydrate by drinking, only to lose it all by vomiting. The schoolroom is turned into a quiet battle scene without the blood but with the silent desperation of those suffering from the heat, regretting their earlier bursts of speed that robbed them of the strength to continue. We work until the aid station shuts down at midnight.

15

It is a warm, drenching rain through which I run, the trees dripping, the mud splashing on my feet and legs as I stride down the trail. My Gore-Tex jacket has kept only my chest and back dry; my head, my legs, and my feet are soaked. It's late afternoon, and I've already been running well over an hour. Despite the rain, I've filled my water bottle twice already, and I have at least another forty-five minutes of trail to cover in the park. Just another training run, I tell myself, but let's not get hurt. I silently calculate the placement for each foot as it falls amid the rocks.

I turn down a narrow, uneven part of the trail, running downhill, picking up speed. I wonder if I will feel this good after the first hours of Western States, now only about a month away. Probably not, I tell myself, turning my mind once more to my feet, the trail in front of me, the rocks, the dripping trees, and the distance I must cover today.

The last year has been a blur of mostly work and a little research mixed with training for the race. Last July, less than four weeks after discovering myself in remission, I did a six-hour run on a one-kilometer dirt track. Hoping to run a total of thirty kilometers, I surprised myself by running over forty. In early September, I completed a fifty-mile run in less than nine and a half hours, qualifying for the race.

I am still without sign of relapse, and Ellis has given me his cautious approval. Even my parents, initially aghast that I would consider running Western States, have accepted my resolve.

I know that running the race will be like surviving my illness. I have been blessed with the support of my family, my friends, and my colleagues, but in the end, I am the one who has had to put up with discomfort and pain. The procedures, the surgeries, the chemotherapy for my leukemia, all of these were watched by others as I went through them. I could not expect any more from them than they gave me: their acknowledgment of my illness, their witness to my diagnosis and my personal fight against it. The race soon to come will be the same, for if I am to complete it, it must be my own power that moves my legs hour after hour. I will have a crew to greet me at the checkpoints, to have clean socks and replacement shoes, a long-sleeved shirt for the night, batteries for my light. I will have a pacer, someone to accompany me from the sixty-two-mile mark in Foresthill to the finish in Auburn. But I will have to put the one hundred miles of trail under my feet, carrying my own water and food, step by step. The only one who can run my race is the same person who endured my leukemia. The saying in ultrarunning is "pain is inevitable, suffering is optional"; it is true for more than ultrarunning.

My crew will be good. I've known Al since I entered medical school. Nick helped me make it up and over a high pass in the Himalayas five years ago. Jen is the wife of my closest colleague in Sacramento. Evan, who will be my pacer for the last thirty-eight miles, has been my friend for twenty-five years, and he's actually done the race several times. His experience and advice have already been invaluable.

My crew will not include the one person I want there most of all. Karin has a family reunion in Montana the same weekend as the race. She told me only a month ago by phone. I tried to sound upbeat. "Sounds like it'll be fun. I'm sorry you can't make it to the race."

"The kids have really looked forward to going, and I've got to go with them. They're too young to travel alone. I wish I could be in the crew . . . I just can't."

"It's okay. It's okay." It was easy to rationalize. She was right, of course. The kids are definitely too young to travel alone by plane to Montana. And her place is with them, not me. I'm sure she knew I was lying.

Suddenly, the rock beneath my descending left foot moves, turns into a frog, and leaps off the trail. I cannot stop, for the trail is too steep, and I know I'll probably fall if I make any sudden turns. But I know the frog is safe. I finish my run in time for a quiet dinner alone and look ahead to the race I will run.

It is Saturday morning, June 30. The race is only a few hours old. We all waited in the darkness before the start, milling around the chairlifts at the base of Squaw Valley. Several times I walk-jogged back to the room I'd stayed in at the lodge for the last few days, giving me a chance to acclimatize and rest before the race. I took a few extra moments alone in the room before the race, to talk with myself. I told myself that I deserve to be here, that I will finish, that I will be careful. My parents hadn't arrived, although they promised to be there at the start; knowing my father is traditionally late, I wasn't concerned with their absence when the starting gun, actually a Springfield rifle, blasted out and echoed off the mountain walls. Turning quickly to say my good-byes and hug my crew, I ran off near the back of the pack of 350. We climbed up the face of Squaw, our run rapidly becoming a medium walk on a trail often only one or two people wide. Passing was considered unnecessary; this was no time to gain a few seconds of time, for we all wound up walking most of the steep climb. When we reached the top, the race would still have nearly ninety-five miles to go, plenty of distance to pass or be passed. The temperature was only about forty degrees at the start, and the cool was a friendly comfort; the canyons will be hotter when we finally get to them. At Emigrant Pass on the top of Squaw, the wind coming over the Sierras hit us in the face. I turned around and saw the view I'd waited years to see: the summer sun rising over the Sierras guarding the eastern side of Lake Tahoe, now a shimmering blue nearly three thousand feet below.

With only about fourteen miles run, I have my first fall. Running downhill, the trail becoming more scree than dirt, my eyes and mind wander for only a moment. I find myself momentarily airborne and horizontal before landing hands and hip first into the stones. I hear voices of the few runners around asking if I'm all right as I get up, wipe the stones out of my abraded hands, and start down the trail again. I wash my cuts using a little water from my bottle and keep moving. I remind myself to wash off my hands at the next aid station and pay more attention to the unforgiving trail. It could be worse, I tell myself. It could have happened where a fall would put me down a canyon.

I pull into Robinson Flat, the thirty-mile mark, near noon. Even though that means I ran the distance of a marathon along the way in the incredibly slow time of about six hours, it still means that I am on pace to actually finish the race in less than twenty-four hours, good enough to get a silver belt buckle. But I realize that hot canyons and major climbs are still in front of me. My crew meets me and communally hands me a cold coke as I sit. They lie, telling me how good I look; I lie back, telling them how good I feel. After the less than five minutes it takes to down the drink, I will myself upright and start out again, heading down a trail that becomes increasingly hot and sun exposed, the dust rising on my legs. The temperature is well over eighty degrees now, and the hottest part of the day and the race are miles away.

Only a few miles later, I've run down into one canyon and up the other side. The trees open up from the trail, and I see for the first time the vista of French Meadows far below. I stop as if pulled up by a chain, staring at the expanse of trees in the valley several miles wide. The sky is so blue that I feel as if my hand could go through it, rippling into night. The sun, slightly ahead of me in the sky, will get to the finish long before I do. My feet feel the heat, blisters starting to form that will, I'm sure, require several stops with the podiatry volunteers at the aid stations. But I don't care. I know now that I have been training for this race since I was a kid, next to last in the first time trial of cross-country in tenth grade, unwilling to give up. I know that I have been kneaded and folded into this place, tempered by the ordeal of leukemia for the last three and a quarter years. I look once more, for a moment, at the valley stretching below, knowing that Auburn is miles beyond. I look back up to the sky, say a silent thanks, then turn back to the trail, smile, and start running toward the horizon.

ACKNOWLEDGMENTS

I wish to thank the physicians, nurses, technicians, and research scientists who made my survival a possibility. I am grateful for the nourishing support of many dear friends and colleagues, only a few of whom could be included in this book; they made my survival a reality. My family and my wife, Kristen, have made my survival worthwhile.

The patients and parents whom I've served in Sacramento, California, and Pittsburgh, Pennsylvania, have been a source of inspiration, strength, and continuing education for me.

I thank my cross-country coaches through my high school and college years, especially Jim Davis, who allowed me to succeed or fail as a runner on my own. Norm Klein gave me a place in the greatest race imaginable.

Denise Marcil, my literary agent, read my article published in *Newsweek* and convinced me to write this book. Her support, patience, and prodding led me to continue to work when it seemed as though I'd never finish.

My editor, Erika Goldman, was unflinching in telling what worked and what didn't, what to cut and what to keep.

I've had encouragement in my writing from many, especially Lee Gutkind, who first introduced me to the term *creative nonfiction*.

ABOUT THE AUTHOR

Geoffrey Kurland, M.D., is a pediatric pulmonologist at Children's Hospital of Pittsburgh and professor of pediatrics at the University of Pittsburgh. This is his first book.